KIDS LOVE MISSOURI

Your Family Travel Guide to Exploring "Kid-Friendly" Missouri

500 Fun Stops & Unique Spots

Michele Darrall Zavatsky

Dedicated to the Families of Missouri

In a Hundred Years...It will not matter, The size of my bank account...The kind of house that I lived in, the kind of car that I drove...But what will matter is...That the world may be different Because I was important in the life of a child.

- author unknown

© Copyright 2018, Kids Love Publications

For the latest major updates corresponding to the pages in this book visit our website:

www.KidsLoveTravel.com

All rights reserved. No part of this book may be reproduced or transmitted in any form or by any means, electronic or mechanical, including photocopying, recording or by any information storage and retrieval system without the written permission from the authors, except for the inclusion of brief quotations in a review.

Although the authors have exhaustively researched all sources to ensure accuracy and completeness of the information contained in this book, we assume no responsibility for errors, inaccuracies, omissions or any other inconsistency herein. Any slights against any entries or organizations are unintentional.

- **REMEMBER:** Museum exhibits change frequently. Check the site's website before you visit to note any changes. Also, HOURS and ADMISSIONS are subject to change at the owner's discretion. Note: _FAMILY ADMISSION RATES_ generally have restrictions. If you are tight on time or money, check the attraction's website or call before you visit.

- **INTERNET PRECAUTION:** All websites mentioned in KIDS LOVE MISSOURI have been checked for appropriate content. However, due to the fast-changing nature of the Internet, we strongly urge parents to preview any recommended sites and to always supervise their children when on-line.

- **EDUCATORS:** There are suggestions for finding FREE lessons plans embedded in many listings as helpful notes for educators.

KIDS ♥ Missouri ™   Kids Love Publications, LLC

TABLE OF CONTENTS

General Information..Preface
(Here's where you'll find "How to Use This Book", Maps, Tour Ideas, etc.)

Chapter **1** – CENTRAL AREA **(C)**..1

Chapter **2** – NORTH EAST AREA **(NE)**...29

Chapter **3** – NORTH WEST AREA **(NW)**..83

Chapter **4** – SOUTH EAST AREA **(SE)**...133

Chapter **5** – SOUTH WEST AREA **(SW)**......................................163

Activity Index..200
(Amusements, Animals & Farms, Museums, Outdoors, State History, Tours, etc.)

State Detail Map

(With Major Routes and Cities Marked)

Chapter Area Map
(Chapters arranged alphabetically by chapter name)

HOW TO USE THIS BOOK

(a few hints to make your adventures run smoothly:)

BEFORE YOU LEAVE:

- ☐ Each chapter represents a two hour radius area of the state or a Day Trip. The listings are by City and then alphabetical by name, numeric by zip code. Each listing has tons of important details (pricing, hours, website, etc.) and a review noting the most engaging aspects of the place. Our popular Activity Index in back is helpful if you want to focus on a particular type of attraction (i.e. History, Tours, Outdoor Exploring, Animals & Farms, etc.).
- ☐ Begin by assigning each family member a different colored highlighter (for example: Daniel gets blue, Jenny gets pink, Mommy gets yellow and Daddy gets green). At your leisure, begin to read each review and put a highlighter "check" mark next to the sites that most interest each family member or highlight the features you most want to see. Now, when you go to plan a quick trip - or a long van ride - you can easily choose different stops in one day to please everyone.
- ☐ Know directions and parking. Use a GPS system or print off directions from websites.
- ☐ Most attractions are closed major holidays unless noted.
- ☐ When children are in tow, it is better to make your lodging reservations ahead of time. Every time we've tried to "wing it", we've always ended up at a place that was overpriced, in a unsafe area, or not super clean. We've never been satisfied when we didn't make a reservation ahead of time.
- ☐ If you have a large family, or are traveling with extended family or friends, most places offer group discounts. Check out the company's website for details.
- ☐ For the latest critical updates corresponding to the pages in this book, visit our website: www.kidslovetravel.com. Click on *Updates*.

ON THE ROAD:

- ☐ Consider the child's age before you stop at an exit. Some attractions and restaurants, even hotels, are too formal for young ones or not enough adventure for teens.
- ☐ Estimate the duration of the trip and how many stops you can afford to make. From our experience, it is best to stop every two hours to stretch your legs or eat/snack or maybe visit an inexpensive attraction.
- ☐ Bring along travel books and games for "quiet time" in the van. (see tested travel products on www.kidslovetravel.com) As an added bonus, these "enriching" games also stimulate conversation - you may get to know your family better and create memorable life lessons.

ON THE ROAD: *(cont.)*

- ☐ In between meals, we offer the family snacks like: pretzels, whole grain chips, nuts, water bottles, bite-size (dark) chocolates, grapes and apples. None of these are messy and all are healthy.
- ☐ Plan picnics along the way. Many Historical sites and State Parks are scattered along the highway. Allow time for a rest stop or a scenic byway to take advantage of these free picnic facilities.

WHEN YOU GET HOME:

- ☐ Make a family "treasure chest". Decorate a big box or use an old popcorn tin. Store memorabilia from a fun outing, journals, pictures, brochures and souvenirs. Once a year, look through the "treasure chest" and reminisce. "Kids Love Travel Memories!" is an excellent travel journal and scrapbook template that your family can create (available on www.kidslovetravel.com).

WAYS TO SAVE MONEY:

- ☐ Memberships - many children's museums, science centers, zoos and aquariums are members of associations that provide FREE or Discounted reciprocity to other such museums across the country. AAA Auto Club cards offer discounts to many of the activities and hotels in this book. If grandparents are along for the ride, they can use their AARP card and get discounts. Be sure to carry your member cards with you as proof to receive the discounts.
- ☐ Supermarket Customer Cards - national and local supermarkets often offer good discounted tickets to major attractions in the area.
- ☐ Internet Hotel Reservations - if you're traveling with kids, don't take the risk of being spontaneous with lodging. Make reservations ahead of time. We don't use non-refundable, deep discount hotel "scouting" websites (ex. Hotwire) unless we're traveling on business - just adults. You can't cancel your reservation, or change them, and you can't be guaranteed the type of room you want (ex. non-smoking, two beds). Instead, stick with a national hotel chain you trust and join their rewards program (ex. Choice Privileges) to accumulate points towards FREE night stays.
- ☐ State Travel Centers - as you enter a new state, their welcome centers offer many current promotions.
- ☐ Hotel Lobbies - often have a display of discount coupons to area shops and restaurants. When you check in, ask the clerk for discount pizza coupons they may have at the front desk.
- ☐ Attraction Online Coupons - check the websites listed with each review for possible printable coupons or discounted online tickets good towards the attraction.

> Check out these businesses / services in your area for tour ideas:

AIRPORTS - All children love to visit the airport! Why not take a tour and understand all the jobs it takes to run an airport? Tour the terminal, baggage claim, gates and security / currency exchange. Maybe you'll even get to board a plane.

ANIMAL SHELTERS - Great for the would-be pet owner. Not only will you see many cats and dogs available for adoption, but a guide will show you the clinic and explain the needs of a pet. Be prepared to have the children "fall in love" with one of the animals while they are there!

BANKS - Take a "behind the scenes" look at automated teller machines, bank vaults and drive-thru window chutes. You may want to take this tour and then open a savings account for your child.

CITY HALLS - Halls of Fame, City Council Chambers & Meeting Room, Mayor's Office and famous statues.

ELECTRIC COMPANY / POWER PLANTS - Modern science has created many ways to generate electricity today, but what really goes on with the "flip of a switch". Because coal can be dirty, wear old, comfortable clothes. Coal furnaces heat water, which produces steam, that propels turbines, that drives generators, that make electricity.

FIRE STATIONS - Many Open Houses in October, Fire Prevention Month. Take a look into the life of the firefighters servicing your area and try on their gear. See where they hang out, sleep and eat. Hop aboard a real-life fire engine truck and learn fire safety too.

HOSPITALS - Some Children's Hospitals offer pre-surgery and general tours.

NEWSPAPERS - You'll be amazed at all the new technology. See monster printers and robotics. See samples in the layout department and maybe try to put together your own page. After seeing a newspaper made, most companies give you a free copy (dated that day) as your souvenir. National Newspaper Week is in October.

PETCO - Various stores. Contact each store manager to see if they participate. The Fur, Feathers & Fins™ program allows children to learn about the characteristics and habitats of fish, reptiles, birds, and small animals. At your local Petco, lessons in science, math and geography come to life through this hands-on field trip. As students develop a respect for animals, they will also develop a greater sense of responsibility.

PIZZA HUT & PAPA JOHN'S - Participating locations. Telephone the store manager. Best days are Monday, Tuesday and Wednesday mid-afternoon. Minimum of 10 people. Small charge per person. All children love pizza – especially when they can create their own! As the children tour the kitchen, they learn how to make a pizza, bake it, and then eat it. The admission charge generally includes lots of creatively made pizzas, beverage and coloring book.

KRISPY KREME DONUTS - Participating locations. Get an "inside look" and learn the techniques that make these donuts some of our favorites! Watch the dough being made in "giant" mixers, being formed into donuts and taking a "trip" through the fryer. Seeing them being iced and topped with colorful sprinkles is always a favorite with the kids. Contact your local store manager. They prefer Monday or Tuesday. Free.

SUPERMARKETS - Kids are fascinated to go behind the scenes of the same store where Mom and Dad shop. Usually you will see them grind meat, walk into large freezer rooms, watch cakes and bread bake and receive free samples along the way. Maybe you'll even get to pet a live lobster!

TV / RADIO STATIONS - Studios, newsrooms, Fox kids clubs. Why do weathermen never wear blue/green clothes on TV? What makes a "DJ's" voice sound so deep and smooth?

WATER TREATMENT PLANTS - A giant science experiment! You can watch seven stages of water treatment. The favorite is usually the wall of bright buttons flashing as workers monitor the different processes.

U.S. MAIN POST OFFICES - Did you know Ben Franklin was the first Postmaster General (over 200 years ago)? Most interesting is the high-speed automated mail processing equipment. Learn how to address envelopes so they will be sent quicker (there are secrets). To make your tour more interesting, have your children write a letter to themselves and address it with colorful markers. Mail it earlier that day and they will stay interested trying to locate their letter in all the high-speed machinery.

MISSION STATEMENT

At first glance, you may think that this is a book that just lists hundreds of places to travel. While it is true that we've invested thousands of hours of exhaustive research (*and drove over 3000 miles in Missouri*) to prepare this travel resource…just listing places to travel is not the mission statement of these projects.

As a child, I was able to travel throughout the United States. I consider these family times some of the greatest memories I cherish today. Quite frankly, I felt that most children had this opportunity to travel with their family. However, as we started our own family, we found that wasn't necessarily the case. We continually heard friends express several concerns when deciding how to spend "quality" and "quantity" family time. 1) What to do? 2) Where to do it? 3) How much will it cost? 4) How do I know that my kids will enjoy it?

Interestingly enough, as I reflect on experiences with my family trips, many of the fondest memories were not made at an expensive attraction, but rather when it was least expected.

It is my belief and mission statement that if you as a family will study and use the contained information to create family memories, these memories will grow more well-rounded children. Our ultimate mission statement is, that your children will develop a love and a passion for quality family experiences that they can pass to another generation of family travelers.

We thank you for purchasing this book, and we hope to see you on the road (*and hear your travel stories!*) God bless your journeys!

Happy Exploring, Michele

General State Agency & Recreational Information

Call *(or visit websites)* for the services of interest. Request to be added to their mailing lists.

> **MISSOURI TOURISM**: www.visitMO.com
>
> **MISSOURI STATE PARKS & HISTORIC SITES**: https://.mostateparks.com. State Park Activity Sheets: http://mostateparks.com/kids.htm. History & Heritage Teachers Guides: http://www.dnr.mo.gov/shpo/educawar.htm.
>
> **KANSAS CITY TOURISM**: www.visitkc.com
>
> **MISSOURI AGRICULTURAL SEASONAL FARMS**: www.agrimissouri.com/pdf/agritourismmap.pdf
>
> **ST. LOUIS TOURISM**: www.explorestlouis.com

Central Area

Chapter 1
Central (C)

QUICK LOOK...

Ozarks - Caves, Creatures & Cabins

Boom Towns - Wild West Began

Candy, Honey, Ham & Cheese Tours

Funny Body & Animal Works

Castles on Cliffs

Arrow Rock
- Arrow Rock State Historic Site

Blackwater
- Blackwater

Boonville
- Boone's Lick State Historic Site
- Old Cooper County Jail

California
- Burgers' Smokehouse

Camdenton
- Bridal Cave
- Dinospace Adventure
- Ha Ha Tonka State Park

Columbia
- University Of Missouri
- Shakespeare's Pizza
- State Historical Society Of Missouri
- The Candy Factory
- Finger Lakes State Park
- Boone County Historical Museum & Visitors Center
- Rock Bridge Memorial State Park
- For The People Pow Wow
- Heritage Festival
- Shryocks Annual Corn Maze

Columbia (Hartsburg)
- Hartsburg Pumpkin Fest

Fort Leonard Wood
- Museum Complex At Fort Leonard Wood

Fulton
- Winston Churchill Memorial & Library

Jefferson City
- Central Dairy
- Jefferson Landing State Historic Site
- Missouri Highway Patrol Safety Education Center
- Missouri State Capitol Complex
- Runge Conservation Nature Center
- Missouri Veterinary Museum

Kaiser (Lake Of The Ozarks)
- Lake Of The Ozarks State Park

Knob Noster
- Knob Noster State Park
- Whiteman Air Force Base Open House

Lake Ozark
- Bagnell Dam
- Lake Ozark Amusements

Lake Ozark (Four Seasons)
- Lodge Of The Four Seasons

Lebanon
- Bennett Spring State Park
- Lebanon Midway Speedway

Linn Creek
- Big Surf Waterpark

Marthasville
- Deutsch Country Days

Osage Beach (Lake Of The Ozarks)
- Osage Beach Amusements
- Main Street Music Hall
- Tan-Tar-A Resort
- Lake Of The Ozarks Holiday Light Park

Osage City
- Clark's Hill-Norton State Historic Site

Pittsburg
- Pomme De Terre State Park

Sedalia

For updates & travel games visit: **www.KidsLoveTravel.com**

Central Area

- Bothwell Lodge State Historic Site
- Katy Depot And Railroad Heritage Museum
- Missouri State Fair

Versailles
- Jacob's Cave

Warsaw
- Harry S Truman Dam & Reservoir Visitor Center
- Harry S Truman State Park
- Lost Valley Hatchery And Visitor Center

Waynesville
- Old Stagecoach Stop

Williamsburg
- Crane's Museum And Country Store

Travel Journal & Notes:

Sites and attractions are listed in order by City, Zip Code, and Name. Symbols indicated represent: 🍽 Restaurants ⛺ Lodging

ARROW ROCK STATE HISTORIC SITE

Van Buren Street & Van Buren (Hwy 41) **Arrow Rock** 65320
Phone: (660) 837-3330
https://mostateparks.com/park/arrow-rock-state-historic-site
Hours: Daily 10:00am-4:00pm (March-November). Winters only open Friday thru Sunday and winter holiday Mondays. Extended summer hours.
Admission: The Missouri state park system does not charge entrance fees. However, there are fees associated with camping, lodging, tours, museums and certain special events.
Tours: Guided tram tours of the village of Arrow Rock are provided for a nominal fee by the Friends of Arrow Rock.

The spirit of Missouri's frontier years lingers in this quiet, historic village town. You can tour an old jail, courthouse and the home of artist George Caleb Bingham. Dine at the Old Tavern. Sample a delicious, family-style meal in a charming log cabin restaurant. Meals include choice of smoked pork chop, buffalo brisket, country ham, fried or grilled honey-glazed chicken breast accompanied by spinach salad and fruit salad, scalloped potatoes, green beans, homemade breads, fabulous desserts, and coffee/tea/lemonade. This restaurant is guaranteed to be highlight of any tour.

A visitor center, hiking and camping are available. The site's visitor center museum features exhibits that tell about Arrow Rock and the historic "Boone's Lick Country." Visitors can watch a 20-minute video "Arrow Rock: Frontier Town of the Boone's Lick." The kids will like looking at the dioramas of famous people who lived in town. The Bingham Home, built by Missouri's preeminent artist of the 1800s, George Caleb Bingham, has been restored and furnished as it might have been when he lived there. The Huston Tavern, dating back to 1834, stands ready to serve you its traditional hearty fare. The old courthouse, a town doctor's home, a stone jail and other historic buildings are part of a walking tour offered at the site. The Pierre a Flèche (Rock of Arrows) hiking trail is a nearly one and one-half mile loop in the southern half of the site (see site map). The trailhead is in the visitor center parking lot. The River Landing Trail runs along the old warehouse road from town to the river landing - a spot that connected Lewis and Clark's trails and goods traveling the Missouri. So much history moved through this town, it's like walking through a mini-US History lesson in person. Basically, this whole town IS the historic site.

For updates & travel games visit: **www.KidsLoveTravel.com**

Central Area 5

BLACKWATER

125 Main Street (3 miles north of I-70 at exit 89) **Blackwater** 65322

https://blackwatermissouri.weebly.com/
Admission: FREE.
Note: Iron Horse Restaurant serves lunch Weds-Saturday.

As pioneers moved west, little "boom" towns were created. One such town was Blackwater, a common stop for coal and water used by the Missouri Pacific Railroad. After much restoration, you drive into this town and get a feeling you're on the set of a Western movie. Blackwater offers a jail replica, an exact replica of the Missouri-Pacific Depot, country school building, telephone museum, veterans memorial, water gardens and a 10-room, renovated 1887 hotel. You can almost hear the steam whistle or hear the music and voices from the Arcade saloon. Many buildings have been turned into gift shops so there is much browsing for old-fashioned treats involved in your visit.

The Telephone Museum showcases a lifetime collection of telephone memorabilia, including some items dating to the days before direct-dial systems. (Open April-Thanksgiving 9:00am-5:00pm).

BOONE'S LICK STATE HISTORIC SITE

Route 187 (Northwest of Boonville) **Boonville** 65233

Phone: (660) 837-3330 (Arrow Rock)
https://mostateparks.com/park/boones-lick-state-historic-site
Hours: The historic site grounds are open from sunrise to sunset year-round.
Admission: The Missouri state park system does not charge entrance fees. However, there are fees associated with camping, lodging, tours, museums and certain special events.

This is the site of the salt manufacturing business once owned and operated by Daniel Boone's sons, Daniel and Nathan started in 1805. Brine water was poured into iron kettles and heated to boiling on a stone furnace. As the water evaporated, salt crystallized in the bottom of the kettle. The salt was shipped by keelboat on the Missouri River to St. Louis. Salt, which was indispensable at the time for preserving meat and tanning hides, was produced at the site until approximately 1833.

It was Boone who created Boon's Lick Trail through the Saint Charles countryside, out of which grew the Santa Fe Trail and later the Oregon Trail – critical paths for early pioneers seeking a better life in the western United States. A self-guided gravel trail leads down a hillside to the salt springs and an outdoor exhibit explains the history of the site. Picnic sites available. Tour Boone's family home and pioneer village in neighboring Defiance, Missouri.

OLD COOPER COUNTY JAIL

614 East Morgan Street (just a couple miles north of I-70) **Boonville** 65233
Phone: (660) 882-7977 www.friendsofhistoricboonvillemo.org/?page_id=128
Hours: Open for tours Monday-Friday, 9:00am-5:00pm. During summer also open Saturday and Sunday afternoons, 2:00-4:00pm.
Admission: $5.00
Note: Another historic property in town is the HAIN HOUSE (Fourth & Chestnut). For a small fee, you can tour this typical 19th century, single-family dwelling built and owned by one extended Swiss family for 170 years.

The jail was used from 1847 to 1978, longer than any other lockup in Missouri. It housed outlaw Frank James and was the site of many public hangings. Slaves quarried the 2.5 foot thick limestone blocks which they used for construction of the two story building. Ironically, this was the site of slave sales and the round rings bolted to the outer walls of the dungeon rooms held prisoners and slaves shackled by their feet. The graffiti-carved limestone rock walls stand as silent witnesses to a way of life beyond our comprehension. While this site may be a little too deep in late 1800s history for young ones, those who have begun to study US Civil War era history will learn much emotionally.

DID YOU KNOW? Boonville was the site of the first actual clash of arms between Union and pro-Confederate Missouri State Guard troops. Several markers in the town commemorate the First Battle of Boonville on June 17, 1861, and the Second Battle of Boonville in September 1863, as well as Gen. Sterling Price's raid through the town in October 1864.

BURGERS' SMOKEHOUSE

32819 Hwy. 87 (along Moreau River, 3 miles south of town, off Hwy 87)
California 65018
Phone: (800) 345-5185 www.smokehouse.com
Hours: Weekdays 8:00am-5:00pm (yearround except Holidays). Store open Saturdays (late September-before Christmas). Admission: FREE.

Take a tour of this "scented" and artsy smokehouse operated by the Burger family for more than 50 years. The visitors center features dioramas that depict the seasons of the year. Other exhibits display ingredients, pictures, and artifacts that explain the art of meat curing. As you proceed down the hall, you'll end up in the retail store. Tell the receptionist you would like to see the video tour of the smokehouse in the theatre. Now that you know the process, try some samples. If you're still hungry, purchase a sandwich in their shop.

Central Area 7

BRIDAL CAVE

526 Bridal Cave Rd (2 miles north of Camdenton on Highway 5)
Camdenton 65020

Phone: (573) 346-2676 **www.bridalcave.com**
Hours: Daily 9:00am-5:00pm. Closes at 4:00 winter, open until 6:00pm summer.
Admission: $18.00 adult (13+), $9.00 child (5-12).

Legend holds that an American-Indian couple wed at the cave site in the early 1800s. Since then, more than 2,100 couples from around the world have exchanged vows in the stalactite adorned Bridal Chapel. Hour-long tours offer views of giant columns, delicate soda straw configurations and the crystal-clear waters of Mystery Lake. Kind of a spooky place to get married-don't you think?

DID YOU KNOW ? Camdenton is home to several Marinas (near Rte 5, near bridges or at resorts) that have boat rentals - even houseboats. Often a motel or cottages are near the marina.

DINOSPACE ADVENTURE

1163 South Hwy 5 (a mile south of the Hwy 5 and Hwy 54 intersection)
Camdenton 65020

Phone: (573) 346-5516 **www.dinospaceadventure.com**
Hours: Tuesday-Saturday 9:00am-5:00pm (Memorial Day-Labor Day). Friday & Saturday 9:00am-5:00pm (Labor Day-November & March-Memorial Day). Closed December-February.
Admission: General $7.00 (ages 3+).
Educators: wonderful space-related curriculum unit studies (w/activities) are found here: **www.dinospaceadventure.com/starlab.html**

DinoSpace Adventure is a unique combination of science center and theme park with serious exhibits for adults and fun activities for kids. From dinosaurs to outer space and everything in between, it's all here. One exhibit space is called the Bone Room which features a life-size cast of the head of Stan the T-Rex. Outside, the DinoSpace Adventure Park has up to a dozen hands-on activities. Take what you learned in the science museum outside to the fun park launching balls from trebuchets, riding zip lines and pretending that you can overcome dinosaurs. The great beasts have size and teeth and claws...but you have scientific knowledge and technology to defend the village. Your array of weapons, learned from history, range from slingshots to guided missiles.

HA HA TONKA STATE PARK

1491 State Road D **Camdenton** 65020

Phone: (573) 346-2986 **https://mostateparks.com/park/ha-ha-tonka-state-park**
Hours: Daily from 8:00am-sunset.
Admission: The Missouri state park system does not charge entrance fees. However, there are fees associated with camping, lodging, tours, museums and certain special events.

Your family may not have any dragons to slay, but you'll find many wild creatures in a natural setting as you amble toward Ha Ha Tonka Castle located in Ha Ha Tonka State Park, near Camdenton on the Niangua arm of the Lake of the Ozarks. The Castle was built after European-style castles and, after a series of fatal events, what remains are the stark, devastated outside walls that majestically stand on the edge of the cliff. Ha Ha Tonka is a geological wonderland: sinkholes, caves, a huge natural bridge, soaring bluffs, and Missouri's twelfth largest spring. Scenic trails lead thru deep ravines and bowls caused by collapsed caves, past a 100 foot natural bridge and a theater like pit called the Colosseum (used for Native American tribal meetings?). Fifteen miles of trail traverse the park, leading visitors to spectacular scenery, natural wonders and the famous castle ruins. Accessible, paved walkways and rugged, rocky trails provide every hiking experience, from a casual boardwalk stroll to an overnight backpack trip.

DID YOU KNOW ? Ha Ha Tonka State Park is host to several geocache and letterbox sites.

UNIVERSITY OF MISSOURI
Columbia

www.missouri.edu/visitors/

Visit the oldest land-grant university west of the Mississippi and the Historic Francis Quadrangle on the MU Campus, site of the historic MU Columns, and (believe it or not) Thomas Jefferson's original tombstone. Here's some other highlights of a campus visit:

- MIZZOU TIGERS - Faurot Field, football home games.
- MUSEUM OF ART & ARCHEOLOGY - Pickard Hall. http://maa.missouri.edu/. The Museum of Art and Archaeology features major works of art, plus ancient art and artifacts such as death masks. The unique costumes, masks and other special exhibits will surprise and delight most visitors.
- MUSEUM OF ANTHROPOLOGY - Swallow Hall. http://anthromuseum.missouri.edu/. The Anthropology Museum focuses on the native peoples of the country and those in Missouri, as well as the early settlements of

Missouri. The permanent exhibition gallery focuses on American Indian cultures from across North America and on Missouri prehistory, from B.C. to the present. Both museums have special features that kids like - from mummified animals - to American Indian artifacts, and a replica of a settlers cabin.

- ENTOMOLOGY MUSEUM - Agricultural Building.
- BUCK'S ICE CREAM PARLOR ON THE MU CAMPUS, (573) 882-4100. One of Columbia's best kept secrets, Buck's is located on the southeast corner of College & Rollins in Eckles Hall. Here, the MU Food Science Department makes and serves some of the best ice cream and yogurt to be found - Tiger Stripe ice cream, a rich vanilla swirled with chocolate fudge is a Columbia favorite! **http://bucks.missouri.edu/**

SHAKESPEARE'S PIZZA

Columbia - *225 South Ninth Street 65201. Phone: (573) 449-2454 (The District) www.Shakespeares.com.* Note: Another location is at 3304 Broadway Business Park Court, (573) 447-1202. If you want pizza this is the place to go. They sell by the slice during lunch. They also offer subs, salads and garlic bread. Prices range from about $3-5 for lunch and $4-10 for dinner. Go early evening to avoid the crowds. The best part, by reservation, you and up to five friends or relatives can make and bake your own Shakespeare's pizza at the downtown shop, then enjoy watching the pizza bake. Which of their fresh pizza toppings did you choose? The best part is really the tasting!

STATE HISTORICAL SOCIETY OF MISSOURI

1020 Lowry Street (University of Missouri campus) **Columbia** 65201
Phone: (573) 882-7083 or (800) 747-6366
https://shsmo.org/about/columbia/
Hours: Tuesday-Friday 8:30am-4:30pm, Saturday 8:30am-3:00pm.
Admission: FREE.
Note: Downtown Columbia has lots of little shops and restaurants to do a walk-around.
Educators: the best thing about this historical site is their online Education page, especially if you're preparing to write an essay about Famous Missourians.

In Columbia, the most famous painting of the Civil War era hangs at the State Historical Society of Missouri. George Caleb Bingham's "Order No. 11" depicts the Union order to clear the civilian population from Missouri's western counties near the Kansas border. The purpose was to check guerrilla activity in the region, but the harsh measure only served to increase the bloodshed as William Quantrill, "Bloody Bill" Anderson and others raised terror in the hearts of anyone connected with the Union war effort. Outside of this painting, there's not much for kids. Better to visit their online resources or stop in with older youth to physically research state history.

THE CANDY FACTORY

701 E. Cherry Street, downtown **Columbia** 65201
Phone: (573) 443-8222 www.theCandyFactory.biz

Chocolate, candies, milk shakes, all scrumptious treats, what could be better? How about a cookie dipped in chocolate? The Candy Factory takes your favorite snacks and treats, like Oreos, Nutter Butters, potato chips and dips them in chocolate for a sweet treat. The potato chip chocolates are surprisingly good - the perfect blend of sweet and salty. Watch them roll cherry filling or dip caramel apples. Walk down candy cane lane past viewing windows watching a chocolate enrober do its thing or view the goings on in the candy cooking kitchens and chocolate molding room. Call ahead for daily hours and best viewing hours.

FINGER LAKES STATE PARK

1505 E. Peabody Road **Columbia** 65202

Phone: (573) 443-5315 https://mostateparks.com/park/finger-lakes-state-park
Admission: The Missouri state park system does not charge entrance fees. However, there are fees associated with camping, lodging, tours, museums and certain special events.

This old strip mining area is now used for swimming, fishing, and canoeing. Holes left from the strip mining have resulted in excellent swimming lakes and one even has a sandy beach. Note that the swimming holes are extremely deep, and there are no shallow areas. There is also a campground, picnic sites and mountain bike paths.

YOUTH RIDING AREA - This area is located north of the Motocross Track. This small riding area has be set aside for children under the age of 12 years and who are riding ORVs 80cc or under. Adult supervisor is required at all times. On race days, the youth track is closed along with the main track.

BOONE COUNTY HISTORICAL MUSEUM & VISITORS CENTER

3801 Ponderosa Street **Columbia** 65203

Phone: (573) 443-8936 http://boonehistory.org
Hours: Wednesday-Saturday 11:00am-4:30pm & Sunday Noon-4:30pm. Longer summer hours. Call or see website for details.

Tour the Boone County Historical Museum which features a sampler exhibit of the lives and events that shaped the settlement of Boone County - from

For updates & travel games visit: **www.KidsLoveTravel.com**

Daniel Boone and his Boone's Lick Trail to the establishment of the University of Missouri. Each display highlights the Western Expansion along the Trace and on native Americans. Kids find out what broadax is, check out a weaving loom and a collection of antique toys, such as an airplane pedal car. Then go next door to the Maplewood, a 19th Century rural farmstead which features a gracious 2 story home and original outbuildings.

ROCK BRIDGE MEMORIAL STATE PARK

5901 South Hwy. 163 **Columbia** 65203

Phone: (573) 449-7207 https://mostateparks.com/park/rock-bridge-memorial-state-park
Admission: *The Missouri state park system does not charge entrance fees. However, there are fees associated with camping, lodging, tours, museums and special events.*

Geologic formations are the main features of this day-use park, which sits atop Devil's Icebox Cave. Cave tours are only recommended for healthy, strong teens and adults. Trails lead visitors to the natural rock bridge, sinkholes and springs. Nature programs are offered and picnic areas are available. Bats love this area in the summer but only come out to feed at dusk. The Cave trails are also supported by wood boardwalks that meander through the woods and keeps visitors' feet dry inches above the stream that flows through the Rock Bridge. Displays tell visitors more about the cave system and the area's history. Additional information can be gained from using the Devil's Icebox Self-Guiding Trail booklet, which is available for a small fee at the park office.

FOR THE PEOPLE POW WOW

Columbia (Jefferson City) - Boone County Fairgrounds. American Indian traditional dance. Honored guest, Larry Sellers; played Cloud Dancing on the Dr. Quinn, Medicine Woman TV program. American Indian art vendors; Indian fry bread and foods; raffles. Held in the open air, covered pavilion at the Boone County Fairgrounds, rain or shine. All drums are welcome. Limited seating available; bring your own chairs. Free camping and RVs. Small Admission. http://msptv.org/powwows/ (Memorial Day weekend)

HERITAGE FESTIVAL

Columbia - Historic Maplewood Farm in Nifong Park. **http://boonehistory.org/mng/historic-maplewood-house/**. The festival celebrates the history of mid-Missouri with demos and displays of cowboys and a chuckwagon, a Lewis and Clark encampment, Native American teepees, trades people exhibiting their wares, hayrides, storytelling, entertainment stages and lots of kettle corn. (third weekend in September)

SHRYOCKS ANNUAL CORN MAZE

Columbia - 2927 County Road 253 (12 miles east of Columbia on I-70 betw. Exit 137 & 144). Phone: (573) 592-0191. **http://callawayfarms.com/** Fall fun with corn maze featuring 12 acres of corn and over four miles of trails!, plus a three story gumball machine and petting zoo. Allow at least one hour and 15 minutes to get through the maze. Groups will take longer. A portion of all ticket sales benefit the Boy Scouts and Girl Scouts of Mid-Missouri. Hours: Thursday, Friday, and Sunday: 2:00pm-dark Saturday: 10:00am - 10:00pm (flashlight nights). Admission. (starts mid-summer but best in fall)

HARTSBURG PUMPKIN FESTIVAL

Columbia (Hartsburg) - Downtown. **www.hartsburgpumpkinfest.com** This quaint river town brings in over 100 craft vendors and offers a petting zoo, pony rides, food booths and tons of pumpkins and pumpkin-related games and food. Hartsburg is filled with musical entertainment, and tens of thousands of pumpkins. The festival features pumpkin carving, pumpkin pie eating competitions, hayrides in the pumpkin patch, pumpkin painting, apple butter making, and a straw maze. (mid-October weekend)

MUSEUM COMPLEX AT FORT LEONARD WOOD

495 South Dakota Avenue **Fort Leonard Wood** 65473

Phone: (573) 596-0780 www.wood.army.mil/usaes/museum.html
Hours: Monday-Friday 8:00am-4:00pm, Saturday 10:00am-4:00pm. Closed during inclement weather.
Admission: Free

The history and contributions of the military police, Army engineers and chemical warfare units during conflicts dating to the Revolutionary War are on display in a three-museum complex. Land-mine warfare, tactical bridging, demolition and explosives, arms, chemical warfare. Military Police vehicles are on display in the vehicle park located across the street from the museum. Kids think seeing the Army barracks (everything in place) is pretty cool.

WINSTON CHURCHILL MEMORIAL & LIBRARY

501 Westminster Avenue (Westminster College campus) **Fulton** 65251

Phone: (573) 642-3361 **www.churchillmemorial.org**
Hours: Daily 10:00am-4:30pm.
Admission: $8.50 adult, $7.50 senior, $6.50 youth (12-18), $5.50 child (6-11)
Educators: Students trying to get a hold of the character and accomplishments of a great man in the history books may love this curricula online: **www.churchillmemorial.org/schoolprograms/curricula/Pages/default.aspx**.

Central Area 13

In 1946, Sir Winston Churchill made his famous Iron Curtain speech at Westminster College. Interactive exhibits, artifacts and a film focus on one of the 20th century's most well-known statesmen, Winston Churchill. See the podium Churchill used to make that speech and watch a film of him delivering it. Look for his famous top hat (autographed). On the outside and above the museum is the church that was so damaged during the London Blitz in 1940 that it was scheduled to be demolished until Fulton asked that it be shipped to Westminster College so it could be reconstructed as a tribute to Winston Churchill. Visitors can also experience a London air raid through a light and sound show. You won't want to miss the Berlin Wall sculpture "Breakthrough." Doesn't this sound like a fun way to explore the life and character of such a famous historical statesman?

CENTRAL DAIRY

Jefferson City - *610 Madison St. 65101. Phone: (573) 635-6148* **www.centraldairy.biz.** Ice cream has never been so good. Be prepared for a tough decision as you view the flavors behind the long glass window. There are over 40 flavors of ice cream to try and this is the home of the $1.00 triple, hand-dipped cones and unbelievable banana splits. A trip to our hometown dairy for an enormous scoop of ice cream has been a tradition in Jefferson City since the 1930s. Open 10am-6pm daily.

JEFFERSON LANDING STATE HISTORIC SITE

Jefferson Street and Capitol Avenue **Jefferson City** 65101

Phone: (573) 751-2854 **www.mostateparks.com/jeffersonland.htm**
Admission: The Missouri state park system does not charge entrance fees. However, there are fees associated with camping, lodging, tours, museums and certain special events.

Jefferson Landing State Historic Site is significant as a rare surviving Missouri River landing. The Lohman Building, built in 1839, is a sturdy stone structure that served as a tavern and hotel, and in its heyday also housed one of the city's largest warehouse and mercantile businesses. Today, the main floor contains a visitor center with exhibits on transportation. The ground floor of the building still serves as the city's Amtrak train station. Don't you love walking on those brick "cobblestone street" hallways?

MISSOURI HIGHWAY PATROL SAFETY EDUCATION CENTER

1510 East Elm Street **Jefferson City** 65101

Phone: (573) 751-3313 www.mshp.dps.mo.gov
Hours: *Weekdays 8:00am-5:00pm*
Admission: *FREE. Groups of 10 or more people should call for a reservation (573) 526-6149.*

Nowhere in the state of Missouri is there such a comprehensive display of information concerning traffic safety law enforcement, drug abuse and other items relating to the history of the Missouri Highway Patrol. Exhibits focus on the services and responsibilities of the Highway Patrol, both on and off the highways. Test your emergency reaction time and see wreckage of a car crash where passenger's lives were saved wearing seat belts. It seems funny to think patrolmen cased the streets in a 1931 Model A Ford Roadster at one time. See one up close.

MISSOURI STATE CAPITOL COMPLEX

201 West Capitol Avenue **Jefferson City** 65102

Phone: (573) 751-2854 https://mostateparks.com/page/55179/capitol-tours
Admission: *The Missouri state park system does not charge entrance fees. However, there are fees associated with camping, lodging, tours, museums and certain special events.*
Audio Tours: *are downloadable from the Audio Tours link online BEFORE you get there. In a hurry? Self-guided tour maps are available at the Capitol Tour Reservation desk located on the first floor. Hours: 8am-5pm daily (Missouri State Museum).*
Capitol tours are given Monday through Friday every hour on the hour (excluding the noon hour) for walk-in guests. Reservations are required for groups of 10 or more. On Saturdays & Sundays, tours are given at 11:00am and 2:00pm.
Educators: *an audio online site of interviews and facts about former Missouri slaves is at this extension: www.mostateparks.com/statecapcomplex/statemuseum/slaverysechoes.htm.*

STATE CAPITOL - As your family approaches the complex, many notice the Missouri Capitol Building looks a lot like the D.C. Capitol building. Very ominous outside and very stately inside. All four floors of Missouri's Capitol are open to the public. A 45-minute guided tour is the best way to experience the historic and decorative features of the building. Two things you must try to see while on tour (if available, obey signs on doors): Legislature in session (January thru mid-May) and the Mural in the House Lounge. Both are "active" spaces. The mural is colorful and busy but kids love trying to make out the different facial expressions and count how many people are in the mural. Oh, and wouldn't the Governor's office be a handsome room to work in? A walk around the Capitol grounds highlights more of Missouri's history, including

Karl Bitter's bronze relief of the signing of the Louisiana Purchase Treaty, which sits on the terrace overlooking the Missouri River.

MISSOURI STATE MUSEUM - Part of the original Capitol plans called for a ground-floor museum that showcased Missouri's cultural and natural history. Now operated by the Missouri Department of Natural Resources, the Missouri State Museum features exhibits, dioramas and changing displays.

- HISTORY HALL - Be a history detective as you explore the hands-on exhibits and try to answer questions asked along the way. Try on 19th century clothing, design a flag and learn about the equipment soldiers carried during the war. "Slavery's Echoes" is where quotes from interviews with former slaves give first-hand accounts of working conditions, family life, housing and treatment they endured. Also in the display, you'll find "hands-on" artifacts like shackles and clothing, along with an audio stories. Scavenger Hunt: http://www.mostateparks.com/statecapcomplex/statemuseum/se_scavengerhunt.pdf.

- NATURAL RESOURCES HALL - Displays the products of the state's forests, fields and mines. This gallery displays Missouri's natural resources on the south wall, human resources on the north wall and the story of how the two have interacted in the center.

RUNGE CONSERVATION NATURE CENTER
(Mo. Hwy. 179 - 1/2 mile north of Highways 50/63) **Jefferson City** 65102
Phone: (573) 526-5544 **www.facebook.com/pages/Runge-Conservation-Nature-Center/127181780661343**
Hours: (Area) 6:00am-9:00pm. (Buildings) Tuesday, Wednesday, Friday, Saturday: 8:00am-5:00pm, Thursday 8:00am-8:00pm.
Admission: FREE.

Enjoy the wonders of Missouri's habitats and the fish, forest and wildlife resources found in the Show-Me State. There are hiking trails and wildlife habitats outdoors, while the nature center features indoor exhibits. Kids love "Bubba", an enormous model of a bullfrog, the 2500 gallon aquarium full of native state fish and the walk-thru cave. Age a fish using an enormous fish scale and learn how and why we tag fish. Follow a river otter with a tracking device and see a rare swamp rabbit that can swim. This is a great little Missouri natural history stop and it's free.

MISSOURI VETERINARY MUSEUM

2500 Country Club Drive (50 west to Rte 179 exit) **Jefferson City** 65109
Phone: (573) 636-8737 www.movma.org
Hours: Monday-Friday, 9:00am-4:00pm & Saturday by appointment.

The only museum in the United States that is devoted solely to veterinary medicine is located in Jefferson City. On display are veterinary artifacts and instruments, many over 100 years old. The museum houses over 3,500 artifacts dating from the 1st century to present. The interactive museum is appropriate for both children and adults. Hands-on learning center for kids: Visitors touch and explore materials, such as bones, animals skins and hairballs. Other discovery materials are specimens showing stages of a calf embryo and various animal diseases. Be prepared for the unusual such as a hog catcher, huge horse pills and giant syringes. What strange objects does a veterinarian find in a cow's stomach? What did a veterinarian use in 1929 to give Fido his medicine? Discover the answers to these questions at the Veterinary Museum.

LAKE OF THE OZARKS STATE PARK

403 Highway 134 (off Hwy. 54 on Route A)
Kaiser (Lake of the Ozarks) 65047
Phone: (573) 348-2694 https://mostateparks.com/park/lake-ozarks-state-park
Admission: The Missouri state park system does not charge entrance fees. However, there are fees associated with camping, lodging, tours, museums and certain special events. Tours run $4.00-$6.00 (Mid-May thru mid-Sept).

The wooded hills and miles of shoreline provide a getaway from nearby attractions. The park offers camping, camper cabins, a yurt, marinas, beaches, trail rides and hiking trails. The park's visitor center is located at Ozark Caverns, the site of the cave tours. The center features a variety of educational exhibits, particularly displays on the cave environment and animal life within the cave system. (Visitor Center open 11:00am-3:00pm daily except closed in winter).

<u>OZARK CAVERNS</u> - Cave is located in the park and can be explored using handheld lanterns. Guided one hour tours give you a view under the Ozark hills of bats, salamanders and interesting cave formations like the Angel Showers. The spectacular Angel's Shower is among the highlighted sights. The perpetual flow of water seems to spring directly from the rocks above into two massive basins below. Visitors center exhibits about the natural features of the cave. Tours offered 2 - 4 times daily each summer & weekends.

For updates & travel games visit: **www.KidsLoveTravel.com**

Central Area

KNOB NOSTER STATE PARK
873 SE 10 **Knob Noster** 65336

Phone: (660) 563-2424 https://mostateparks.com/park/knob-noster-state-park
Admission: The Missouri state park system does not charge entrance fees. However, there are fees associated with camping, lodging, tours, museums and certain special events.

Dominated by second growth hardwood forest, this park contains restored remnants of open woodlands and grasslands. It has a nature center, small lakes, a campground, hiking trails, an equestrian trail and campground. Several small lakes in the park cater to the fisherman, and non-motorized boats may be used. The nature center is open daily during business hours.

WHITEMAN AIR FORCE BASE OPEN HOUSE

Knob Noster - Highway 23 off Highway 50. Once a year you can visit the home base of the Stealth bomber. Usually held a summertime weekend, the open house is set up so you can climb into older planes, view displays about aircraft and the air force, and see guard dogs, a mobile command station, and other military items. Includes an air show and aerial demonstrations throughout the day. (mid-September weekend)

BAGNELL DAM
1 Willmore Lane **Lake Ozark** 65049

Phone: (900) 451-4117 www.lakeareachamber.com

WILLMORE LODGE VISITORS CENTER & MUSEUM - Lodge serves as offices of the Lake Ozark area Chamber of Commerce and houses a museum with a great big view of the Dam. The visitors center is your first stop when arriving in the area to orient yourself and pick up the latest coupon booklets. The museum exhibits tell about the area before Bagnell Dam was built and the construction of the dam. Occasionally, a guide will offer a short free tour of the dam showing how electricity is generated and how the dam was built. What are the dozens of rooms in this building named after?

BAGNELL DAM - OMA & NOMA DAYS FESTIVAL

Lake Ozark - Experience yesteryear as we celebrate the first crossing of the Bagnell Dam by Oma and Noma Degraffenreid in 1931. Dress in era style clothing and enjoy an old fashioned festival with events such as: outhouse racing, frog jumping, watermelon seed spitting, pie eating contests, to name a few. Held at the south end of Bagnell Dam. www.omanomadays.org. (mid-May weekend)

DID YOU KNOW? The Lake of the Ozarks area has a number of oddities, but one that remains a mystery is on the west side of Highway 5 to State Road 135-3. It's a shoe fence with dozens of shoes of all shapes, styles, and colors on the fence post. Each year it grows and changes as new shoes are added. In the same vicinity is the Cup Tree. Some believe that there was once a natural spring here and people left their cups and mugs for other travelers. While not necessarily sanitary, its intent was quite hospitable and quite colorful with cups and mugs of all colors and sizes dancing in the breeze.

LODGE OF THE FOUR SEASONS

Lake Ozark (Four Seasons) - *315 Lodge of Four Seasons Drive 65049. Phone: (573) 365-3000, (800) THE-LAKE or (888) 265-5500 (reservations)* **www.4seasonsresort.com.** This is a true lodge setting with rock or stone walls, fireplace in the lobby and cozy furnishings. While the main lodge is older, the condos are new and furniture and carpeting in the lodge rooms has been updated recently. This resort area also offers a full-service marina offering boat, water ski and personal watercraft rentals, parasailing, fishing guides, lake cruises, gasoline and a store. They also have a full-service spa on the property. Good for a few days of retreat and recreation in the Ozarks.

BENNETT SPRING STATE PARK

26250 Hwy 64A Lebanon 65536

Phone: (417) 532-4338 (Park Office) or (417) 532-4307 (Lodging)
www.bennettspringstatepark.com
Admission: The Missouri state park system does not charge entrance fees. However, there are fees associated with camping, lodging, tours, museums and certain special events.
Note: Lebanon is a hub for handfuls of canoe rental and guided tours and dozens of family campgrounds.

Bennett Spring, the fourth largest state park in Missouri, has a daily output of over 100 million gallons of water, rising out of a narrow cave. Native Americans were the first to enjoy its beauty and benefits, and referred to it as "Eye of the Sacred One." Bennett Spring was one of Missouri's first state parks. Today it is still one of the most beautiful and most popular in the state's system. Many things draw people here, but the reason that tops the list is the fishing - trout fishing. The hatchery in the park adds fish to the stream daily. Stop in at the hatchery for a quick tour.

For updates & travel games visit: **www.KidsLoveTravel.com**

In addition to fishing, park visitors can enjoy 12 miles of hiking trails, with an abundance of wildlife and wildflowers to be found along the paths. Area outfitters can provide float trips on the Niangua River. The Nature Interpretive Center is a great place to get an overview of the park's wildlife, as well as learn the history of the spring. There's an outdoor swimming pool, tent camping and RV sites, motel rooms, single cabins, duplexes and four-plexes available. Feed you cravings at the rustic C.C.C. Dining Lodge. Built in 1930, the Dining Lodge offers a varied cuisine of just bring in your catch and they will cook it for you!

LEBANON MIDWAY SPEEDWAY

22304 Route B **Lebanon** 65536

Phone: (417) 588-4430 **www.lebanonmidwayspeedway.com**

Spring through fall, race fans can watch the action on this dirt-track speedway in Lebanon. April-September. $5.00-$25.00; ages 10 & younger are FREE. Friday or Saturday nights. Gates open at 5pm. Hot Laps 6:30pm. Racing Starts at 7:30pm.

BIG SURF WATERPARK

954 State Road Y (off Hwy. 54 at State Rt. Y) **Linn Creek** 65052

Phone: (573) 346-6111 **www.bigsurfwaterpark.com**
Hours: Daily, (Memorial Day-Labor Day)
Admission: $31.95 adult (11-59), $26.95 junior (4-10), $22.95 senior (60+). Discounts after 3:00pm.

Big Surf Waterpark – Features 27 acres of water fun including a wave pool, three-story Zambezi Falls water experience, whirlpool spa, rapid rides, body flumes, lazy river and Tropical Splash Island for young children.

DEUTSCH COUNTRY DAYS

Marthasville - Luxenhaus Farm, Highway O. A living history event that takes place on a farm that is home to 19 restored historic buildings. This is the only time the farm is open to the public. Usually 60+ crafts and skills demonstrators share their skills: rugs, crosscut sawing, sheep shearing, natural dyeing, paper marbling, primitive folk-art gourds and kloppelei (bobbin lace). Admission. (third weekend in October) **www.deutschcountrydays.org**

OSAGE BEACH AMUSEMENTS
Osage Beach (Lake of the Ozarks)

- **MINER MIKE'S ADVENTURE TOWN** - 4515 Hwy 54. Admission: http://minermikes.com. Ride packages $8.00-$14.00. Over 100 token operated games are available and must be purchased separately. You may purchase the rides individually, and each ride requires 4 tokens per child. One adult may ride free with a paying child. Open year-round except winter.
- **PIRATES COVE ADVENTURE GOLF** - 5850 US 54. Admission: $7.95 adult, $6.95 child. www.piratescove.net. Your choice of 2 courses, the Captains Course, or the more challenging Blackbeard's Challenge.
- **PUTT N STUFF FAMILY FUN CENTER** - 5440 Highway 54. March - October. Phone: One-stop fun for the family. Two 18-hole mini-golf courses with waterfalls, caves and fans to keep you cool; bumper cars; skee ball; video games; a children's merry-go-round; figure-eight go-cart track with a kiddies' track. http://puttnstuffgolf.com/
- **GRAN RALLY KARTS** - 5730 US 54. Phone: www.granrallygokarts.com.

MAIN STREET MUSIC HALL

1048 Main Street (note GPS address is 5845 Highway 54) **Osage Beach (Lake of the Ozarks)** 65065

Phone: (573) 348-9500 or (800) 348-9501 **www.lakemusichall.com**
Hours: (Showtime) is at 8:00pm. Christmas shows in late November and December are at 7:00pm. Call or see website for latest schedule.
Admission: $22.00 adult, $20.00 senior, $13.00 child (5-12).

The Main Street Music Hall is a live music show that is now in it's 15th season at the Lake of the Ozarks in Osage Beach, Missouri. Located in the Landing On Main Street Shopping Village, the show offers a wide variety of musical enjoyment as well as comedy that is sure to bring a laugh and a smile to people of all ages. The show consists of two hours of current and classic country, gospel, and patriotic songs, as well as a trip through time with their medley of songs from the 1960's through today.

TAN-TAR-A RESORT

494 Tantara Drive (Route KK) **Osage Beach (Lake of the Ozarks)** 65065
Phone: (573) 348-3131 or (800) 826-8272 **www.tan-tar-a.com**

For updates & travel games visit: **www.KidsLoveTravel.com**

Parents who long for the nostalgia of old-fashioned lakeside resorts will appreciate this established resort property. Although the resort has been around a while, their rooms are clean and roomy and the resort is right on the lake. There are two pools at Tan-Tar-A. The larger complex has a large pool that has a maximum depth around 4 ft. There is also a hot tub and a fairly decent water slide for the kids. The spa also has an indoor pool. Other amenities: bowling, horseback riding, boat rentals, tubing, miniature golf, an arcade and hiking trails. There are restaurants on the property but, for convenience, they may be pricey for a family budget. Tan-Tar-A covers quite a few acres with hills, so make sure to use the shuttle service if you don't want to drive around or try to walk to everything. (And speaking of driving around, make sure to grab a map when you check in! If you don't you might get lost). Average basic room rate: $150/night. Recent guests suggest requesting the main building. Every activity (except the pools) requires an additional fee.

- **TROPIC ISLAND CRUISES** - Offers a 90 minute narrated cruise that covers about 2.5 miles of the lake and a good bit of local flavor storytelling. Daily Scenic Cruises: Tuesday-Sunday 3:00-4:30pm. Juices, soft drinks and cocktails available. Public Scenic Cruise Rates: Adults: $16, Ages 4 - 12: $10, 3 & under: Free. www.tropicislandcruises.com.
- **TIMBER FALLS INDOOR WATERPARK** - This indoor waterpark offers four water slides, a lazy river for floating, an activity pool where water basketball and other games are played, and a three-story tree house that dumps water every so often. Hours vary. www.tan-tar-a.com/1/timber_falls.htm. Separate admission: ~$22.00.

LAKE OF THE OZARKS HOLIDAY LIGHT PARK

Osage Beach (Lake of the Ozarks) - Osage Beach City Park. More than 80 giant, animated displays at the Osage Beach City Park. Admission: $10.00 a car. (starts daily weekend before Thanksgiving thru New Years Day)

CLARK'S HILL-NORTON STATE HISTORIC SITE

(I-70 exit 128) **Osage City** 65101

Phone: (573) 449-7402 **www.mostateparks.com/clarkshill.htm**
Admission: The Missouri state park system does not charge entrance fees. However, there are fees associated with camping, lodging, tours, museums and certain special events.

The Lewis and Clark Expedition camped near this site and Clark climbed the hill to see the confluence of the Missouri and Osage rivers. He made observations and took measurements of the rivers from a rock on the hilltop, noting that he passed two Indian Mounds to get to the top. On June 1-3, 1804, they camped at the base of what is now known as Clark's Hill. Today, a half-mile interpretive trail passes American Indian mounds to an overlook of the rivers. The rock where Clark stood and the location of the crew's campsite below can also be seen from the overlook. Interpretive signs along the trail discuss the history of the area. This site is open daylight hours.

POMME DE TERRE STATE PARK
Route 64B **Pittsburg** 65724

Phone: (417) 852-4291 https://mostateparks.com/park/pomme-de-terre-state-park
Admission: The Missouri state park system does not charge entrance fees. However, there are fees associated with camping, lodging, tours, museums and certain special events.

Pomme de terre, French for "potato," can be translated "apple of the earth," which is a fitting interpretation when referring to Pomme de Terre State Park. Visitors can launch a boat and find a quiet cove to fish for bass, walleye, catfish, crappie or even muskie. A fishing pier and marina or one of the park's two public swimming beaches provide a great place to cool off or lounge in the sun. The park offers two hiking trails that wind through several scenic areas and picnic sites in the forest or near the lake. Overnight accommodations include more than 250 campsites, many located near the lake shore, on both sides of the lake.

BOTHWELL LODGE STATE HISTORIC SITE
19349 Bothwell State Park Road **Sedalia** 65301

Phone: (660) 827-0510 https://mostateparks.com/park/bothwell-lodge-state-historic-site
Admission: The Missouri state park system does not charge entrance fees. However, there are fees associated with camping, lodging, tours, museums and certain special events.
Tours: (Castle) $4.00 adult (13+), $3 child (6-12). Monday & Thursday-Saturday 10:00am-4:00pm & Sunday 11:00am-4:00pm (April - mid-September). Weekends & Holiday Mondays 10:00am-4:00pm & Sunday 11:00am-4:00pm (mid-September - March). The last tour begins at 3:00pm.
Educators - Teacher's guides are available to assist school group visits. **https://mostateparks.com/page/55045/teachers-guides**

Between 1897 and 1928, this castle was built for a well-known Sedalia lawyer named John Homer Bothwell. The 12,000-square-foot lodge is constructed atop three caves and was built in four different sections...on the side of a cliff. Not only is the house handsomely appointed, Bothwell Lodge State Historic Site offers nature lovers hiking trails, bike paths, a picnic area and playground equipment for the kids. Guided tours take you through the 3-story house, pointing out the unusual design elements of the owner.

KATY DEPOT AND RAILROAD HERITAGE MUSEUM

600 East Third Street **Sedalia** 65301

Phone: (660) 826-2222 http://**katydepotsedalia.com**
Hours: Monday-Friday 9:00am-4:00pm. Saturday also (April-December).
Note: Folks can rent bikes at the Trailside Café or take a short walk on the Katy Trail to the only tunnel on the trail. $1.00 exhibit admission. Guided tour: $3.00 per person.

The great railroad town of Sedalia is home to the Sedalia Katy Depot, constructed in 1896 on the Missouri-Kansas-Texas (M-K-T or "Katy") line. One of the largest depots between Kansas City and St. Louis, this depot features Henry the telegrapher and Jeanie, a young girl who describes her family's recent trip to the 1904 St. Louis World's Fair. Children can be an engineer for a day and drive a train while learning more about the train station operations at the turn of the last century. The youth activity area also has a place where kids can pretend to sell train tickets. One of the exhibits is a working telegraph. This is also the hub of the visitors bureau where you can find assistance in exploring the rest of the town.

MISSOURI STATE FAIR

Sedalia - State Fairgrounds, Hwy 65 (2503 W. 16th Street). The 11-day fair showcases the best of Missouri agriculture; competitions: professional entertainment; rural lifestyle experiences; hands-on science, technology and innovation; family-friendly amenities for infants to mature adults; and action-packed activities. The Missouri State Fair is the perfect blend of activities for a memorable family outing. The midway carnival includes games and rides for children and thrill seekers of all ages. The nightlife on the fairgrounds kicks up each evening with free music on the Budweiser Stage and music stars performing on the stage of the Grandstand. Admission. **www.mostatefair.com**. (eleven days in August).

JACOB'S CAVE

23114 Highway TT (1 mile off State Highway 5) **Versailles** 65084

Phone: (573) 378-4374 www.jacobscave.com
Hours: 9:00am-5:00pm (Memorial Day - Labor Day), Closes at 4:00pm rest of year.
Admission: $18.00 adult, $9.00 child (4-12).

Known for its reflecting pools, ceiling sponge-work, prehistoric bones and one of the world's largest geodes. Find evidence of ice ages and three earthquakes.

HARRY S TRUMAN DAM & RESERVOIR VISITOR CENTER

15968 Truman Road **Warsaw** 65355

Phone: (660) 438-7317 or (660) 438-2216 (Visitor Center)
www.nwk.usace.army.mil/Locations/District-Lakes/Harry-S-Truman-Lake/
Hours: 9:00am-5:00 (summer). Closes at 4:00pm spring & fall. (March-October). Closed winters.

Atop Kaysinger Bluff, the center offers spectacular views of the lake, dam and the city of Warsaw. Exhibits using touch screens conveying history and culture of Osage Valley and the process of turning the moving energy from water to electricity are available. The theater offers a must-see short movie on Osage Valley history and construction of the dam. Wildlife and water safety videos are also available for viewing. The staff will be available to answer questions and to provide Annual Day Use Passes, water safety materials, lake area brochures and maps.

HARRY S TRUMAN STATE PARK

28761 State Park Road **Warsaw** 65355

Phone: (660) 438-7711 https://mostateparks.com/park/harry-s-truman-state-park
Admission: The Missouri state park system does not charge entrance fees. However, there are fees associated with camping, lodging, tours, museums and special events.

Surrounded by water on three sides, this park encompasses the tip of a peninsula that juts into Truman Lake. Water activities such as swimming, boating and fishing are featured, as are a marina, boat ramps, hiking trails and campgrounds. Hiking trails wind through the woods and out to rocky overlooks, offering breathtaking views of the lake and an occasional glimpse of the abundant wildlife. Fox, coyote, deer, wild turkey and beaver make their homes in the forest and grasslands of Truman State Park. Anglers of all skill levels will be challenged to hook a variety of fish in the lake's cool, clear waters.

For updates & travel games visit: **www.KidsLoveTravel.com**

LOST VALLEY HATCHERY AND VISITOR CENTER

28232 Hatchery Avenue (located east of Highway 65 at the Truman Dam access road on County Road 620 just NE of Warsaw) **Warsaw** 65355
Phone: (660) 438-4465 www.facebook.com/pages/Lost-Valley-Fish-Hatchery/167823733230770
Hours: (Visitor Center) Tuesday-Saturday 9:00am-4:00pm (year-round).

The Lost Valley Fish Hatchery is the largest state-owned, warm water hatchery in Missouri and one of the largest in the nation. The hatchery houses a large visitors center, where guests can learn about the fish. A variety of exhibits focusing on fishing and aquatic themes include an over-sized native Missouri mussel model, a model of hatchery water flow, how to legally measure fish, computer games, fishing line knot- tying, and many other demonstrations and displays. The visitor may view the hatchery production room from two large windows inside the visitor center. A scenic pullout on the access road overlooks most of the rearing ponds and a portion of Truman Lake. Fishing for youth 15 years of age and younger is allowed in a pond on site during Visitor Center hours. Tackle and bait are available at the Visitors Center. There is no charge for fishing or the use of the equipment or bait.

OLD STAGECOACH STOP

(Downtown - On the east side of the square, in the middle of the block on Linn Street, sits the white two-story Old Stagecoach Stop) **Waynesville** 65583

Phone: (573) 762-9683 or (573) 435-6766 www.oldstagecoachstop.org
Admission: FREE.
Tours: Saturday 10:00am-4:00pm (April-September). A tour with a guide in-period costume takes about 45 minutes.
Note: FROG ROCK is at 300 Historic Route 66. This huge rock is painted as a frog (named W.H. Croaker) and overlooks the city of Waynesville. Frog Fest is held in the frog's honor the first full weekend in May. Laughlin Park is not far away and has a spring for trout fishing, swimming or visitors can utilize the park's walking trail.

Built in 1854, the Old Stagecoach Stop is a 10-room-house museum where every room is NOT set up in the same time period. Each of the rooms has been restored to a different use or era in the building's history. It was used as a Civil War hospital, hotel, boarding house and dentist's office. The building is a two story structure. There are ten rooms, nine restored to various periods in the building's history (1854-now).

OLD SETTLERS DAY

Waynesville - The Old Stagecoach Stop sponsors this Old Settlers Day. It is the oldest city festival. Events are scheduled in the City Park, one block west, along with food and craft vendors. (last Saturday in July).

CRANE'S MUSEUM AND COUNTRY STORE

10665 Old Hwy 40 **Williamsburg** 63388

Phone: (573) 254-3311 www.cranesmuseum.org

The country store has lots of old-time and classic clothing and assorted gifts. Serves one-meat-one-cheese $1.00 dollar sandwiches.

The 1800s regional history museum displays rare toys, American Indian artifacts, primitive hardware and tools, a recreated 1929 White Eagle gas station and Victorian items. Marlene's Restaurant is an extension of Crane's Museum. Marlene's offers a full-service cafe environment serving sandwich plates for around $5.00 as well as an Old-Fashioned Ice Cream Parlor. Museum charges small admission to folks 10 and older. Open daily.

North East Area

Chapter 2
North East (NE)

QUICK LOOK...

Mark Twain Adventures

Lewis & Clark Explorations

The Mighty Mississippi

Gateway Arch & MonstroCity

Land of Museums (many FREE)

Alton, IL
- National Great Rivers Museum

Athens (Revere)
- Battle Of Athens State Historic Site

Ballwin
- Castlewood State Park

Clarksville
- Clarksville Visitor Center, River Heritage Center

Defiance
- Daniel Boone Home And Boonesfield Village

DeSoto
- Washington State Park

East St. Louis, IL
- Gateway Geyser
- Gateway Grizzlies

Eureka
- Route 66 State Park
- Six Flags St. Louis
- Wild Canid Survival & Research Center (Wolf Sanctuary)
- Yogi Bear's Jellystone Park Camp Resort

Festus
- The Pumpkin Patch

Florida
- Mark Twain Birthplace State Historic Site & Park

Glencoe
- Wabash Frisco And Pacific Steam Railway

Grafton, Il
- Pere Marquette State Park & Visitors Center
- Raging Rivers Waterpark

Gray Summit
- Purina Farms
- Shaw Nature Reserve

Hannibal
- Adventures Of Tom Sawyer Diorama Museum
- Big River Train Town
- Cameron Cave
- Hannibal Tours
- Mark Twain Boyhood Home Complex
- Mark Twain Cave Complex
- Mark Twain Dinette
- Mark Twain Himself
- Mark Twain Riverboat
- Molly Brown Birthplace & Museum
- Ole Planters Restaurant
- Sawyer's Creek Fun Park
- Paddlewheel Popcorn & Candy Company
- Tom Sawyer Days

Hartford, IL
- Camp River Dubois, Lewis & Clark State Historic Site

Hermann
- Deutschheim State Historic Site & Museum

Imperial
- Mastodon State Historic Site

Kahoka
- Clark County Mule Festival

Kirksville
- Still National Osteopathic Museum
- Thousand Hills State Park
- Shrine Pro Rodeo

La Grange
- Wakonda State Park

For updates & travel games visit: **www.KidsLoveTravel.com**

North East Area

La Plata
- Jackson Country Connections

Macon
- Long Branch State Park

Mexico
- Audrain Historical Society Museum Complex
- Binders Hilltop Apple And Berry Farm

Monroe City
- Mark Twain Landing

Montgomery City
- Graham Cave State Park

Robertsville
- Robertsville State Park

St. Charles
- Fast Lane Classic Cars
- First Missouri State Capitol State Historic Site
- Katy Trail State Park
- Lewis And Clark Boat House And Nature Center
- Rt Weiler's Restaurant
- Fete De Glace Ice Carving Competition
- Lewis And Clark Heritage Days
- Festival Of The Little Hills

St. Louis
- Double Key Treasure Hunts
- Flamingo Bowl
- HealthWorks
- Eat-Rite Diner
- Eugene Field House & St. Louis Toy Museum
- Gateway Arch
- Gateway Arch Riverboat Cruises
- St. Louis Cardinal's Busch Stadium Tours
- The Old Courthouse
- City Museum
- Scott Joplin House State Historic Site
- St Louis Blues Hockey
- Union Station
- Soulard Market
- Crown Candy Kitchen
- Bob Kramer's Marionnette Theater
- Earthways Center
- Ted Drewes Frozen Custard
- Forest Park
- Missouri Botanical Garden
- St. Louis Art Museum
- St. Louis Science Center
- St. Louis Zoo
- Missouri History Museum
- Miniature Museum Of Greater St. Louis
- Museum Of Transportation
- Grant's Farm
- America's Incredible Pizza Company
- Suson Park
- Old Chain Of Rocks Bridge
- The Hill
- St. Louis Storytelling Festival
- Celebrate St. Louis - Fair St. Louis
- St. Louis Holiday Magic

St. Louis (Chesterfield)
- Faust Park

St. Louis (Fenton)
- Swing-A-Round Fun Town

St. Louis (Ferguson)
- Challenger Learning Center - St. Louis

St. Louis (Hazelwood)
- Big Foot 4 X 4 Inc.
- St. Louis Mills Mall, Sportstreet

St. Louis (Kirkwood)
- Magic House: St. Louis Children's Museum
- Powder Valley Conservation Nature Center
- Laumeier Sculpture Park

St. Louis (Lemay)
- Jefferson Barracks Historic Park

St. Louis (Maryland Heights)
- Aquaport

- Thies Farm & Greenhouses

St. Louis (University City)
- Fitz's American Grill & Bottling Co.

St. Louis (White Haven)
- Ulysses S. Grant National Historic Site

Troy
- Cuivre River State Park

Valley Park
- World Bird Sanctuary

Wayland
- Iliniwek Village State Historic Site

West Alton
- Jones - Confluence State Park

Wildwood
- Babler Memorial State Park
- Hidden Valley Ski Resort

For updates & travel games visit: **www.KidsLoveTravel.com**

North East Area   31

Sites and attractions are listed in order by City, Zip Code, and Name. Symbols indicated represent: 🍽 Restaurants   🛏 Lodging

RIVER FERRIES OVER THE MISSISSIPPI RIVER INTO ILLINOIS

www.greatriverroad.com/SecondaryPages/ferries.htm
Note: If you are planning a visit to any of the ferries in the Middle Mississippi Valley and believe the ferries might not be operating due to flood conditions or ice please call the numbers below for current information.

Early American ferries consisted of rafts, rowboats and horse boats that could cross rivers where demand for transportation existed but where there weren't any easy crossings. The advent of railroads and bridges put most ferries out of business and motorized vessels replaced the earlier forms of transportation of those that survived. For modern travelers, the remaining ferries in operation can save time as well as providing scenic river views.

GOLDEN EAGLE FERRY - (618) 396-2535. This ferry takes vehicles across the Mississippi River between the small town of Golden Eagle in Calhoun County in Illinois and St. Charles County in Missouri. To reach the Golden Eagle Ferry from Pere Marquette State Park or Grafton, cross the Brussels Ferry and continue on County Road 1 until you see the signs directing you to the ferry. From the Missouri side of the Mississippi River take MO-94 to County Road B north of St. Charles. Take CR-B west to Golden Eagle Ferry Road. Take Golden Eagle Ferry Road to the ferry. Daily from 8:00am-9:00pm. Toll fees: Car or pickup truck $8.00 one-way or $15.00 round trip. Motorcycles $5.00, $4.00 bicycles or $3.00 pedestrians.

GRAFTON FERRY - (636) 899-0600. The Grafton Ferry is located on the Illinois side at the foot of Illinois Route 3, just upriver of the Grafton public boat ramp. On the Missouri side, it terminates just off of Grafton Ferry Road alongside the St. Charles County Airport. From there it is a short ride to highway 94 and about 10 miles to the St. Charles city line. Toll Fees: $8.00 one way, $5.00 for motorcycles, $4.00 for bicycles, & $3.00 for pedestrians with reduced rates for round trips. Daily except major winter holidays.

NATIONAL GREAT RIVERS MUSEUM

2 Lock and Dam Way, Melvin Price Lock & Dam Illinois Route 3 intersects I-270 approx. two miles east of the Mississippi River. Take IL Route 3 North to Hwy 143 west 2 miles) **East Alton, IL 62024**

Phone: (877) 462-6979 **www.meetingoftherivers.org**
Hours: Daily 9:00am-5:00pm except major winter holidays.
Admission: FREE.
Tours: Free tours of the Melvin Price Locks and Dam are conducted daily at 10:00am, 1:00pm and 3:00pm. Also explained are what causes floods, with emphasis on the Great Flood of 1993 and how the Corps of Engineers fights these destructive acts of nature, and what future strategies are being developed to limit their impact.
Educators: They have a in-house link (**www.meetingoftherivers.org/html/teacher_resources.html**) to an amazing array of simple and in-depth lessons, games and projects related to navigation and water science of great rivers-all presented on a very teachable level.

The Museum features state of the art interactive displays and exhibits that help visitors understand the many aspects of the Mississippi River and how humans interact with it. A large model of the bluffs of the region is in the center of the museum and provides info on the various wildlife from prairie plants and trees to birds and other animals. An aquarium displays the various species of fish that inhabit the Mississippi River. Stir river sediment banks; make a stairway of water; or make your own map. One display explains how the Mississippi has been used as a highway, not only by humans but by migrating waterfowl, and chronicles the different types of vessels used from canoes to steamboats to modern day barges. The Pilot House simulator allows visitors to see what it's like to guide a 1,000 foot tow of barges under a bridge or through a lock. We took on the challenge (harder than it seems) of steering a barge as a parent/child team and finally successfully made it through. This activity, and the dam tour, are the kids' favorites. It sure is eventful when a big barge comes through during the 45-minute lock tour!

BATTLE OF ATHENS STATE HISTORIC SITE

Hwy. CC **Athens (Revere) 63465**

Phone: (660) 877-3871 **https://mostateparks.com/park/battle-athens-state-historic-site**
Admission: The Missouri state park system does not charge entrance fees. However, there are fees associated with camping, lodging, tours, museums and special events.
Tours: Tours of the Thome-Benning House are offered free of charge. From April through early October, they are available Wednesday-Sunday 10:00am-4:00pm. Friday-Sunday rest of October.

The Battle of Athens State Historic Site interprets the battle, town history, and contains buildings that were part of the once-thriving town. Today, the historic

For updates & travel games visit: **www.KidsLoveTravel.com**

North East Area

site encompasses much of the former town of Athens. Several buildings have been preserved and are undergoing restoration. Foremost is the Thome-Benning house, locally known as "the Cannonball House," which still exhibits two holes made through the kitchen walls by a cannonball during the battle. Visitors can tour the house, visit the Thome mill ruins, participate in guided tours of the historic town site or take advantage of numerous recreation opportunities. There are hiking trails, a lake for fishing, picnic areas, a playground, a campground and 1.5 miles of Des Moines River frontage.

CASTLEWOOD STATE PARK

1401 Kiefer Creek Road **Ballwin** 63021

Phone: (636) 227-4433   https://mostateparks.com/park/castlewood-state-park
Admission: The Missouri state park system does not charge entrance fees. However, there are fees associated with camping, lodging, tours, museums and special events.

The Meramed River, with limestone bluffs towering above it, flows through this park, making it popular for canoeing and fishing. The park is great for day-use activities like picnicking, hiking, mountain biking and horseback riding. River Scene Trail: this three-mile loop is the most spectacular trail in the park and highlights the park's most memorable features. The trail climbs to and then traverses a series of bluffs overlooking the Meramec River. It then goes down a long wood staircase that takes you from the top of the bluffs to the valley below. From there, the trail takes you through an up-close and personal look at the river and the bottomland surrounding it. Along the way, you will pass panoramic vistas, remnants of the historic resort era and floodplain forest. This trail is designated for hiking and bicycling (hiking only on the bluff portion).

CLARKSVILLE VISITOR CENTER, RIVER HERITAGE CENTER

204 North 2nd Street **Clarksville** 63336

Phone: (573) 242-3132   www.clarksvillemo.us/visitorscenter.html
Hours: Friday-Monday 11am-4pm.
Note: While kids may not be interested in shopping in historic downtowns, they may like Clarksville. Several varied artists have set up shop here such as: Clarksville Glassworks, Bee Naturals, The Bent Tree Gallery, Dawn of Creation Art Studio and the Great River Pottery and Wood Shop. You'll find these working artist shops on First and Second Streets. Often, the artist is in residence to demo their work.

500 foot bluffs overlook the Mississippi River. This Center contains large displays and hundreds of items and artifacts relative to the various cultural societies that lived along the Mississippi, Illinois and Missouri rivers.

Displays span the last 100 years, but the emphasis is on tools and equipment used during 1870-1970 period by the families living along the rivers. Displays include commercial and sport fisheries, the mussel-shell pearl button industry, water fowling, furbearer harvesting, family fish markets, vintage boats and outboard motors, and a typical river man's workshop.

The center has a viewing platform with a spotting scope. It looks out onto the Mississippi River, and the U.S. Lock and Dam #24, providing a close vantage point to view all river boat and barge traffic and a 'front row seat' in the midst of one of the largest winter migrating areas for the bald eagles.

EAGLE DAYS

Clarksville - Visitors Center. Special exhibits, guided eagle-viewing tours and live eagle exhibits. Every winter bald eagles come to this town to fish along the river bluffs and around the locks. FREE. (late January weekend)

HISTORIC DANIEL BOONE HOME AT LINDENWOOD PARK

1868 Highway F (I-70 or Hwy 40-61 to Hwy. 94 south then 5 miles west on Hwy F) **Defiance** 63341

Phone: (636) 798-2005   http://sccmo.org/1701/The-Historic-Daniel-Boone-Home
Hours: Daily 9:00am-5:00pm. Sunday 11:30am-5:00pm.
Admission: (1-hour tour) $8.00 adult, $6.00 senior (55+), $5.00 child (5-12).
Tours: Tours start on the hour. FREEBIES: Previsit Activity Sheet: www.danielboonehome.com/docs/2013/PreVisitActivitySheet.pdf

This site offers visitors a look at life as a frontiersman. The Boone Home is nearly 200 years old and it's where Daniel Boone lived later in life and died. Costumed guides give one hour tour of the home and the 19th century village buildings focusing on Boone family history and life on the frontier. (Buildings available in the village are the schoolhouse, dressmaker's shop, carpenter's shop, Old Peace Chapel, general store, grist mill, and home of Squire Boone.) In the school house, students can quickly pretend they are a pioneer student. Before each tour there is a 10 minute video of Daniel Boone's Life shown in the theater.

WASHINGTON STATE PARK

13041 State Hwy 104   **DeSoto** 63020

Phone: (636) 586-0322   https://mostateparks.com/park/washington-state-park
Admission: The Missouri state park system does not charge entrance fees. However, there are fees associated with camping, lodging, tours, museums and special events.

For updates & travel games visit: **www.KidsLoveTravel.com**

North East Area

This park was once a ceremonial ground for prehistoric Indians. Today, petroglyphs - American Indian rock carvings - are a special attraction. These carvings, or petroglyphs, are believed to have been made around A.D. 1,000 and give clues to the lives of the prehistoric Indians who once inhabited this part of Missouri. In addition to a lodge, there are quaint stone hiking shelters, a picnic pavilion, and the beautifully laid stone slabs that make up the 1,000 Steps Trail. The three hiking trails at Washington State Park provide every experience, from an easy stroll with bluff-top views of the river to a vigorous excursion through 10 miles of rugged Ozark terrain. The park offers a pool, float trips, cabins, hiking and backpacking trails, a store and camping.

GATEWAY GEYSER

185 W. Trendley Avenue (Front Street and Trendley Avenue)
East St. Louis, IL 62201

Phone: (618) 346-4905 www.hydrodramatics.com/gateway_geyser.htm
Hours: The Geyser Fountain runs from April thru October. It usually runs a few times a day at Noon, 3:00pm, 6:00pm, 9:00pm daily, but only for 15 minutes. Schedule subject to change. Admission: FREE.

Currently the tallest fountain in the world, the Gateway Geyser rises as a testimonial to the engineering expertise and 16-year effort of Hydro Dramatics. Soaring to nearly 630-feet, the geyser's height mirrors that of St. Louis' famed Gateway Arch, located directly across the Mississippi River. The center fountain is complemented by four auxiliary fountains, which represent the four rivers that converge in the St. Louis area. The "park" setting around the geyser is FREE of charge to wander through.

GATEWAY GRIZZLIES

GCS Stadium (I-70 exit IL 3 south. The stadium faces riverfront St. Louis)
East St. Louis, IL 62206

Phone: (618) 337-3000 www.gatewaygrizzlies.com

The Gateway Grizzlies minor league baseball team plays in the outdoor GCS Stadium. The 6,000 seat stadium includes reserved box seats, picnic table seats (for families/groups), general and lawn seats. This stadium is the area's own "field of dreams," It's minor league baseball at its finest in a small venue and for a small price. Game tickets run $6.00-$12.00. There's a kids zone area where children can climb and play ball on their "turf." They get the kids involved on the field and every week there are theme nights.

ROUTE 66 STATE PARK

97 North Outer Road **Eureka** 63025

Phone: (636) 938-7198 https://mostateparks.com/park/route-66-state-park
Hours: Visitor Center: 9:00am-4:30pm daily (April thru October). Weekends only (November to mid-December). Closed winters.
Admission: The Missouri state park system does not charge entrance fees. However, there are fees associated with camping, lodging, tours, museums and certain special events.

In Eureka, the 419-acre Route 66 State Park includes picnic areas, walking trails and a visitor center offering a peek into the past with artifacts and displays from the route's 82-year history. Route 66 State Park showcases the history and mystique of a highway that has been called "The Main Street of America."

Bridgehead Inn, a 1935 roadhouse, serves as Route 66 State Park's visitor center. It houses Route 66 memorabilia and interprets the environmental success story of the former resort community of Times Beach, which once thrived on the location of the park. A gift shop, specializing in hundreds of Route 66 items, is also located in the visitor center building. Although the kids may only recognize the black-n-white Route 66 road signs on display, they'll have fun looking at the corny neon signs and pictures.

SIX FLAGS ST. LOUIS

4900 Six Flags Road (I-44 exit 261) **Eureka** 63025

Phone: (636) 938-4800 www.sixflags.com/stlouis
Hours: Vary by season. Open daily in summer 10:30am-9:00pm. Hurricane Harbor closes at 8:00pm. Call or visit website for Spring/Fall hours.
Admission: $66.99 General, $51.99 (child under 48"). Ages 2 and under are FREE. Significant online discounts are available. Parking $15.00. Additional fees for some concerts and special events.

Six Flags St. Louis continues its tradition of bringing new thrills to the popular theme park. Admission to the park also includes the Hurricane Harbor water park for the same price. The water park has expanded with the exciting Wahoo Racer attraction. Six Flags has also added a spectacular nighttime parade, appropriately named "Glow in the Park" and several live stage shows. The littlest visitors will enjoy pint-sized rides and friendly characters in Looney Tunes Town while bigger brothers and sisters can experience more than 100 rides and attractions throughout the park. Special events including Fright Fest in October and the Country Fair in the fall extend the season of fun well beyond summer.

For updates & travel games visit: www.KidsLoveTravel.com

North East Area

ENDANGERED WOLF CENTER

6750 Tyson Valley Road (Washington University property, 20 miles southwest of ST. Louis) **Eureka** 63025

Phone: (636) 938-5900 www.endangeredwolfcenter.org
Admission: $15 adult, $12 child (4-14).
Tours: The Tour is a 1.5 hour guided walking tour of the wolf enclosures. The walk is outdoors and a 1/2 mile round trip. Public tours are offered Fridays, Saturdays and Sundays. On a public tour you are grouped with other visitors. Public tours start at 1:00pm. Optional Tours are available at additional cost and start at 9:30am. Advance Reservations are required.
FREEBIES: a free download of the WolfQuest: Survival of the Pack computer game is available here: *www.endangeredwolfcenter.org/educational-resources/*

The place was founded in the 1970's to help promote the survival of the wolf, which has become endangered all over the world. The original founder was Wild Kingdom host Marlin Perkins. All fees you are charged go directly to this effort. The tour begins indoors with a movie as well as other hands-on activities while learning about the evolution of the wolf through fossils, paw prints and old pelts Outside, endangered wolves are born and reared on the property for reintroduction to the wild. Your guide will lead you on the trail to view the wolves and African wild dogs and swift foxes that live in their own packs in natural areas. (FYI wear comfortable shoes, flip flops are not the appropriate footwear for this trek.) Evening campfire programs share how wolves communicate - with live "sound bites."

YOGI BEAR'S JELLYSTONE PARK CAMP RESORT

5300 Fox Creek Road **Eureka** 63025

Phone: (800) 861-3020 www.eurekajellystone.com

Conveniently located just ¼ mile from the gate of Six Flags and nestled among 35 wooded acres; this family resort offers all the fun and adventure of a back-to-nature vacation combined with first class resort amenities including FREE WIFI, pool, mini-golf, video arcade, train rides, arts & crafts, a variety of outdoor games, and daily character visits from Yogi Bear. A full time Rec Director is on hand. Exciting theme events and planned activities change weekly.

The large campground has sites for all sizes of RVs or the resort's cozy cottages. Each cottage sleeps six and features two bedrooms, kitchen, bath, and sitting area. A covered dining porch and outdoor grill make family picnics a breeze. Plus, each cottage has a fire pit so your family can end the perfect day roasting S'mores and telling tales around the campfire. Hookups are around $30 and cabins range from $80-$120 per night.

SANTA'S MAGICAL KINGDOM

Eureka - Yogi Bear's Jellystone Park is transformed into a magical paradise that includes a thirty-five-acre display of animated scenes, spectacular special effects, and millions of lights celebrating the holiday season.

THE PUMPKIN PATCH

Festus - 14560 Dry Fork Road. **www.albesm.com/pumpkinpatch/pumpkinpatch.html** Phone: (636) 931-3901. In the fall, there's a corn maze, children's train rides, apple butter making and weekend wagon rides down to the pumpkin patch. Wagon ride and corn maze free. (pumpkin patch begins late September thru October)

MARK TWAIN BIRTHPLACE ST HISTORIC SITE

37352 Shrine Road **Florida** 65283

Phone: (573) 565-3449 https://mostateparks.com/park/mark-twain-birthplace-state-historic-site

Admission: The Missouri state park system does not charge entrance fees. However, there are fees associated with camping, lodging, tours, museums and certain special events.

Tours: From November through March, the museum is open Friday through Sunday from 10:00am-4:30pm with the exception of Thanksgiving, Christmas and New Year's days. Tours are offered during these times. The museum is closed Monday through Thursday. Summertime, the museum is open daily. A fee of $2.50-$4.00 is charged for the tours.

Note: near town (24000 Route 107, in the Mark Twain Lake area) is GRANDMAS COUNTRY MUSIC SHOW featuring live country music on the first, third and fifth Saturdays of each month. Kiddies FREE. Admission for those over 10.

The two-room cabin where Samuel Langhorne Clemens was born is on-site, surrounded by a modern museum with memorabilia of Mark Twain, the name Clemens adopted as a writer. Exhibits and audio visual programs dot the perimeter of the cabin (indoors). They have a handwritten manuscript of the Adventures of Tom Sawyer on display. The Visitors Center has a bird watching station for waterfowl. The park overlooks Mark Twain Lake and offers fishing, boating, hiking trails, campsites and swimming beaches.

WABASH FRISCO AND PACIFIC STEAM RAILWAY

109 Grand Avenue (Old State Road & Washington Street) **Glencoe** 63038

Phone: (636) 587-3538 **www.wfprr.com**
Hours: The Railroad is open every Sunday, May through October rain or shine. Trains start their scheduled departures from the station at 11:00am with trains departing about every 20 minutes. The final train leaves at 4:15pm. The ride is a two-mile round trip lasting about 30 minutes and travels along the scenic Meramec River.

For updates & travel games visit: **www.KidsLoveTravel.com**

Admission: A $4.00 donation is asked per ticket. Children 3 years & under ride free.

Just outside of St. Louis is this 12-inch-gauge miniature steam railroad that takes passengers on a two-mile round trip ride along the scenic Meramec River every Sunday, May through October. The ride takes only about 30 minutes. Afterwards, picnic at the tables near the station. Perfect place to bring that young model train fan.

PERE MARQUETTE STATE PARK VISITORS CTR

Illinois Route 100 (take the ferry over from St. Charles to Grafton)
Grafton, IL 62037

Phone: (618) 786-3323 or (618) 786-2331 (Lodge)
https://www.dnr.illinois.gov/Parks/Pages/PereMarquette.aspx
Admission: Admission to Illinois State Parks is FREE. Camping and lodge fees apply for overnights.
Tours: The Sam Vadalabene Bike Trail runs from this State Park to the City of Alton, approx. 20 miles. The entire trail is paved and a map is available showing the location of historic sites, restaurants, and local attractions.
Note: The Lodge consists of both new facilities as well as those constructed by the CCC. Native stone and rustic timbers of the original Lodge blend with the new to provide first class accommodations in an historical setting. The mammoth stone fireplace in the lobby soars to a roof height of 50 feet. There are 50 spacious guest rooms and 22 stone guest cabin rooms. Among the facilities available are a restaurant, gift shop, indoor swimming pool, whirlpool, game room and tennis court.

Pere Marquette State Park comprises over 8,000 acres making it Illinois' largest state park. Named for Jacques Marquette, a French missionary who was a member of a European expedition led by Louis Joliet. They were the first Europeans to reach the confluence of the Mississippi and Illinois rivers. A large stone cross located east of the main park entrance along Route 100 commemorates their historic landing. The park is famous for the beauty of its fall colors and as a home for bald eagles in the winter. In addition to the spectacular views of the Illinois and Mississippi rivers from several scenic overlooks (can you find the Piasa Bird?), visitors can take advantage of a variety of year-round recreational activities, including hiking, biking, horseback riding, camping, fishing, boating, and taking part in interpretative programs. The Visitor Center welcomes you with a three-dimensional map of the park, a 300-gallon aquarium, and a wealth of other displays and exhibits concerning the Illinois River, wildlife habitats, local history and geology. Pere Marquette Lodge provides elegant dining, with a Sunday brunch that draws people from Missouri as well as Illinois. The dining room seats 150 people and offers a choice of family style dining or selections from the menu. Many comment that this is a nice haven to escape to quiet nature.

RAGING RIVERS WATERPARK

100 Palisades Parkway (along Great River Road, take Grafton ferry or bridge to Alton) **Grafton, IL** 62037

Phone: (618) 786-2345 www.ragingrivers.com
Hours: Daily 10:30am to 6:00pm or later (Memorial Day Weekend-Labor Day).
Admission: $21.95-$25.95 per person (age 3+). Save $5.00 after 3:00pm. Parking $5.00.
Note: Locker rooms, showers, concessions. No coolers.

Raging Rivers WaterPark is cool when it's hot! Form the zoomin' Cascade Body Flumes, to the tube (or tubeless) wave pool, to a lazy Endless River, there's something for everyone. SwirlPool is a two-bowl attraction that's really 3 rides in one. Slide quickly down the tunnel flume, spin swiftly in the giant vortex, then drop into a deep pool of water. (for the more daring, try this ride at night) The milder Runaway Rafts Ride takes you on a 600 foot long journey down the hillside and then thru swift water and wild rapids. Or, ride the tubed Shark Slide that floats down a flume into a catch pool. Itty Bitty Surf City and TreeHouse Harbor are for the younger set.

PURINA FARMS

200 Checkerboard Drive (I-44 west past Six Flags over Mid-America to the Gray Summit exit. Turn right onto Hwy 100) **Gray Summit** 63039

Phone: (314) 982-3232 www.purinafarms.com
Hours: Daily 9:30am-3:30pm. Wagon rides 10am-3pm.
Admission: Free admission and parking, however, a nominal fee may be charged for special events.
Note: Purina Farms Store to pick up Purina mementos or breed-specific sculptures, ornaments and shirts. Snack bar.

Purina Farms combines a tourist center and two canine competition areas. Show and field events as well as hands-on activities and exhibits reinforce the bond between pets and their people. The Visitors Center hosts regularly scheduled obedience shows and grooming demonstrations. Plus, the center has interactive stations like Scent Boxes (lets you smell how a dog smells things) and Vision displays show the differences between your vision and that of dogs and cats.

Instead of just displaying Purina products and benefits, the complex features more of a petting zoo. Kids can pet Purina's own dogs and cats, milk a cow, and play in the hayloft at the Farm Animal Barn. The Pet Center building's key attraction is a 20-foot-tall, multilevel cat house, complete with windows, stairways, rocking chairs and other furnishings, creating a feline paradise. A staircase surrounding the structure provides visitors with an eye-level view of the cat house's inhabitants. Kind of a huge dollhouse (cat house) that you can walk around!

The Canine Competition Center is designed specifically for field and test competition with a spacious arena for herding trials and tests, lure coursing and whippet races.

SHAW NATURE RESERVE
Hwy. 100 & I-44 **Gray Summit** 63039

Phone: (636) 451-3512 **www.shawnature.org**
Hours: (Nature Reserve) Daily, 7:00am until sunset. (Visitor Center) Monday-Friday 8:30am-4:30pm, Saturday & Sunday 9:00am-5:00pm. (Bascom House) Monday-Sunday 10:00am-4:00pm.
Admission: $5.00 adult, $3.00 senior (65+) & students, Child 12 & under-FREE
Tours: April – October. Weekdays: 10 a.m. to 4 p.m., departing every hour on the hour. Weekends: 9:30 a.m. to 4:10 p.m., departing every 40 minutes.

The Nature Reserve is dedicated to returning the land to its condition before European-style agriculture. Plant scientists are actively reintroducing "heritage" plants to this reserve to grow alongside almost 1,000 species of native plants. Glades are the "crown jewels" of habitat preservation at the nature reserve. Glades are sunny areas where rock is at the surface, so the land can't be used for crops. The starting point of the woodland trail system, trails departing here lead visitors through glades, prairie, woodlands, and bottomland forests, and provide access to the Meramec River. Restrooms, drinking water, and a sheltered picnic area are available.

If you want a "Little House on the Prairie" feel, take the tram tours. The narrated wagon ride travels the 3 mile Trail House Loop Road, with stops at the Trail House and wetland bus stop. $4.00 per person. It's a great way to shorten the hike to the river or to the wetlands if you have small children or non-hikers in your group. Get off at either stop and get picked up later. You'll feel like a pioneer heading west as you hear about comparisons to early pioneer life and what living conditions were like. Would you rather live in a teepee or a sod house? Near the end of the trail, you'll see a real sod house built into the side of an earthen mound.

ADVENTURES OF TOM SAWYER DIORAMA MUSEUM

323 N. Main Street (next to historic Grant's Drug Store, down the hill and around the corner from the Mark Twain Home and Museum.)
Hannibal 63401

Phone: (314) 221-3525
Hours: Monday-Friday 8:00am-6:00pm, Saturday & Sunday 9:00am-5:00pm.

An excellent overview of Mark Twain's The Adventures Of Tom Sawyer can be seen in these sixteen hand carved scenes. Art Sieving spent five years creating these dioramas, his painstaking artistry evident in every detail. Look for the scene of tom whitewashing the fence, tom and Becky on Jackson's Island and then in a cave. A candy shop is in the front portion of the building.

BIG RIVER TRAIN TOWN

320 N 3rd Street **Hannibal** 63401

Phone: (573) 221-1966. https://www.facebook.com/Big-River-Train-Town-116314118392860/
Hours: 10am-5pm daily. Small admission.

All Aboard! To Train Town. Where toy trains come alive. New and Vintage toy trains. Take a journey to a time where the Golden Age of railroading and toy trains were a part of most everyone's life. So stroll back and enjoy our operating and interactive layouts, along with toy train memorabilia and a depot store. Bring your camera and smiles. Open Daily.

CAMERON CAVE

300 Cave Hollow Road (1 mile South of Hannibal on Highway 79)
Hannibal 63401

Phone: (573) 221-1656 www.marktwaincave.com
Hours: Daily 9:00am-6:00pm (most days). Open until 8:00pm most summer days. 10:00am-4:00pm (November-March).
Admission: $20.95 adult, $12.95 child (6-12), $5.00 child (5 and under). Additional fees for other activities and tour upgrades.
Tours begin at Mark Twain Cave Visitors Center.

Visit the Northern Hemisphere's most complex cave, Cameron Cave, Missouri's newest show cave. You'll see the cave nearly as it was when first discovered. This lantern guided tour takes you through this complex maze cave. The tour last 1 ½ hours and several visitors on the tour will carry lanterns. This is a natural cave with no artificial or artistic lighting. Guests lanterns casting shadow (and light) on formations makes this cave feel like you're in a mystery

North East Area   43

novel. Don't a lot of the formations look like honeycombs? There are only 3 maze type caves in North America and two of them are right here!

HANNIBAL TROLLEY
220 N Main Hannibal 63401

Phone: (573) 221-1161. Admission Charged. Call for current rates.

Along the Mississippi River you come across a little town that Mark Twain made famous. Twain grew up here on the banks of the river and featured this town in some of his best-loved stories. Just as the trolleys that once "clanged" their bells along Hannibal's streets, the Hannibal Trolley Company also serves as transportation to and from some of Hannibal's attractions. 60 minute tour hits all the important stops in town. You may depart and re-board our trolley at the Mark Twain Cave, Sawyer's Creek, Rockcliffe Mansion, and the depot. Trolleys run open air in summer months and are enclosed in early spring and late fall.

MARK TWAIN BOYHOOD HOME COMPLEX
120 North Main Street Hannibal 63401

Phone: (573) 221-9010 www.marktwainmuseum.org
Hours: Daily, 9:00am-5:00pm (April-early January). Daily 10am-4pm (winter).
Admission: $12.00 adult, $10.00 senior (60+), $6.00 child (6-17).
Tours: There are a total of 8 properties to see. We suggest at least 90 minutes to view all of the buildings.
Educators: Wonderful creative writing and reading comprehension for various ages is found under the Education icon>For Teachers>Lesson Plans. Note: Annually on Memorial Day weekend in September, Main Street Hannibal honors Mark Twain and his literary works with a Twain literature-inspired theme festival. Festival goers are encouraged to dress in theme attire.

A tour of the museum properties includes the actual buildings that inspired many famous scenes in Samuel Clemens' (pen name Mark Twain), most well-known novels, including The Adventures of Tom Sawyer and Adventures of Huckleberry Finn. The museum includes 8 properties where young Sam Clemens lived, played and had the adventures he would later use as inspiration for his stories. The Interpretive Center, located directly behind the Mark Twain Boyhood Home, begins the visitor experience.

Visitors may then visit the Huck Finn House, a reproduction of the home of Tom Blankenship, the young boy Twain knew in his youth and later labeled as the model for Huckleberry Finn.

Visitors are then directed to the Boyhood Home, the house that inspired Twain's imagination. Life size white figures of an adult Twain residing in each room give visitors the feeling of returning with Twain to the boyhood home of his memories. Visitors can almost imagine a young Sam Clemens sneaking out the window, like Tom in The Adventures of Tom Sawyer. Be sure to notice the stairwell going to the second floor at the inside of the house, and then remember Tom Sawyer sneaking in to overhear Aunt Polly and the others planning the boys' funeral. On summer afternoons, Mark Twain re-enactors begin conversations with guests, in character.

Across the street stands the Becky Thatcher House, the childhood home of Laura Hawkins, immortalized in The Adventures of Tom Sawyer as Becky Thatcher. There is a Children's Play Discovery Area as well, where children can dress up as Becky or Tom would have in the mid-1800s or play some games that were also popular in that time period, such as checkers. The site also serves as a bookstore with a large selection of Twain's books and many children's classics and souvenirs.

Next door is the Justice of the Peace Office. This is J.M. Clemens Law Office where Samuel Clemen's father presided as Justice of the Peace. The courtroom here provided the inspiration for the trial scene in Tom Sawyer. Samuel's dad died when he was 11 and he was taken from school and placed in the office of the Hannibal Courier as a printer's apprentice.

The next museum building is Grant's Drug Store. It is set up like an old drug store in Sam Clemens' day with bottles of herbs and treatments arranged on shelves.

The Museum Gallery, located on Main Street just two blocks south of the Boyhood Home holds a wealth of Twain artifacts, exhibits featuring scenes from five of Twain's most popular books as well as a replica steamboat pilot house. The first floor features five of Twain's books. You can walk through a simulated cave as Tom Sawyer or sit on a raft similar to the one that took Huck Finn down the river. Actual artifacts include Mark Twain's writing desk, white linen coat, top hat and well-worn pipe. Upstairs is more of an art gallery with many drawings done by Norman Rockwell as illustrations of editions of Tom Sawyer and Huckleberry Finn books. Although he left Hannibal in 1853, Clemens didn't begin writing "The Adventures of Tom Sawyer" until 20 years later.

After your day in Hannibal, we promise your kids will feel like they were dropped into the middle of Twain's books. Don't be surprised if your kids act

For updates & travel games visit: **www.KidsLoveTravel.com**

out scenes from Twains tales as they wander the old-fashioned town streets.

DID YOU KNOW? For a $10.00 contribution to the endowment fund they will let you sign the whitewashed fence outside.

MARK TWAIN CAVE COMPLEX

300 Cave Hollow Road **Hannibal** 63401

Phone: (573) 221-1656 **www.marktwaincave.com**
Hours: Daily 9:00am-6:00pm most spring & fall days. Open until 8:00pm (summer). Daily 10:00am-4:00pm (November-March).
Admission: $18.95 adult, $9.95 child (6-12), $4.00 (5 and under). Upgraded tours available at additional fees.
Tours: Allow 60-90 minutes for tour.
Note: Walkways are level and smooth and there are no steps. Persons of any age can easily make the tour. Bring a light wrap as the cave is 52 degrees year around. Wear sensible walking shoes and be sure to bring your camera. Just a few steps away across the creek from the Visitor Center is Sticks and Stones and a sluice where kids of all ages can pan for semi-precious gemstones (extra fee). MARK TWAIN CAVE CAMPGROUNDS are on location for RV or tent camping w/ hookups, showers, playground. **www.marktwaincave.com/campground.html**.

Samuel Clemens explored the cave as a child, and later, under the pen name of Mark Twain, wrote about his adventures. Mark Twain wrote, "By and by somebody shouted, "Who's ready for the cave? Everybody was. Bundles of candles were procured and straight away there was a general scamper up the hill." The historic tour begins with a video presentation which explains the geology of caves and how this particular cave was discovered. An experienced guide will escort you on a one-hour tour featuring points of interest mentioned in five of Mark Twain's writings. Visit the Mark Twain Cave where Tom and Becky got lost while running from Injun Joe. Other formations to look for are Aladdin's Palace and the Cathedral. The cave was also a hideout for the notorious outlaw Jesse James and provided refuge for slaves seeking freedom via the Underground Railroad. What is really a dull cave suddenly is full of intrigue as stories are woven and images conjured up in kids minds.

MARK TWAIN DINETTE

Hannibal - *400 N. 3rd Street (Historic District next to Mark Twain Home) 63401. Phone: (573) 221-5511.* **https://marktwaindinette.com/** Lunch and dinner buffet daily plus a large menu to choose from. Saturday & Sunday Breakfast Buffet, full menu upon request. Outdoor seating available. Breakfast w/ super buffets on weekends, burgers, tenderloin, catfish specialty for dinner. Try the homemade root beer. Open daily 6:00am-9:00pm.

MARK TWAIN HIMSELF

Planter's Barn Theater, 319 North Main Street **Hannibal** 63401

Phone: (573) 231-0021 or (866) 492-0021 **www.heritagestage.com**
Hours: Call or visit website for current schedule.
Admission: $16.00 adult, $14.00 senior & child.

Just a few steps from the Mark Twain Boyhood Home and Museum is a live, one man show that captures Twain's humor and satire. Performing on the 1849 stage in a barn on Dead Man's Alley (same stage as Clemens played), the actor Twain returns to the bank of the Mississippi River. Laugh along with Tom Sawyer and catch a glimpse of America through the eyes of Huckleberry Finn. Seasonally they put on a show titled A Shepherd's Tale (Christmas season), all presented by veteran actor Richard Garey. Served with lots of laughter and a Victorian Tea of cake, cookies, coffee, and tea, this is great theater.

MARK TWAIN RIVERBOAT

100 Center Street (foot of Center Street at the Mississippi River - Center Street Landing) **Hannibal** 63401

Phone: (573) 221-3222 **www.marktwainriverboat.com**
Hours: (Sightseeing) Daily @ 11:00am, 1:30pm & 4:00pm (Memorial Day week-Labor Day), Daily @ 1:30pm & 4:00pm (September & October). Boarding begins 30 minutes before departure.
Admission: (Sightseeing) $20.00 adult (13+), $12.00 child (5-12).
Tours: Various cruises available but the Sightseeing tour features commentary on river history, legends, and sights. This cruise features an open snack bar with sandwiches and beverages. No reservations are required for the sightseeing cruises.

To Mark Twain, the most exciting aspect of growing up in Hannibal was living just two blocks from the Mississippi River, and there was nothing he was prouder of in later years than his career as a riverboat pilot. Today a nostalgic riverboat named after Twain plies the mighty river giving visitors the opportunity to experience a taste of "Life on the Mississippi." During the day, the Mark Twain Riverboat offers One Hour Sightseeing Cruises.

MOLLY BROWN BIRTHPLACE & MUSEUM

600 Butler Street **Hannibal** 63401

Phone: (573) 221-2477 **www.visitmollybrown.com**
Hours: Thursday, Friday, Saturday eacn summer 10am-4pm.
Admission: $4.00 adult, $3.00 child.

Did you know Molly Brown was on her way to Hannibal when the Titanic went down? Come learn more about this "Unsinkable" heroine of the Titanic…a woman of means who still had a Midwestern mentality to work hard to survive

For updates & travel games visit: **www.KidsLoveTravel.com**

(she coordinated rowing activities to keep the lifeboat moving and keep the frightened women warm). The story circulated that when first interviewed by reporters in New York, they asked to what she attributed her survival. "Typical Brown luck," she supposedly said, "We're unsinkable." The label stuck, and she became a national celebrity. Visit the place where America's most fascinating rags to riches story began on July 18, 1867. Just a few short blocks from downtown, Margaret (Molly) Tobin Brown's original Irish immigrant's cottage is restored to its 1860's condition. One of six children of John and Johanna Tobin, Molly lived and worked in Hannibal until age 18. She rose to fame after moving to Colorado and marrying J.J. Brown who, seven years later, struck the largest vein of gold known at that time! View her home as it might have been when she was a girl and explore a little Titanic memorabilia as well.

OLE PLANTERS RESTAURANT

Hannibal - *316 N Main Street 63401. Phone: (573) 221-4410.* A Main Street staple for more than 30 years, Ole Planters has a full-service lunch and dinner menu, specializing in hickory smoked pork and beef, homemade tenderloins and unforgettable homemade pies. Ask about the famous guests who have stopped by to grab a bite. Lunch/Dinner most days. Closed Tuesday and Sunday nights. Closed January-February.

SAWYER'S CREEK FUN PARK

11011 Hwy 79 south (across from Mark Twain Cave, one mile south of downtown) **Hannibal** 63401

www.sawyerscreek.com
Hours: Open daily at 10:00am.

The Fun Park features an 18 Hole Miniature Golf Course in a beautiful garden setting, Bumper Boats in the Fish Pond (feed the fish), Bounce House, Fast Pitch, Water Wars and a Too Too Twain for the little ones. Each activity has a pay to play fee or you can buy all-play wristbands. The Sweet Shop features homemade fudge and candy, ice cream, fresh caramel corn, and snacks.

- **RIVERVIEW CAFÉ** - Relaxing atmosphere featuring a "Taste of Hannibal". Enjoy a sandwich for lunch or the large Soup and Salad Bar. Dinner selections include everything from catfish to steaks. Top it off with a delicious homemade dessert or your favorite beverage. Every table has a great view of the Mississippi River...in season you can dine inside or on their river view deck.

PADDLEWHEEL POPCORN & CANDY COMPANY

Hannibal - *121 North Main St., downtown 63491.* ***https://www.facebook.com/Paddlewheel-Popcorn-181939521849128/.*** Phone: (573) 221-0880 Delicious popcorns and hard-to-find candies make Paddlewheel Popcorn the one-stop shop to satisfy that sweet tooth. What we like best about this store is they've named their gourmet popcorns after characters. For example: Becky Thatcher (vanilla sugar), Huck Finn (slingshot zing cheddar cheese), Injun Joe (hot and sweet cinnamon), or Tom Sawyer (troubly, bubbly buttery caramel).

TOM SAWYER DAYS

Hannibal - Downtown. *www.hannibaljaycees.org*. A Hannibal tradition for over 50 years. The National Tom Sawyer Days celebration focuses on family fun. Visitors can watch or join in many of the activities. The town Mark Twain grew up in plays host to the National Fence Painting Championships, the Tomboy Sawyer competition, a frog-jumping contest (you can rent a frog if you didn't bring your own), Mississippi Mud Volleyball, entertainment, food and then a big fireworks display on July 4th. (days leading to July 4th)

CAMP RIVER DUBOIS, LEWIS & CLARK STATE HISTORIC SITE

IL 3 & New Poag Road (take I-270 over the River to IL. Then head north on IL 3) **Hartford, IL** 62048

Phone: (618) 251-5811 **www.campdubois.com**
Hours: Wednesday-Sunday 9:00am-5:00pm.
Admission: FREE.
Educators: Lesson Plans about the Lewis & Clark expedition are found on links on the For Teachers page of the website.

On May 14, 1804, Captain Meriwether Lewis wrote, "The mouth of the River Dubois is to be considered the point of departure." Visit the Lewis and Clark Interpretive Center, a replica of the 1803-04 winter encampment, and the Lewis and Clark Monument at this facility. The space tells the story of how the Corps of Discovery assembled equipment, supplies and men at Camp River Dubois.

In the Convergence Theater an original 15-minute, high definition film, "At Journey's Edge," is shown every 20 minutes. Highlighting the tour is the "Cutaway Keelboat," a 55-foot long replica of the keelboat Lewis had built in Ohio. The boat has been cut in half revealing how it was filled with "tools of every description." This is the room where kids can really explore! Be sure to ask the front desk for the scavenger/stamp hunt sheet. As you explore and log your provisions and usefulness, try to determine whether you would be able

For updates & travel games visit: **www.KidsLoveTravel.com**

to pack and organize as well as these folks. Try it.

Finished packing? Now venture outside towards the reconstruction of the camp. The volunteers act as guides to the fort where visitors can view the sleeping quarters of the men and the main building that served as guardhouse, storehouse, and the Captain's quarters. Be sure to behave so you don't get 100 lashings. The Camp often had visitors, many who provided information about the west. Today you are invited to visit and share as many may have done before. We promise, this historic site sparks a kids' sense of adventure.

DEUTSCHHEIM STATE HISTORIC SITE & MUSEUM

109 W. 2nd Street (west of Market Street / Hwy. 19) **Hermann** 65041
Phone: (573) 486-2200 **https://mostateparks.com/park/deutschheim-state-historic-site**
Admission: The Missouri state park system does not charge entrance fees. However, there are fees associated with camping, lodging, tours, museums and certain special events.
Tours: Tours are given daily at 10:00am, 12:30pm and 2:30pm. (April-October), Thursday-Sunday Only (November-March). Tours fee: $3.00-$5.00 (age 6+).

Deutschheim State Historic Site captures the culture and heritage of the German people who migrated to Missouri in the mid- to late-19th century. Tours of the Strehly and Pommer-Gentner houses, along with two period gardens, focus on the culture of German immigrants and German Americans across Missouri. Tour Deutschheim's buildings and experience the daily life of German Americana the way it really happened 150 years ago.

While the New Germany was never achieved in Hermann or any other part of the U.S., the German language has been the first one spoken by many Missourians right up into the 1950s. Before farming became industrialized, travelers always knew when they had come to a German American district by the barns and the distinctive haystacks. Workers in some industries and in dairies and gardens wore wooden shoes as recently as the 1960s. Once even windmills could be found in some places, and half-timbered buildings are still common. Other traditions have lasted: foods like home-made wurst (sausages) and the making of sauerkraut, wine, beer, and Christmas cookies like Lebkuchen and Springerle are still part of the lives of many German Americans.

MASTODON STATE HISTORIC SITE

1050 Charles J. Becker Drive (I-55 to Exit 186/Imperial/Kimmswick, heading west) **Imperial** 63052

Phone: (636) 464-2976 https://mostateparks.com/park/mastodon-state-historic-site

Hours: The park trails are open sunrise to sunset. The museum is the highlight of your visit, however. Open 9:00am-4:30pm Monday-Saturday and Noon-4:30pm Sunday (mid-March thru mid-November). Closed Tuesday-Thursday and opens at 11:00am other days during winter.

Admission: The Missouri state park system does not charge entrance fees. However, there are fees associated with the museum (small admission for folks age 16+) and certain special events.

Archaeological excavations found Paleo-Indians hunted the American mastodon here during the ice age. Bones of mastodons and other now-extinct animals were first found here in the early 1800s. A slide show is started every half hour. The museum dioramas detail these discoveries with placards explaining the difference between animals today vs. Prehistoric times. They display a prehistoric beaver skull and a modern beaver skull. The prehistoric beaver's skull was about twice if not three times the size of the modern beaver. A full-size replica of a mastodon skeleton highlights the exhibits. The area gained fame as one of the most extensive Pleistocene ice age deposits in the country and attracted scientific interest worldwide. Archaeological history was made at the site in 1979 when scientists excavated a stone spear point made by hunters of the Clovis culture (14,000 - 10,000 years ago) in direct association with mastodon bones. This was the first solid evidence of the coexistence of people and these giant prehistoric beasts. The site's museum displays ancient artifacts, fossils and a mastodon skeleton replica.

A day use area is available for picnics and hikes to explore the same land where the lives of Native Americans and mastodons once intertwined. It's like the movie "Ice Age" come to life!

CLARK COUNTY MULE FESTIVAL

Kahoka - Route EE, Clark County Fairgrounds. The Clark Co. Mule Festival is a three day mule show. It includes crafts; a flea market; trail rides; and souvenirs. Enjoy Mule Polo and Team penning Friday, 6:00pm, Saturday and Sunday, 10:00am and a Mule Rodeo Saturday, 7:00pm. Food, drink, and camping available on the grounds. Phone: (660) 727-2490. Admission. (third full weekend in September) **www.clarkcountymulefestival.com**

STILL NATIONAL OSTEOPATHIC MUSEUM

800 W. Jefferson Street (Museum is located inside the Tinning Education Center, which is the glass-fronted building ahead on the right as you enter the campus grounds) **Kirksville** 63501

Phone: (660) 626-2359 **www.atsu.edu/museum**
Hours: Monday-Friday 8:00am-5:00pm, Saturday 10am-5:00pm.
Admission: FREE.

Home of the founding Osteopathic School. Osteopathy is an approach to healthcare that emphasizes the role of the musculoskeletal system in health and disease. Artifacts span 150 years of the evolution of osteopathic medicine and include the log cabin where Dr. Andrew Still was born and the original two-room classroom building of the American School of Osteopathy, founded in 1892. Young kids may not get too excited about a human bones museum but they are attracted to many of the tools early doctors used, the bright red manipulation table, and sensor-activated audio systems that present interpretive glimpses into the Still family's frontier life and the earliest years of the ASO. The main gallery also contains a fully-dissected human nervous system—one of only four such dissections known to exist. While it may be gross to weak stomachs, curious kids tend to *"ooh and aah"*.

THOUSAND HILLS STATE PARK

20431 State Hwy. 157 **Kirksville** 63501

Phone: (660) 665-6995 or (800) 334-694
https://mostateparks.com/park/thousand-hills-state-park
Admission: The Missouri state park system does not charge entrance fees. There are fees associated with camping, lodging, tours, museums, etc.

Nestled in the hills of northern Missouri, this park is centered around Forest Lake. It offers cabins, a marina, dining, a beach, camping, and hiking and mountain biking trails. A shelter along one trail protects an 1000-year-old American Indian petroglyphs. The dining lodge at Thousand Hills State Park serves a wide selection of excellent foods. Water recreation is a highlight of Thousand Hills State Park's outdoor activities. The lake and its 17 miles of shoreline make it popular for fishing, water skiing, paddle boating, canoeing and motor boating. At the marina, you can rent all types of boats including paddle boats, kayaks, canoes, fishing boats and pontoons.

SHRINE PRO RODEO

Kirksville - NEMO Fairgrounds. Largest rodeo in this part of state has barrel racing, saddle bronc riding, calf roping, steer wrestling, team roping and bull riding. (third weekend in June)

WAKONDA STATE PARK

32836 State Park Road **La Grange** 63448

Phone: (573) 655-2280 https://mostateparks.com/park/wakonda-state-park
Admission: The Missouri state park system does not charge entrance fees. However, there are fees associated with camping, lodging, tours, museums and certain special events.

Located on the Mississippi River flyway, this park is noted for bird-watching. It features six lakes, a rare sand prairie, hiking and mountain biking trails, Missouri's largest natural sand beach, recreational trailers and camping. The clear lake waters attract thousands of waterfowl such as Canada geese, snow geese, mallards, snowy egrets and great blue herons during the migratory seasons (note: during migratory season, Agate Lake is closed to boating. Often the trail around the lake is closed, too). The lakes also offer anglers a chance at catching largemouth bass, bluegill, crappie and catfish. Two of the lakes have boat ramps. Non-motorized jon-boats and canoes can be rented.

JACKSON COUNTRY CONNECTIONS

La Plata - 28496 Nature Lane (zip code: 63549). www.jacksoncc.info/. Good ol' family fun, country style. You'll find hayrides, corn and bale mazes, a bounce house, a corn cannon and a pumpkin patch. (September & October).

LONG BRANCH STATE PARK

28615 Visitor Center Road **Macon** 63552

Phone: (660) 773-5229 https://mostateparks.com/park/long-branch-state-park
Admission: The Missouri state park system does not charge entrance fees. However, there are fees associated with camping, lodging, tours, museums and certain special events.

Located along Long Branch Lake, this park combines wooded areas and restored rolling prairie. The park offers a wheelchair-accessible fishing dock, a sand swimming beach, boat slips and ramps, a store, hiking trails, picnic sites and a campground. Near one of the picnic shelters is a one-mile trail that leads to the lake where benches await, providing a great spot to sit.

North East Area 53

AUDRAIN HISTORICAL SOCIETY COMPLEX
501 S. Muldrow (in Robert S. Green Park) **Mexico** 65265
Phone: (573) 581-3910 **www.audrain.org**
Hours: Tuesday-Saturday 10:00am-4:00pm, Sunday 1:00-4:00pm. Often closed in January.
Admission: $5.00 adult, $3.00 child (12 and under).

The complex has an antebellum mansion named Graceland, that's fully furnished with period pieces, the American Saddlebred Horse Museum, the Audrain Fire Brick Museum, a country school, country church and stables. A unique feature of the church is the original theater-style seating. The country school is set up just like it would have been in 1903 with a slate backboard, desks, schoolbooks, and such. And, for horse lovers, the American Saddlebred Horse Museum, is the oldest in the nation. Every famous horse or rider from these parts is prominently featured. And what is "fire brick"? Audrain also became known as the "Fire Brick Center of the World." The importance of fireclay lay in its capacity to withstand extremely high temperatures without changing form or deteriorating. This type of brick was the most significant industry in the counties history. It became obsolete in 2002.

BINDERS HILLTOP APPLE AND BERRY FARM
24688 Audrain Road 820 **Mexico** 65265
Phone: (573) 581-1415 **www.facebook.com/Apples-Alpacas-223403851335785/**

More than 50 colorful alpacas are on-site. Tour the alpaca barn and get close to the animals. Or, come out to get some fresh produce...apples, peaches and blackberries in July; you pick the apples. The Farm store offers organic produce in season, apple products and alpaca apparel. You might want to purchase a bag of apple chips to snack on the way home. Summer and Fall are the best times to visit.
THE U-PICK APPLE TOUR: Tours are offered on Monday, Tuesday and Wednesdays, mornings or afternoons. $4.50 per person. Minimum of 10 (or $45.00 charge is applied to smaller groups). Start in the apple orchard, then go to the honey bee yard. Students get to pick an apple without having to climb on ladders - how? Why are bees so important to apple farmers? Next watch the ducks play or the guineas in their wanderings around the farm. Head over to the pond and finally end up over by the alpacas. Kids get to pet a baby alpaca, feeling their soft fiber. Now that you've picked some apples, you'll get a chance to make it into apple juice. Samples and activity sheets are sent home. (mid-August until mid-October).

MARK TWAIN LANDING

42819 Landing Lane **Monroe City** 63456
Phone: (573) 735-9422 or (877) 700-9422 **www.marktwainlanding.com**

At Mark Twain Landing, all RV sites include a 40-foot cement pad and patio area, full hookups with water, sewer, and electric, BBQ grill and picnic table. The cabins are only one half mile from Spalding Beach and boat ramp on Mark Twain Lake. They have over 250 RV and tent camping sites, cabins, and even a motel. At the Playland they have go carts, bumper boats, miniature golf and much more. Come splash around in their Water Park where you will be able to ride the waves in one of Missouri's largest wave pools that tops out at 500,000 gallons! You can scream through the space bowl at speeds approaching 35 mph; then race down any of four water flumes! You can relax a little as you float around in the Lazy River. The waterpark is an extra fee of $20.00+ per person. At night, gather around the fire ring or grab a snack at the diner.

GRAHAM CAVE STATE PARK

217 Hwy. TT **Montgomery City** 63361
Phone: (573) 564-3476 **https://mostateparks.com/park/graham-cave-state-park**
Admission: The Missouri state park system does not charge entrance fees. However, there are fees associated with camping, lodging, tours, museums and special events.

Nestled in the hills above the Loutre River in Montgomery County, Graham Cave State Park features an unusual sandstone cave that contained evidence that rewrote history books. Once used for shelter, Graham Cave became historically significant when archaeologists discovered how long ago human occupancy had occurred. Radiocarbon dating has shown it was inhabited thousands of years ago. Graham Cave Trail is a walking trail that leads to the main feature of the park, Graham Cave, and the interpretive shelter. It also connects with Fern Ridge Trail. The paved path from the parking lot to Graham Cave has a high degree of incline. Today, visitors are allowed in the entrance of the cave, where interpretive signs point out interesting discoveries. The park also offers picnic areas, camping, Loutre River access and hiking trails.

ROBERTSVILLE STATE PARK

902 State Park Drive (5 miles east of I-44 on Route O near the junction of Route N) **Robertsville** 63072
Phone: (636) 257-3788 **https://mostateparks.com/park/graham-cave-state-park**
Admission: The Missouri state park system does not charge entrance fees.

For updates & travel games visit: **www.KidsLoveTravel.com**

North East Area

With the Meramec River and Calvey Creek along its border, this park attracts many kinds of waterfowl. The 1,225-acre park features a variety of outdoor activities for visitors of all ages, including canoeing and fishing in the adjoining Meramec River. Facilities include a boat-launching area on the river, a picnic area with two shelters, hiking trails, a playground and a campground. For those wishing to spend a night or more in the park, well-shaded basic and electric campsites are nestled among the wooded hills.

FAST LANE CLASSIC CARS
427 Little Hill Blvd. **St. Charles** 63301

Phone: (636) 940-9269 www.fastlanecars.com
Hours: Monday 9:30am-7:00pm, Tuesday-Thursday 9:30am-6:00pm, Friday 9:30am-7:00pm, Saturday 9:30am-5:00pm.
Admission: FREE.

Corvettes, Cameros, Mopars, Mustangs, street rods and more. See the shine of freshly polished chrome and smell the aroma of a Hemi warning up for a turn around the block. See an authentic Shelby Mustang. Many of these cars are available for auction sale so the museum for looking is FREE.

FIRST MISSOURI STATE CAPITOL STATE HISTORIC SITE
200-216 S. Main Street **St. Charles** 63301

Phone: (636) 940-3322 https://mostateparks.com/park/first-missouri-state-capitol-state-historic-site
Tours: The Missouri state park system does not charge entrance fees. However, there are fees associated with camping, lodging, tours, museums and special events. Tour Fees $4.50 adult, $3.00 child (6-17). Tours: Monday-Saturday 10:00am-3:00pm ends with 3:00pm tour. Sunday Noon-3:00pm ends with the 3:00pm tour (April-October). No tours on Mondays rest of year and Sunday & Monday in January & February.

Missouri's first legislators met here from June 4, 1821 to Oct. 1, 1826, to reorganize Missouri's territorial government. Tours are given of the restored building, including the governmental chambers, a residence and a dry goods store. For a nominal fee, visitors can take a guided tour through the actual restored and furnished rooms where Missouri state government was created and first practiced. The Peck Bros. Dry Goods Store contains examples of merchandise needed in the 1820s, with furs on display to show visitors the importance of the once-thriving fur trade. Admission is free to the historic site's interpretive center, which offers two floors of exhibits and an orientation show. Any families with kids in grades 4+ would be recommended to take the wonderful, interesting ranger tours.

HISTORICAL CHILDREN'S FESTIVAL

St. Charles - First Missouri State Capitol - Come live and play as children in the 1820's did. Hear interesting stories on Missouri's struggle for statehood. Hands on activities include: butter churning, quill pen writing, cow milking, candle dipping, baby farm animals, hearth cooking, storytelling, period games, re-enactors, and much more. (third Saturday in May)

KATY TRAIL STATE PARK
St. Charles 63301

Phone: (800) 334-6946 **https://mostateparks.com/park/first-missouri-state-capitol-state-historic-site**
Admission: The Missouri state park system does not charge entrance fees. However, there are fees associated with camping, lodging, tours, museums and special events.

At 225 miles, this park is the longest rail-trail conversion in the nation and runs from St. Charles to Clinton. There are 12 different trailheads in this region, including those in Hermann, Marthasville, Augusta, and St. Charles. If hiking, biking or bird watching are more your style, head out on the Katy Trail **www.katytrail.showmestate.com** or any number of dozens of trails in the area for some of the most spectacular scenery in the Midwest. Towering bluffs, flowing rivers and emerald green fields define the landscape and entice the senses in the area known as America's breadbasket. Fishing is also excellent in the area and many places sell equipment and bait. For the adventurous, consider camping out under the stars just like the pioneers and the Native American Indians did. Many campgrounds are in the area.

LEWIS AND CLARK BOAT HOUSE & NATURE CTR
1050 Riverside Drive (Bishop's Landing) **St. Charles** 63301

Phone: (636) 947-3199 **www.lewisandclarkcenter.org**
Hours: Monday-Saturday 10:00am-5:00pm, Sunday Noon-5:00pm.
Admission: $5.00 adult, $2.00 child (under 17).
FREEBIES: Be sure to ask for kids activity sheet to complete for prizes.

The Lewis & Clark Boathouse and Nature Center is situated on the banks of the Missouri River and is home to the Discovery Expedition of Saint Charles and its authentically reproduced keelboat and pirogues. The building is also home to the recently expanded Lewis & Clark museum which houses detailed dioramas of the great adventure and many hand-on exhibits of life in the area in 1804, from its wildlife to its architecture. Look for an early "laptop" desk, a bullboat and dress up clothes. Your kids will understand historical styles of building as they peer through windows of four half-scale buildings each showing different architectural styles of the 1700 and 1800s.

For updates & travel games visit: **www.KidsLoveTravel.com**

North East Area

The nature trail winds through a woodland area, and a typical wetland marsh. Also, depending on weather and river conditions at different times of the year, you can enjoy re-enactors providing demonstrations on the boats outside.

EMBASSY SUITES HOTEL

St. Charles - Convention Center Plaza 63303. http://embassysuites.hilton.com. Phone: (800) Embassy. Rates: $141.00 plus. Each suite is beautifully decorated with a private bedroom and spacious living room. All suites are fully equipped with two televisions, a refrigerator, microwave, coffee maker, two telephones with data ports, high-speed Internet access and a well-lit dining/work table. Price also includes cooked-to-order breakfast and nightly manager's reception.

LLYWELYN'S PUB

St. Charles - 100 N Main Street 63301. www.llywelynspub.com Historic area. Kids Menu includes: Grilled Cheese, Mac & Cheese, Mini Corndogs, Two Mini Burgers, Chicken Tenders, Pizza, or Kids Fish. All are served with a kids drink (excluding Fitz's) Fries, chips, fruit cup, or veggie sticks and Oreos for $5.49. Parents, you must try Welsh Potato Chips or Welsh Rarebit to start, flatbreads w/Guinness for lunch or traditional Irish fare of Bangers & Mashed, Shepherds Pie or Irish Stew for a filling dinner.

LITTLE HILLS RESTAURANT & WINERY

St. Charles - 501 S Main Street 63301. www.littlehillswinery.com Wait until you see their Children's Menu: typical chicken tenders, grilled cheese, mac and cheese, burgers but also pot roast or a chicken tender bowl with mashed potatoes and corn. Avg. $5.00-$6.00. Special items for adults are highlighted on the main menu – including specialty steak and chicken dishes plus dinner "bowls."

RT WEILER'S RESTAURANT

St. Charles - 201 N Main Street 63301. www.rtweilers.com. Phone: (636) 947-1593. . Serving lunch and dinner daily, the name of the restaurant was meant to mimic the name of a rather large breed of dog. The kids menu has PB & J, grilled cheese, chicken strips, etc. served in an authentic doggie dish. Family owned: 15 TV's, Hand Cut Steaks, Fried Chicken to BBQ and Homemade Desserts. Moderately priced and great fun for the whole family. Lunch, Dinner and Entertainment.

FETE DE GLACE ICE CARVING COMPETITION

St. Charles - 100 to 200 blocks of North Main Street. **https://www.facebook.com/Fete-de-Glace-St-Charles-Ice-Festival-101518709973161/** Watch professional ice carvers bring the art to life in a competition using chain saws, power grinders, sanders, cold chisels, hand saws, and irons from 9:30am-3:30pm. This competition is judged and juried by the crowd. Coffee and hot chocolate will be available & nearby fire pits to warm up. (last weekend in January)

LEWIS AND CLARK HERITAGE DAYS

St. Charles - Frontier Park. Authentic reenactment of Lewis & Clarks encampment in 1804 prior to embarking on the exploration of the Louisiana Purchase. Saturday 9:30am-5:00pm & Sunday 10:00am-4:00pm. Parade, church service Sunday, walk through encampments; plus weapon demonstrations in the afternoons, boat replicas, museum tours, crafts & foods of 1804, children's games, period music and more. (third weekend in May)

FESTIVAL OF THE LITTLE HILLS

St. Charles - Frontier Park and Main Street. www.festivalofthelittlehills.com. The largest festival of the year, activities include over 300 craft booths, with some demonstrations by crafts people and artisans. Also includes numerous food & beverages booths along with live music and other entertainment and Kids Corner. (third full weekend in August)

DOUBLE KEY TREASURE HUNTS

(ordered online) **St. Louis**

www.doublekeytreasurehunts.com
Admission: $77.00-$129.00 per kit.

Double Key Treasure Hunts creates complete treasure hunt packages in a sackcloth bag using real antique items from the 1800s to the early 1900s. To solve the clues, you'll visit various places around St. Louis by decoding the treasure written instructions and artifacts. A family, kids party, extended family can all help with one hunt as it's self-contained and you don't need outside assistance. What a great way to engage your kids in historical places you might have just peeked in for a quick look before. Now the kids are motivated to explore and they notice every square inch of the building trying to solve a part of the query.

FLAMINGO BOWL

St. Louis - *1117 Washington Avenue, downtown 63101. Phone: (314) 436-6666. www.FlamingoBowl.net. Hours: Best 3-6pm weekdays, Noon-6pm weekends for children. Admission: Children (12 & under) $3.00/game everyday* *until 6:00pm. Reservations are available – please inquire. Shoe rental $3.00.* Twelve lanes of bowling with an Art deco design and flamingo theme. During daylight hours, the place is family friendly and kids like the foods offered - mostly appetizers, sandwiches and pizza. Average sandwich is $8.00. Fun environment to bowl and snack while downtown. 🍽

EAT-RITE DINER

St. Louis - *622 Chouteau Avenue 63102. Phone: (314) 621-9721. Hours: Breakfast, Lunch & Dinner.* No reservations and no tables in this near downtown diner...you have to hope one of the dozen counter stools are open. A second diner is located South of St. Louis at 5513 South Lindbergh Blvd and a third diner is located Southwest of St. Louis at 1059 Gravois Road. The Eat-Rite Diner near the old, now closed MacArthur Bridge is a Route 66 Tradition. This diner has been sitting on the corner of Chouteau and 7th for 60 years! This small classic diner has seen a lot of action in that time and it still serves up a quick meal. It's a dinky little place but a classic diner experience.

EUGENE FIELD HOUSE & ST. LOUIS TOY MUSEUM

634 South Broadway **St. Louis** 63102

Phone: (314) 421-4689 **www.eugenefieldhouse.org**
Hours: Wednesday-Saturday 10:00am-4:00pm, Sunday Noon-4:00pm.
Admission: $10.00 adult, $5.00 child (7-16).

A National Historic Landmark, the Eugene Field House is the home of Roswell Field, the attorney for Dred Scott and his son, Eugene, "the children's poet." Eugene Field was a St. Louis children's poet, famous for such poems as 'Little Boy Blue' and 'Wynken, Blynken and Nod'. The famous children's poet's downtown row house is filled with antique toys and fascinating traveling exhibits. The combination of the miniature toys museum with the displays and information on the Fields and the Scotts really help to keep the kids interested. History is weaved in as interactive displays show the lives of slave kids or the installation Narrative Voices tells about the Dred Scott case.

GATEWAY ARCH

(St. Louis riverfront, last Missouri exits off Interstates) **St. Louis** 63102

Phone: (877) 982-1410 **www.gatewayarch.com**
Hours: Generally 8:00am-9:00pm summers. Shorter hours rest of year (close at 5:00pm).
Admission: $13.00 adult, $10.00 child (3-15) for tram to the top. Children FREE. Museum of Westward Expansion is FREE. $3.00-$7.00 Movie fees apply for showings of Documentary Movie. Visiting the Gateway Arch in the summer? That's peak season for visits to the nation's tallest monument and "Journey to the Top" tram tickets sell out fast. Guarantee your ride for the day and time you want by ordering tickets in advance via online.
Security Checks: at one or more points before entering an exhibit space, you must allow some extra time to pass thru a security checkpoint.
FREEBIES: Click on the web icon: The Arch Experience. Then click Fun Stuff for an Arch quiz and a game to construct the Arch.

The imposing Gateway Arch, America's tallest monument, is a must see attraction. The Arch and Old Courthouse sit on riverfront land where the original Route 66 passed by - forging a trail to the American West. Take a ride to the top of the Arch - 630 feet high over the Mississippi - which was built as a monument to President Thomas Jefferson's dream of a continental United States.

Tram Ride to the Top is a two-part multimedia exhibit where riders board trams to the top. Begin your tour with our new, interactive pre-boarding exhibits featuring 60s era animation and Gateway Arch trivia. The ride feels like a somewhat slower version of a carnival Ferris wheel. Although the "pods" you ride on are painted soothing robin egg blue, the "ride" is like a futuristic adventure in the dark (except for your lighted pod). You'll catch the frontiersmen's sense of adventure, for sure! (Note: visitors with claustrophobia or "fear of heights" may have trouble with this ride. If in doubt, ask an attendant to let you try a pod first). From the top of the monument, you'll get a 30-mile panoramic view of the river and St. Louis far below. We took pictures of everything - even the funky pods you ride to the top.

As you're waiting for your timed ticket tram tour to the top, why not meander around the base of the museum. You'll step back in time to see buffalo, covered wagons, Native American teepees, Lewis & Clark expedition dioramas and many other artifacts from America's western beginnings in St. Louis. To keep it interesting for the young-ins, look for these animatronic figures - Thomas Jefferson; William Clark; a buffalo soldier; and a 1846 Overlander woman preparing to head west.

For updates & travel games visit: **www.KidsLoveTravel.com**

GATEWAY ARCH RIVERBOAT CRUISES

800 North First Street (riverfront, below the Gateway Arch) **St. Louis** 63102

Phone: (877) 982-1410 **www.gatewayarch.com/experience/gateway-arch-riverboat-cruises10**
Admission: (Sightseeing) $20.00 adult, $8.00 child (3-15). Other tours are available. Call or see website for cruise schedule.
Tours: (Sightseeing 60 minutes) Daily 1:30pm, Weekends Noon & 1:30pm. Added times during peak season. Reservations required.

The Gateway Arch Riverboats, two replica steamboats, explore the Port of St. Louis daily. After the boat ride, you can rent bikes on the dock and explore the Riverfront Trail or roll through downtown to see the sights.

ST. LOUIS CARDINAL'S BUSCH STADIUM TOURS

700 Clark Street (purchase tickets at Gate 5 windows on Clark Street)
St. Louis 63102

Phone: (314) 345-9565 (tour line)
http://stlouis.cardinals.mlb.com/stl/ballpark/ballpark_tours.jsp
Admission: $18.00 adult, $16.00 senior (60+), $14.00 child (<15).
Tours: (During Season) Public tours offered at 9:30am, 11:00am, 12:30pm, and 2:00pm. No Tours During: Dates of afternoon home games (tours are available during days of home night games). Dates of special events at the ballpark. (Off-Season) Tours will be offered daily throughout the off-season at 11:00am and 1:00pm. Tours depart from Gate 5 (on Clark Street). Tours last one hour and end at Gate 3 (near the Stan Musial statue). Tours normally include the following stops: a Party Room, the Redbird Club, the Press Box, the Cardinals Club, and the Cardinals Dugout, the Broadcast booth, as well as other unique areas in the ballpark.

Aspiring athletes can swing away like a big league ballplayer in the Family Pavilion at Busch Stadium. Open before and during Cardinals baseball games, the attraction offers a batting challenge, pitching areas and other interactive activities. Fred Bird, the Cardinals mascot, roams the ballpark to interact with kids during their baseball adventure.

- TOUR: Tour the Cardinals' home and host of the All-Star Game in 2009. The tour lasts one hour and provides an in-depth look at the Cardinals' home. Tours normally include the following stops: a Party Room, the Redbird Club, the Press Box, the Cardinals Club, and the Cardinals Dugout, as well as other unique areas in the ballpark. One of baseball's all-time greats, Hall of Famer Stan "The Man" Musical, played his entire career for the St. Louis Cardinals. Thirty-seven Cardinals plus the late broadcaster Jack Buck and former Cards' broadcaster Harry Caray have been inducted into the Baseball Hall of Fame at Cooperstown, New York.

ST. LOUIS CARDINAL'S

- BUDGET NOTE: It's a steal! The St. Louis Cardinals offer "First Pitch Tickets." Starting at 9:00am on a regular season game day, the first 275 customers at the Busch Stadium Eighth Street ticket window can purchase a voucher entitling the fan to receive two tickets at $5.60 each later that day. The tickets -- a virtual grab bag of locations returned to the ticket office by Cardinals players, the visiting club, sponsors and others - may be for anywhere within the ballpark, from field or terrace level to standing room only. Ten minutes before game time - at 7:00pm sharp for a 7:10pm. game -- fans will be asked to produce their picture I.D. and voucher at the "First Pitch Tickets" sign at Gate 5 to claim their tickets and enter Busch Stadium. Tickets will be in sealed envelopes and distributed on a completely random basis.

THE OLD COURTHOUSE

11 North 4th Street **St. Louis** 63102

Phone: (314) 655-1700 www.nps.gov/jeff/planyourvisit/och.htm
Hours: Daily 8:00am-4:30pm. Extended summer hours.
Admission: FREE.
Educators: Teacher Activity Guides: www.nps.gov/jeff/forteachers/teacher-activity-guides.htm

St. Louis' Old Courthouse, now part of the Jefferson National Expansion Memorial, was the site of the first two trials of the Dred Scott anti-slavery case, in 1847 and 1850, which led to the Supreme Court decision that helped ignite the Civil War. Your kids might be familiar with the names from U.S. History class, but have you been to the courthouse where Scott, a slave, sat after he successfully sued to earn his freedom? Walk the halls where the Scotts' battle for freedom began (roughly 300 other people sued to earn their freedom at the courthouse, too), view a display about the trial or watch a video featuring an interview with one of the Scotts' descendants. The east steps facing the Gateway Arch were the scenes of slave auctions before the war and where, in 1859, Grant freed his only slave. If your kids have studied the slavery issues leading to the Civil War, they will find this particularly interesting and moving to be walking along the same hallways as the courageous slaves did years ago.

CITY MUSEUM
750 North 16th St St. Louis 63103

Phone: (314) 231-CITY (2489) **www.citymuseum.org**
Hours: Monday-Thursday 9:00am-5:00pm, Friday-Saturday 9:00am-midnight, Sunday 11:00am-5:00pm. (closed Monday & Tuesday - Labor Day thru March)
Admission: $14.00 General (ages 3+). Additional $5.00 fee for The Roof. Parking $10.00 cash only.
Educators: grade appropriate questions and games are found under: Group Activities/Educational. FREEBIES: Coloring Pages and Scavenger Hunts are on the Educational page at the bottom. Print them off before you arrive.

See the world's only completely recycled museum when you visit the art-filled playground of City Museum -- an intriguing mix of history, architecture and whimsy. You know you're there when you walk up to the building and see the bus...dangling about three stories above your head. Or, the giant pencil poking out of another wall of the exterior. Anyway, inside is even more bizarre than outside. With endless places for kids to climb and play, these artsy structures are irresistible to children. Everything here is made from recycled materials so nothing is uniform or "new." You'll see kids race through Enchanted Caves as parents try to keep up behind them (entrance to the 10 story slide is here). The City Express departs at the whim of the engineer and at the request of the kiddie crowd. At one-eighth the size of a regular locomotive, the ride takes passengers under a bridge, through a cosmic tunnel and to an even tinier train. Check out the World Aquarium. Sharks, stingrays, reptiles and fish of all kinds, from almost every ocean, sea, lake and river in the world, are found here. Next, swim through thousands of rubber balls, write your name with the world's largest pencil or climb through MonstroCity, a monstrous montage of monkey bars and unusually placed objects along the way. Swinging on a bridge hundreds of feet above the pavement was about when we (the parents) gave out and just followed the shortest path back down to the ground level benches to observe. Note: a flashlight may be helpful.

SCOTT JOPLIN HOUSE STATE HISTORIC SITE
2658A Delmar **St. Louis** 63103

Phone: (314) 340-5790 **https://mostateparks.com/park/scott-joplin-house-state-historic-site**
Admission: The Missouri state park system does not charge entrance fees. However, there are fees associated with camping, lodging, tours, museums and special events.
Tours: Monday-Saturday tours are offered every hour between 10:00am-4:00pm (March-October - last tour at 3:00pm). Closed Sunday and Monday in February. The site is closed November-January. Tour fees are $6.00 adult, $4.00 child (6-17).

Scott Joplin was a visionary in music. His ability to combine musical styles earned him the moniker "The King of Ragtime." The sounds of Joplin's music still fill the air at this home, where Joplin lived with his wife, Belle, and produced some of his better-known works, including the "The Entertainer" (featured in the movie, "The Sting,"). Lit by gaslight, and appropriately furnished for 1902, the Joplin flat where many ragtime classics were composed awaits your visit. To create a feel for the times, the park has recreated what they call the new Rosebud Café, which interprets a café or music hall that would have been in existence during Joplin's era. You can sneak a peak in there. The music makes your toes tap, doesn't it?

ST LOUIS BLUES HOCKEY

1401 Clark Avenue (Scottrade Center, downtown) **St. Louis** 63103

The St. Louis Blues are the only NHL team to appear in the playoffs every year during the 1980s and 1990s. Since joining the National Hockey League in 1967, the Blues have missed the Stanley Cup Playoffs only five times. Today's team takes to the ice at the 20,000-seat Scottrade Center downtown. http://blues.nhl.com/

UNION STATION

1820 Market Street (Downtown) **St. Louis** 63103

Phone: (314) 421-6655 www.stlouisunionstation.com
Hours: Monday-Saturday 10:00am-9:00pm, Sunday 10:00am-6:00pm.

This landmark features more than 80 shopping venues along with a food court, street performers, light shows, a train park, an aquarium, a 200 foot Ferris wheel, and a self-guided tour brochure of The Best of St. Louis memorabilia. Most of the stores and restaurants are unique and specialized - great gift shopping and fun souvenirs.

SOULARD MARKET

730 Carroll Street **St. Louis** 63104

Phone: (314) 622-4180 www.soulardmarket.com
Hours: Wednesday-Friday 8:00am-5:00pm, Saturday 6:00am-5:00pm.

This open-air market, with more than 90 vendors, has been serving the St. Louis area for more than 200 years. Vendors provide fresh produce, meats, fish, poultry, baked goods and spices. There's also craft booths on Saturdays.

For updates & travel games visit: **www.KidsLoveTravel.com**

Kids might like to try some new types of foods at the many cafes serving snacks and meals.

CROWN CANDY KITCHEN

St. Louis - *1401 Saint Louis Avenue (Old North Street neighborhood) 63106. Phone: (314) 621-9650* **http://crowncandykitchen.net/** *Hours: Daily opens at 10:30am- closing at 8:00.* Crown Candy's menu not only includes their delicious 1904 World's Fair style sundaes, but lunch and dinner options. Whether you're in the mood for a thick stacked sandwich, chili, a giant gourmet frank, a salad or a bowl of soup - and don't forget about their desserts - exquisite selection of candy, malts and shakes. Crown Candy Kitchen also makes chocolates, including chocolate hash—marshmallows covered in chocolate and topped with pecans. Think you can drink 5 malts or shakes in 30 minutes? If you do, you, and others (Man vs. Food) get them free (plus a t-shirt). And the average price for most everything you can order? About $5.00.

BOB KRAMER'S MARIONNETTE THEATER

4143 Laclede Avenue (Located in the heart of Saint Louis's Central West End, just minutes west of the Arch) **St. Louis** 63108

Phone: (314) 531-3273 **www.kramersmarionnettes.com**
Hours: Showtimes are Monday-Saturday 10:00am and 1:00pm, Sunday 1:00pm. Admission: $14.00 adult, $12.00 senior & child (1-12). Holiday shows slightly higher. Reservations are required for all shows.

Tour the workshop, get an one hour demonstration of puppetry arts and manufacturing and then watch a performance. Your family will learn all kinds of things about the marionettes, how they are made, the process in which the parts are created, assembled, and what all is required to go into a show. The shows are a lot of fun to watch. The stories are wholesome, old-fashioned tales like "<u>Peter And The Wolf</u>", "<u>Hansel And Gretel</u>", and "<u>Toyland</u>". The neatest thing that happens is when their mouths open and they start to sing. It very unique to see a wooden puppet sing as though it was on a Broadway stage. Kids are mesmerized.

TED DREWES FROZEN CUSTARD

St. Louis - 6726 Chippewa (Rte 66) 63109. www.teddrewes.com. Phone: (314) 481-2652 Note: Across the street from Ted Drewes is the Donut Drive In, a Route 66 icon still serving up cakey glazed donuts. This is a St. Louis tradition of arguably the best custard in the world and a sweet stop along Route 66. Opened in 1929, Ted Drewes has served frosty "concretes" to generations of hungry travelers and long lines of loyal St. Louisans. The frozen vanilla custard shakes are blended with fruits, nuts, candies and other flavors and served so concrete-thick they're handed to customers upside down. Sample an "All Shook Up" blended with peanut butter and bananas in honor of Elvis or have a little "Cardinal Sin" mixed with tart cherries and hot fudge. Bunny-cretes-a carrot cake concoction-show up around Easter and it's not fall unless you have a Pumpkin-crete, which is custard blended with a slice of pumpkin pie. Don't let the crowds scare you away. Lines, which are longest on summer nights after Cardinals baseball games or theatre performances in Forest Park, move at an amazing pace.

FOREST PARK

Government Drive St. Louis 63110

Phone: (314) 289-5300

Introduce the kids to Broadway musical theatre...for free. Take advantage of the first come, first served free seats - there are 1,200 available for every performance -- at The Muny in Forest Park, the nation's oldest and largest outdoor theatre. Each summer, the 12,000-seat theatre offers a seven-week season of musicals starring nationally known performers, from late June until early August. Biking is fun on the 7.5-mile path around the park's perimeter, and the kids can pedal or paddle small boats around the park's refurbished lakes from the Boat House. In winter, the whole family can lace up their skates and take to the ice at the park's Steinberg Rink, and sledding is permitted down Art Hill when Mother Nature provides the white stuff. A favorite is climbing on the whimsical giant turtle sculptures in Turtle Playground.

GREAT FOREST PARK BALLOON RACE

St. Louis - Forest Park - Balloon Glow on Friday night, Balloon Race on Saturday. FREE. www.greatforestparkballoonrace.com. Central Field in Forest Park. (mid-September weekend)

North East Area 67

HEALTHWORKS

1100 Macklind Ave (Laclede's Landing) **St.** Louis 63110

Phone: (314) 241-7391 http://hwstl.org/
Hours: Tuesday-Saturday 9:00am-4:30pm, Sunday Noon-4pm.
Admission: $7.00 general.

Kids most enjoy The Interactive Dude, pretend medical office, pharmacy and market, or the Kitchen. The theaters specialize in programs on the importance of good dental and overall health, and focuses its efforts on children and teens. Features are a three-foot-tall set of lighted teeth and age-appropriate videos. Their newest production is the Healthy Hollow state-of-the-art puppet show. Before you leave try the Beam interactive gaming floor in the lobby.

MISSOURI BOTANICAL GARDEN

4344 Shaw Blvd. **St.** Louis 63110

Phone: (314) 577-5100 www.mobot.org
Hours: Daily 9:00am-5:00pm.
Admission: $12.00 adult (13+) Age 12 and under FREE. (Children's Garden open April-October) $5.00 (ages 3-12). Adults no extra charge for Children's Garden. Resident discounts available.
Tours: narrated tram tours offered April thru October for $3.00; guided walking tours are offered year-round and are included with garden admission.

Stroll through 79 acres of landscaped display gardens, indoor conservatories and historic structures. Check out these garden scenes in particular:

- CLIMATRON - The Climatron at the Missouri Botanical Garden, built in 1960, was the world's first climate-controlled geodesic dome designed as a greenhouse. Today, it houses a re-created rain forest filled with plants and uses E-feron glass to help it use solar energy more efficiently.
- JAPANESE GARDEN - Largest Japanese Garden in North America.
- CHILDREN'S GARDEN - Wander through kid-sized plantings that you can re-create back home or get temporarily "lost" inside the Garden's tall Victorian maze.

CHINESE CULTURE DAYS

St. Louis - Missouri Botanical Garden. The event features a Grand Parade with 70-foot dancing dragon, martial arts, Chinese calligraphy, painting and authentic regional cuisine. Enjoy T'ai Chi and tea tasting in the Grigg Nanjing Friendship Garden, where special tours focus on the symbolism of many plant species and architectural details. Admission. (second or third weekend in May)

GARDENLAND EXPRESS

St. Louis - Missouri Botanical Garden. One of St. Louis's most beloved holiday traditions returns with Gardenland Express, the Garden's annual holiday flower and train show. Admission. (Thanksgiving time thru New Years Day).

ST. LOUIS ART MUSEUM

1 Fine Arts Drive (Forest Park) **St. Louis** 63110

Phone: (314) 721-0072 **www.slam.org**
Hours: Tuesday-Sunday 10:00 am–5:00pm, Friday open until 9:00pm.
Admission: FREE. Admission to featured exhibitions vary.

This art museum prides itself on having more than 30,000 works from nearly every culture and time - Oceanic, pre-Columbian, Chinese, 19th-20th century European and American, and a large collection of 20th century German paintings. Kids always look for the small Egyptian room with the authentic mummy. Artsy families take note of free, hands-on art activities, family tours with complimentary guidebooks, artist demonstrations and performances every Sunday afternoon from 1:00pm-4:00pm. The family-friendly theme changes monthly.

ST. LOUIS SCIENCE CENTER

5050 Oakland Avenue **St. Louis** 63110

Phone: (314) 289-4400 **www.slsc.org**
Hours: Monday-Saturday 9:30am-4:30pm, Sunday 11:30am-4:30pm. Extended summer hours.
Admission: General admission for many exhibits, FREE. Fees for some special events and shows.
Note: A four-story Omnimax Theater and a Planetarium are on the premises. Showtimes and fees are posted online.

The Saint Louis Science Center in Forest Park brings the world of learning to life with hands-on activities. Visitors of all ages can explore the "gene scene" and cast their vote on the ethical issues of genetic engineering, or build a replica of the Gateway Arch. Get a feel for what it's like to live, work and play on the International Boeing Space Station, then use radar guns to clock the speed of cars zooming beneath the enclosed bridge spanning I-64. Here at the St. Louis home of the X-Prize, the Planetarium offers the state-of-the-art Boeing Space Station where kids can see what it is like to live and work in space. Watch an OMNIMAX® large screen movie, visit the Exploradome to see traveling exhibits, touch a tornado or be amazed at the roaring, life-size animatronic dinosaurs. This science center includes more than 700 hands-on exhibits and the Life Science Lab. The Discovery Room is an area just for

For updates & travel games visit: **www.KidsLoveTravel.com**

kids aged 3-7 to explore a range of interactives with magnets, a water table, and dress up at the medical area or native American area. FREE 10-minute science demo shows run every hour.

ST. LOUIS ZOO

One Government Drive **St. Louis** 63110

Phone: (314) 781-0900 or (800) 966-8877 **www.stlzoo.org**
Hours: Daily 9:00am-5:00pm. Extended summer hours.
Admission: FREE, but there are charges to do things like visit the children's zoo, the sea lion or stingray shows, ride the carousel or ride the train. Parking is $11.00 at the Zoo's North Lot on Government Drive and South Lot on Wells Drive.
Miscellaneous: there are many cafes throughout the property, some sit down.
Educators: Teacher Lesson Plans: **www.stlzoo.org/education/forteachers/teacherlessonplans.htm**

The St. Louis Zoo is home to over 18,000 exotic animals; many are rare and endangered. Visit Fragile Forest, Penguin and Puffin Coast and the Children's Zoo. Catch a Sea Lion Show, pet a stingray or ride the Zooline Railroad. The more interactive St. Louis Zoo offers kids the chance to pet guinea pigs and goats and see naked mole rats up-close and personal. There's a large colony of meerkats -- and an active family of small Fennec foxes with huge ears. A popular stop for zoo visitors is the Fragile Forest, a habitat for great apes that provides a refuge for endangered orangutans and chimpanzees. Don't miss the Cypress Swamp exhibit, which is housed in the refurbished 1904 World's Fair flight cage, the Penguin & Puffin Coast and the Conservation Carousel as well. At the Zoo's River's Edge, you can get an eye-to-eye view of river-dwelling hippos and the elephant family.

The Children's Zoo also has a "Just Like Me" play area where children can climb a giant spider web or dig like an aardvark in a sandbox. The indoor space is divided into desert, forest, water and backyard, and kids can crawl through the Frog Surround, climb a cool tree house or "drive" a jeep through a savannah.

DID YOU KNOW ? The Zoo, a pioneer in the use of open enclosures, placing animals in natural environments without bars, is again on the cutting edge of technology with the "The Living World" education center. "The Living World" is the first center to use live animals and high technology together to teach about the diversity of life.

MISSOURI HISTORY MUSEUM

5700 Lindell Boulevard (at Lindell and DeBaliviere in Forest Park)
St. Louis 63112

Phone: (314) 746-4599 www.mohistory.org
Hours Daily 10:00am-5:00pm. Open until 8:00pm on Tuesday.
Admission: General admission to the Museum is FREE. Some fees are charged for special exhibits.
Note: Restaurant and shop are on-site.

This museum invites guests to participate in the past, present and future. The museum traces the early history of the state of Missouri and its major commercial center, St. Louis, through a variety of exhibits including "Seeking St. Louis". Check out exhibits on everything from Charles "Lucky" Lindbergh to more artifacts from explorers Lewis & Clark and a look at the storied 1904 World's Fair. You'll learn how St. Louis' McDonnell Douglas Corporation (now Boeing) designed and built the first space capsule. The Eads Bridge (nearby going over the Mississippi) was the first arched steel truss bridge in the world (naysayers said it was impossible) and the engineer who built it also built the St. Louis, the first ironclad boat built in America. This is a great place for people who are interested in American History. The Forest Park Metrolink Station is close to this museum.

MINIATURE MUSEUM OF GREATER ST. LOUIS

4746 Gravois Avenue **St. Louis** 63116

Phone: (314) 832-7790 www.miniaturemuseum.org
Hours: Wednesday-Saturday 11:00am-4:00pm, Sunday 11:00pm-4:00pm.
Admission: $7.00 adult, $6.00 senior (62+) & student (13-18), $4.00 child (2-12). Discount coupons available on website.

The Miniature Museum of Greater St. Louis is home to permanent and rotating exhibits of dolls and dollhouse furniture. The dollhouses and miniature replicas include some historical scenes, a shopping center, the "old Cathedral," a Trading Post, a 1927 Armory, roomboxes and vignettes of all eras. What kids may notice most is the miniature figures are posed as if they are really lounging watching TV in the living room, shopping at the local grocer, eating in the kitchen or mess hall, or exchanging goods in the middle of the wilderness.

MUSEUM OF TRANSPORTATION

2967 Barrett Station Road **St. Louis** 63122

Phone: (314) 965-6885 http://transportmuseumassociation.org/
Hours: Monday-Saturday 9:00am-4:00pm, Sunday 11:00am-5:00pm. (March-Oct).

For updates & travel games visit: **www.KidsLoveTravel.com**

North East Area

Reduced hours (rest of year). Admission: $10.00 adult, $5.00 senior & child (3-12).
Tours: Public guided tours are available on days of operation. Children's Tours: June-early August, Wednesdays at 10:15am. Appropriate for Pre-K - 2nd Grade. There is lots of walking. No reservations
FREEBIES: Ask for the I Spy Scavenger Hunt at the front desk. Educators: this online page has several different games or activities: http://transportmuseumassociation. org/classroom.html

Get your kicks on Route 66 by visiting St. Louis' Museum of Transportation. It's home to more than 300 moving vehicles including locomotives, streetcars, aircraft, test cars, and automobiles. Many of the historic transportation pieces housed at the museum were experimental vehicles in their time, and several are the only examples remaining in existence. The passenger car collection includes the 1964 Bobby Darin "Dream Car" and a 1901 St. Louis car - a four-seat, single or two-cylinder engine vehicle with tiller steering. Another display features a portion of the Coral Court Motel - St. Louis' infamous Route 66 rendezvous spot that offered drive-in units. The museum includes a miniature train ride for the kids.

GRANT'S FARM

10501 Gravois Road **St. Louis** 63123

Phone: (314) 843-1700 **www.grantsfarm.com**
Hours: Saturday 9:00am-3:30pm, Sunday 9:30am-3:30pm (mid-April - late August). Weekends only each fall. Admission: The admission to Grant's Farm, tram rides and all shows is FREE, but there is an $12.00 parking charge.

At the onset of the Civil War in 1861 Grant reported to Army headquarters in St. Louis, beginning a wartime career that eventually would lead to the White House. Although Ulysses S. Grant was not a farmer, he, at one time, attempted to become a civilian and work normal jobs for a time. He soon learned he was better suited for the military. Today the ex-President's two-story cabin is on display at Grant's Farm, an animal preserve on the estate of the Busch brewing family of St. Louis. A fence made of Civil War gun barrels surrounds a portion of the estate near the cabin.

The real draw here is the farm animals. The property houses more than 1000 animals representing more than 100 different species from six continents. See baby Clydesdales, watch amazing dogs and enjoy bird and elephant behavior shows. A trackless train carries families around the farm's wildlife preserve and stops at the petting zoo. Several times each day (summer) or weekend (fall & spring), the farm hosts Education or Encounter shows - many with elephants. Horse-lovers will be drawn to the Clydesdales. There are also plenty of deer and zebra roaming the grassland.

AMERICA'S INCREDIBLE PIZZA COMPANY

St. Louis - 5254 S Lindbergh Blvd   63126.   *www.stlouisincrediblepizza.com*. Here you'll find an incredible all-you-can-eat buffet featuring fresh pizza, pasta, soup, salad and the best desserts in town. Enjoy your meal in one of our four themed dining rooms: the Gymnasium, the 50's Diner, the Family Room, and the Starlite Drive-In complete with old movies showing. Then, hop into some fun at The Fairgrounds, where you'll find indoor Go-Karts, Bumper Cars, Glow-In-The-Dark Mini Golf, Mini Bowling, and a huge Game Room where you can redeem tickets for incredible prizes. All of this is completely indoors so there's no fear of poor weather ruining the day. Open daily for lunch and dinner until dark.

SUSON PARK

6059 Wells Road   **St. Louis** 63128

Phone: (314) 638-2100   www.co.st-louis.mo.us/parks/suson.html
Hours: Daily 10:30am-5:00pm (April-September). Closes at 3:00pm (October - March).

Country living is just around the corner at the Suson Park animal farm display. Most breeds of farm animals are represented for urban dwellers to see and enjoy, from the draft horses that helped plow our soil to examples of the modern cattle breeds. A lake is available for fishing. Free admission. (goats, pigs and chickens - cows and horses are in the barn on weekends).

OLD CHAIN OF ROCKS BRIDGE

10950 Riverview Drive (just below I-270, north of downtown St. Louis)
St. Louis 63137

www.nps.gov/nr/travel/route66/chain_of_rocks_bridge_illinois_missouri.html
Hours: Daily 9:00am-dusk.
Note: Follow the city's Riverfront Trail, a hiking and biking path, from the Old Chain of Rocks Bridge to the Gateway Arch.

The Old Chain of Rocks Bridge, at 5,353 feet long, is one of the world's longest bicycle and pedestrian bridges. The Bridge spans the Mississippi River and provides a vital link in the bi-state trail system, connecting to the St. Louis Riverfront Trail in Missouri and the MCT Confluence Trail in Illinois. The Bridge, once part of the beloved Route 66, has a rich history and is on the National Register of Historic Places. Located north of downtown, the bridge was Route 66's original crossing over the Mississippi River at St. Louis. The span, which is one of the longest pedestrian and biking bridges in the world, is open to visitors every day. From the bridge, you'll see stunning views of downtown

St. Louis and the city's whimsical castle-like water intake towers from high over the Mississippi. Route 66 themed bump-out, full-span pedestrian lighting, Missouri-side restrooms, benches, bike racks and interpretive plaques. Parking available on either side.

EAGLE DAYS AT THE OLD CHAIN OF ROCKS BRIDGE

St. Louis - Old Chain Of Rocks Bridge. This FREE public program gives visitors the opportunity to view wintering bald eagles in a natural habitat. Educational eagle program repeated every 20 minutes; Viewing scopes on the Bridge permit close-ups of eagles Lewis & Clark re-enactors interact with the public and acquaint visitors with aspects of their 1804-06 expedition, the Corps of Discovery; View St. Louis area birds through hands-on exhibits by St. Louis Audubon volunteers; Get your photo taken in the replica of an eagle's nest. Bring your binoculars and dress to stay warm. Note: Programming is at both Bridge entrances and in the middle of the Bridge. It is about a 1/2-mile walk to the middle of the Bridge for assisted eagle viewing and programming in the warming tent.

THE HILL

The Loop, along the St. Louis Walk of Fame **St. Louis** 63139

- **RIGAZZI'S RESTAURANT** - Toasted ravioli - sample the appetizer that originated on the Hill.
- **BLUEBERRY HILL** - *www.blueberryhill.com*. Some more toasted ravioli but they also have Cheddar Cheese Balls as an appetizer. Locals name it as the place for burgers - the famous 7oz hamburger with cheddar (soft spread). Their burgers avg. under $7.00 and nothing is over $12.00. In addition to its reputation for food and music, the restaurant is known as home to the world's best jukebox and eclectic collections that range from Chuck Berry's guitar to Howdy Doody items and vintage lunchboxes. After you place your order, play some pinball or video games.

ST. LOUIS STORYTELLING FESTIVAL

St. Louis - University of Missouri - St. Louis. ***http://stlstorytellingfestival.org/index.php/about***. 30-40 pro storytellers converge from across nation to perform in various locations around area. FREE. (first weekend in May).

CELEBRATE ST. LOUIS - FAIR ST. LOUIS

St. Louis - Downtown by the Arch. *http://celebratestlouis.org/Celebrate/index.cfm*. This annual Fourth of July event has a Parade, Air Show, K-Town Kids Zone, Local and national entertainment and Nationally recognized fireworks displays each night. FREE. (July 3rd and 4th). Following the Fourth of July fesKviKes, the celebraKon will conKnue throughout the month of July with the LIVE on the Levee concert series.

ST. LOUIS HOLIDAY MAGIC

St. Louis - The America's Center convention complex. Celebrate the holidays at Holiday Magic. The family-friendly show features unique shopping, dazzling holiday lights and decorations, indoor carnival rides and live entertainment. Admission. (first weekend in December).

FAUST PARK

15185 Olive Blvd. (Located one mile north of Highway 40/64)
St. Louis (Chesterfield) 63017

Phone: (314) 615-8328   https://www.facebook.com/FaustPark/

This is the home of three attractions for kids: the BUTTERFLY HOUSE, the HISTORICAL VILLAGE and the ST. LOUIS CAROUSEL. While the Historical Village typically is only open to tour groups, the buildings can be viewed from the outside using a free self-guided tour booklet available at the Seed Visitor Center. The Butterfly House has more than a 1,000 live, tropical butterflies flying freely in the 8,000-square-foot glass conservatory. Watch a butterfly emerge from a chrysalis, visit the outdoor Butterfly Garden, or enjoy indoor insect exhibits. (open year-round for $4.00-$6.00 per person). Next, take a ride on a fully restored, hand-carved 1920s Dentzel carousel with 67 animals and two chariots. ($2.00/ride, open February-December).

DID YOU KNOW ? If you wear bright colors, the resident butterflies are more likely to land on you for a quick, up-close experience.

SWING-A-ROUND FUN TOWN

335 Skinker Lane   St. Louis (Fenton) 63026

Phone: (636) 349-7007   www.swing-a-round.com
Hours: Monday-Thursday 10:00am-9:00pm, Friday-Saturday 10:00am-11:00pm, Sunday 11:00am-9:00pm.
Admission: Pay per activity with prices ranging from $1.00-$6.50. Discount packages available.

North East Area

Feel the need for speed? Swing-A-Round Fun Town is stocked with Go-Karts, bumper boats, batting cages and an arcade, and miniature golf pros will like the links at the amusement center. Fun centers are located in St. Charles and other neighboring cities, too.

CHALLENGER LEARNING CENTER - ST. LOUIS

205 Brotherton Lane (one mile north of I-70 off Florissant Road - next to McCluer South-Berkeley High School) **St. Louis (Ferguson)** 63135

Phone: (314) 521-6205 www.challengerstl.org
Hours: Public programs are available and hours are subject to change. Please call or visit website for most updated schedule.
Admission: $15.00 for public programs when available.
Tours: Brief training session, 2-hour mission, recommended for ages 11 and up.

The center provides hands-on space science education programs and features a replica space station and Mission Control center. Participants partake in a simulated space mission. Advance reservations required; check online calendar.

BIG FOOT 4 X 4 INC.

6311 N. Lindbergh Blvd **St. Louis (Hazelwood)** 63042

Phone: (314) 731-2822 www.bigfoot4x4.com
Hours: (Store) Monday-Friday 9:00am-5:00pm, Saturday 9:00am-1:00pm.
Admission: FREE.

The BIGFOOT® monster trucks have thrilled millions of fans in stadiums and arenas around the world, on television and in the movies. You can explore the world of "The Original Monster Truck®" where it all started, at BIGFOOT 4x4 Inc., the "Home of BIGFOOT," in St. Louis Missouri. The showroom also houses some truly great Bigfoot souvenirs, apparel and collectibles. Visiting Bigfoot 4x4 Inc. is an adventure in itself and includes a tour of the factory or the repair shop that makes the infamous monster trucks. It features more than 20 years of monster truck history and displays the world's largest collection of monster truck memorabilia. Before you leave, be sure to get a group picture standing in the wheel of just one monster machine.

ST. LOUIS MILLS MALL - SPORTSTREET

5555 St. Louis Mills Blvd **St. Louis (Hazelwood)** 63042
Phone: (314) 227-5900 www.stlouismills.com

St. Louis Mills is a retail and entertainment destination that offers a dynamic mix of value-priced shopping and interactive experiences, unique to St. Louis. With 12 anchor stores, including Missouri's only Cabela's, and over 160 specialty retailers, restaurants and entertainment venues, a mini express trackless train, plus a children's play area, there's something for everyone.

- SKATEPARK - www.plan-nine.net
- ICE ZONE - www.icezone.com
- NASCAR SPEEDPARK - www.nascarspeedpark.com
- PUTTING EDGE - www.putting-edge.com

MAGIC HOUSE: ST. LOUIS CHILDREN'S MUSEUM

516 S. Kirkwood Road (one mile north of I-44) **St. Louis (Kirkwood)** 63122
Phone: (314) 822-8900 www.magichouse.org
Hours: Monday-Saturday 9:30am-5:30pm. Friday until 9:00pm. Sunday 11:00am-5:30pm (Memorial Day-Labor Day). Tuesday-Thursday Noon-5:30pm, Friday Noon-9:00pm, Saturday 9:30am-5:30pm, Sunday 11:00am-5:30pm. (Labor Day-Memorial Day).
Admission: $11.00 (ages 1+).

Hands-on, the Magic House, St. Louis Children's Museum is a three-story facility set in a lovely Victorian home that tests minds and imaginations with plenty of "please touch" activities for everyone from babies to adults. Visit The Magic House to transform your silhouette into a kaleidoscope of color; lift yourself with a pulley; freeze your shadow on a wall; experiment in a water playground; make a three-dimensional impression of yourself; and zoom down a three-story slide! The static electricity ball is a favorite. Kids touch it and it makes their hair stand on end (they can even take a funny picture for a $3.00 fee). The popular attraction, which features indoor and outdoor play and learning areas, also hosts Seasonal favorites, such as Toddler Traffic Town and Sandcastle Beach, and traveling exhibits are always popular at the ever-changing Magic House. We like that each station is simple and clear and the settings for role-playing are very realistic. Best for kids ages 1-11.

For updates & travel games visit: **www.KidsLoveTravel.com**

POWDER VALLEY CONSERVATION NATURE CTR

11715 Cragwold Road (off I-44 at Geyer, then make the angled-back left onto Cragwold and follow the long winding road until you're parallel to I-270) **St. Louis (Kirkwood) 63122**

Phone: (314) 301-1500 https://nature.mdc.mo.gov/discover-nature/places/powder-valley-cnc
Hours: (Trails) 8:00am-dusk, open longer in summer. (Building) Tuesday-Saturday 8:00am-5:00pm. Gift shop closes at 4:30pm.

Most families start at the Nature Center. Kids wander around the displays about nature and bugs. They also have a big bee hive. Live animals include turtles and snakes. You can help feed aquarium fish at 2pm on Saturdays. Three hiking trails are all good for the novice; they're paved and they start from the parking lot. Sloping rocky woods are a haven of wildflowers, towering trees and tangled vines.

LAUMEIER SCULPTURE PARK

12580 Rott Road **St. Louis (Kirkwood) 63127**

Phone: (314) 615-5278 **www.laumeier.com**
Hours: (Park) Daily, 8:00am to sunset with the exception of Christmas Day and the Thursday before the annual Art Fair in early May. (Museum Gallery & Shops) Tuesday-Friday 10:00am-5:00pm, Saturday-Sunday Noon-5:00pm.
Tours: During regular Museum Shop hours visitors can rent iPods and take audio tour that highlights the collection. Also From Spring to Fall, free docent-led tours are available the first and third Sundays of each month from May-October. One-hour tours depart from the Museum Shop at 2:00pm. FREE

Head west for Laumeier Sculpture Park for free art of another kind. The open air "museum" features a fascinating - and sometimes whimsical - world-class collection of more than 70 modern sculptures. The 105-acre campus includes indoor galleries and exhibitions of paintings, ceramics, glass and photography related to the outdoor sculpture program, as well as an outdoor garden. Each August the park brings in tons of sand for fantasy sand castle. Mid-December is winter solstice with fire/ice sculptures.

JEFFERSON BARRACKS HISTORIC PARK

345 North Road (End of South Broadway south of Kingston in south St. Louis County) **St. Louis (Lemay) 63125**

Phone: (314) 638-2100 www.stlouisco.com/ParksandRecreation/ParkPages/JeffersonBarracks
Hours: (grounds) 8:00am to one half hour past sunset (Museum buildings) open from Noon-4:00pm Wednesday-Sunday.

Jefferson Barracks was a U.S. Army military post from 1826-1946 and for many years was the most important station on the frontier. As a result, more officers who would become generals of both armies served here before the Civil War than at any other place. The museum buildings date back to the 1850s and the site is now a park operated by St.Louis County and offers a Visitors Center and many historical events.

DID YOU KNOW ? The first successful parachute jump from an airplane took place at St. Louis' Jefferson Barracks in 1912.

WORLD WAR II WEEKEND

St. Louis (Lemay) - Jefferson Barracks - WWII Weekend is one of the largest and oldest WWII reenactment events in the St. Louis area. It has been held at for more than 25 years. This event is hosted by the U.S. 2nd Ranger Infantry Battalion of St. Louis, a unit that is more than 32 years old, to honor all those who have served in the US Armed Forces. There are living history camps daily, containing up to 350 re-enactors. Three battles will be staged. http://2ndrangers.org/wwii_weekend.php. FREE. (last weekend in April)

LIVING HISTORY HAYRIDES

St. Louis (Lemay) - Jefferson Barracks - Jefferson Barracks was a military base from 1826-1946. The hayrides travel through the park, stopping as camps of soldiers from the Revolutionary War, Civil War, and World War II. Re-enactors help you travel through the past. Admission (May & Sept wknds)

AQUAPORT

2344 McKelvey Road **St. Louis (Maryland Heights)** 63043

Phone: (314) 738-2599 www.marylandheights.com/index.aspx?page=97
Hours: Saturday-Thursday 11:00am-7:00pm, Friday 11:00am-8:00pm (late May - mid-August). Only open on weekends after mid-August.
Admission: $15.00 adult (16+), $10.00 senior (62+) & youth (4-15). Resident discounts available.

A family fun, four-acre water park that includes six water slides, a lazy river, children's pool, family leisure pool and the Extreme Bowl. Food, refreshments, lockers and free parking available.

THIES FARM & GREENHOUSES

St. Louis (Maryland Heights) - *www.thiesfarm.com*. 3120 Maryland Heights Expy. Each fall, this farm transforms itself into Pumpkinland. The farm-based play area entertains little ones with cable gliders, slides, tunnels, obstacle courses, a suspended bridge, petting zoos, a cornfield maze and wagon rides. Each season brings new fruits to pick and purchase.

For updates & travel games visit: **www.KidsLoveTravel.com**

North East Area

FITZ'S AMERICAN GRILL & BOTTLING CO.

St. Louis (University City) - 6605 Delmar Blvd 63130. Phone: (314) 726-9555 ***www.FitzsRootBeer.com***. Hours: Open daily at 11:00am. Closing will vary between 9:00pm and Midnight depending upon season/day of week. Field Trips:You and your class can see how root beer is made, learn about the neighborhood, and enjoy an activity Wednesday, Thursday, Friday mornings by appointment. This is the place where root beer floats rule. Enjoy a meal and watch the bottling process at Fitz's, which began selling its famous root beer at Fitz's Drive-In in 1947. Noted for incredible smoothness and thick, creamy texture, Fitz's Root Beer was served in mugs and quickly became the root beer of choice among St. Louisans. The recipe is a closely guarded secret but they do reveal one secret - they still use pure cane sugar in the formula. Call ahead for bottling schedules. A full menu is offered, from 15 different gourmet hamburgers to delicious salads, pizzas and entrees. Special kids meals and treats are offered. Each Kids Meal is served up in a mini-auto. Most every plate is under $10.00.

ULYSSES S. GRANT NATIONAL HISTORIC SITE

7400 Grant Road **St. Louis (White Haven)** 63123

Phone: (314) 842-3298 **www.nps.gov/ulsg**
Hours: Daily 9:00am-5:00pm.
Admission: Entrance into the site is FREE. Visits inside the Main House are also FREE, however, tickets (time-specific "calling cards") are required, and are available at the Visitor Center.
Tours: Free interpretive visits to the Main House are usually offered every 30 minutes beginning at 9:30am. Typically the last house visit of the day begins at 4:00pm.
*Note: Grant's Farm is just down the street. You can park at Grant's Farm, with plenty of parking, and walk to the Ulysses S. Grant NHS via a public walking trail. Educators: Reading History Cards (small lessons) are found here: **www.nps.gov/ulsg/forkids/tradingcards.htm***

The property Grant considered his family home for four decades, White Haven, at the Ulysses S. Grant National Historic Site, commemorates the life, military career and presidency of Grant, as well as his wife, Julia Dent Grant. The 9.65-acre site contains six structures including the main house and a visitor center. There's a short movie to set the scene, a tour guide then gives you an overview about the house and then visitors can make their way around the house and grounds at their leisure. While the house is nice, kids may gravitate to the interactive exhibits in the museum (it's located in the historic stable). The displays really give you the sense he loved family life.

DID YOU KNOW? After his presidency, Grant planned to retire to the home but sold it to pay off a debt just before his death in 1885.

CUIVRE RIVER STATE PARK

678 State Route 147 **Troy** 63379

Phone: (636) 528-7247 **https://mostateparks.com/park/cuivre-river-state-park**
Admission: The Missouri state park system does not charge entrance fees. However, there are fees associated with camping, lodging, tours, museums and special events.

This park encompasses much of the rugged, wooded terrain that surrounds Big Sugar Creek in the southern Lincoln Hills. A stroll through the park in the spring when many woodland wildflowers are in bloom or in the fall when the prairie grasses tower over your head is an outdoor delight. It includes a lake, a visitor center, hiking and equestrian trails, and campsites.

WORLD BIRD SANCTUARY

125 Bald Eagle Ridge Road **Valley Park** 63088

Phone: (636) 225-4390 www.worldbirdsanctuary.org
Note: While you're in town, stop at the WHITTLE SHORTLINE RAILROAD (**www.woodentrain.com**) for a look at the 15-foot-long train table designed so little engineers can try out the merchandise. Parents hang out on benches while the kids play with the trains.

At the World Bird Sanctuary, the kids can learn about some of the most majestic creatures of the wild - eagles, hawks and other birds of prey. Live displays feature bald eagles, owls, hawks, falcons, vultures, parrots, reptiles and more. There are hiking trails throughout the sanctuary's 305-acre wooded property. Picnic tables available. FREE. Hours: Daily 8:00am-5:00pm.

ILINIWEK VILLAGE STATE HISTORIC SITE

(2 miles north of Wayland on Hwy. 27, take gravel roads to site)
Wayland 63472

Phone: (660) 877-3871 **https://mostateparks.com/park/iliniwek-village-state-historic-site**
Admission: The Missouri state park system does not charge entrance fees. However, there are fees associated with camping, lodging, tours, museums and certain special events.

This was once the site of a village inhabited by American Indians of the Iliniwek Confederacy. It is the only Illinois village site so far found in Missouri. The historic site interprets the history and daily life of the Illinois Indians and the Jolliet and Marquette expedition of 1673. The Illinois Indians were the first Native Americans that Louis Jolliet and Father Jacques Marquette encountered in present-day Missouri in 1673. At that time, the village contained 300 lodges and perhaps 8,000 people. Evidence of early European contact appears in archaeological finds through glass beads, metal objects and Jesuit trade rings. A short walking trail crosses the site, and the location of an excavated Illinois Indian longhouse is marked to show its size

JONES - CONFLUENCE STATE PARK

1000 Riverlands Way **West Alton** 63386

Phone: (636) 899-1135 https://mostateparks.com/park/edward-ted-and-pat-jones-confluence-point-state-park

Admission: The Missouri state park system does not charge entrance fees.

In 1804, Meriwether Lewis and William Clark began their journey up the Missouri River at the confluence of the two great rivers of North America, the Missouri and Mississippi. Today, visitors can watch as the Big Muddy and Mighty Mississippi merge into one at Edward "Ted" and Pat Jones - Confluence Point State Park. The role that both rivers played in the Lewis and Clark Expedition and the history of the rivers are interpreted at the park in outdoor exhibits. A short interpretive trail takes visitors to the confluence point. NOTE: Heavy rainfall in spring/fall temporarily closes this state park.

BABLER MEMORIAL STATE PARK

800 Guy Park Drive **Wildwood** 63005

Phone: (636-) 458-3813 https://mostateparks.com/park/dr-edmund-babler-memorial-state-park

Admission: The Missouri state park system does not charge entrance fees. However, there are fees associated with camping, lodging, tours, museums and certain special events.

Note: The park also provides experiences for those with special needs at the Jacob L. Babler Outdoor Education Center, a barrier-free resident camp with swimming pool (exclusive to outdoor education center users), cabins and recreation and dining halls.

Located in the St. Louis area, this wooded park in the Missouri River hills features camping, hiking and equestrian trails, a paved bicycle trail, picnic areas, interpretive programs and a visitor center. A visitor center with exhibits illustrates the wonders of the park's natural communities; classrooms and an auditorium are available for special programs. Several special events are offered annually. They include Bug Day.

HIDDEN VALLEY SKI RESORT

17409 Hidden Valley Drive **Wildwood** 63025
Phone: (636) 938-5373 or Snow Report @ (636) 938-6999
www.hiddenvalleyski.com

A resort that is fun for all levels or skiing or snowboarding, with 310 feet of vertical drop. Beginners: a wonder carpet. Advanced: Outlaw Terrain Park

North West Area

Chapter 3
North West (NW)

QUICK LOOK...

The Pony Express & Trails West

Outlaw Jesse James

Presidential Stories

Trains, toys, craft & covered wagons

Fun Places to Eat

KIDS LOVE MISSOURI

Belton
- Belton, Grandview & Kansas City Railroad Co.

Blue Springs
- Burr Oak Woods Conservation Nature Center
- Fleming Park & Blue Springs Lake
- Dogtober Fest

Cameron
- Wallace State Park

Craig
- Big Lake State Park

Grandview
- Truman National Historic Site

Hamilton
- J. C. Penney Museum & Boyhood Home

Higginsville
- Confederate Memorial State Historic Site

Independence
- 1859 Jail, Marshal's Home And Museum
- Adventure Oasis Water Park
- Chicago & Alton Train Depot
- National Frontier Trails Center
- Pioneer Trails Adventures
- Truman Home, Museum And Information Center
- Puppetry Arts Institute
- Cool Crest Family Fun Center
- Strawberry Festival At Vaile Mansion

Jamesport
- Amish Community Of Jamesport

Kansas City
- Arthur Bryant's Barbecue
- Fiorella's Jack Stack Restaurants
- American Royal Museum & Visitor Center

Kansas City (cont.)
- Arabia Steamboat Museum
- City Hall Observation
- City Market
- College Basketball Experience
- Chips Chocolate Factory
- Coterie Theatre
- Crayola Café
- Crown Center
- Fritz's Railroad Restaurant
- Hallmark Visitor Center
- Kaleidoscope
- KC Rail Experience
- National WwI Museum At Liberty Memorial
- Negro Leagues Baseball Museum
- Science City
- Union Station Complex
- Kemper Museum Of Contemporary Art
- Nelson-Atkins Museum Of Art
- Thomas Hart Benton Home And Studio State Historic Site
- Toy And Miniature Museum
- John Wornall House
- Kansas City Chiefs - Arrowhead Stadium
- Kansas City Royals - Kauffman Stadium
- Kansas City Zoo
- Lakeside Nature Center
- Cave Spring Historic Site And Nature Center
- Coco Key Water Resort
- Longview Lake Park
- Shoal Creek Living History Museum
- Oceans Of Fun
- Worlds Of Fun
- Federal Reserve Bank Of Kansas City
- Schlitterbahn Vacation Village Waterpark
- Festa Italiana
- KCriverfest
- Faulkner's Pumpkin Farm
- Kansas City Ballet Presents "The Nutcracker"

For updates & travel games visit: **www.KidsLoveTravel.com**

North West Area

Kansas City (Westport)
- Battle Of Westport

Kansas City, KS
- Great Wolf Lodge
- Renaissance Festival

Kearney
- Jesse James Farm & Museum

Kingsville
- Powell Gardens

Laclede
- Gen. John J Pershing Boyhood Home State Historic Site
- Pershing State Park

Lawson
- Watkins Mill State Park & Site

Lee's Summit
- Missouri Town 1855
- Paradise Park Family Entertainment Center

Lexington
- Battle Of Lexington State Site

Liberty
- Jesse James Bank Museum
- Martha Lafite Thompson Nature Sanctuary
- Carolyn's Country Cousins Farm Pumpkin Patch

Marceline
- Walt Disney Hometown Museum

Maryville
- Mozingo Lake & Recreation

Meadville
- Fountain Grove Conservation Area

Miami
- Van Meter State Park

Mound City
- Squaw Creek National Wildlife Refuge

North Kansas City
- Chappell's Restaurant And Sports Museum

Osborn
- Shatto Milk Company

Platte City
- Pumpkins Etc.

Rushville
- Lewis And Clark State Park

Sibley
- Ft. Osage National Landmark

St. Joseph
- First Street Trolley
- Robidoux Row Museum
- Jesse James Home Museum
- Patee House Museum
- Pony Express Museum
- Remington Nature Center
- Schweizer Orchards
- Trails West Festival
- St. Joe Corn Maze

Sumner
- Swan Lake National Wildlife Refuge

Trenton
- Crowder State Park

Weston
- Snow Creek Ski Area
- Weston Bend State Park

Weston
- Weston Red Barn Farm
- Ferries Over Mississippi

Sites and attractions are listed in order by City, Zip Code, and Name. Symbols indicated represent: 🍴 Restaurants   🛏 Lodging

BELTON, GRANDVIEW & KANSAS CITY RAILROAD CO.

502 E. Walnut St. 10 miles south of the I-470, I-435, US 71 interchange (the Grandview Triangle) **Belton** 64012

Phone: (816) 331-0630 www.beltonrailroad.org
Tours: May thru Fall. $10.00 - $12.00 per person. Fares are for ages 3+. Weekends. Note: Train is neither heated nor air conditioned, we suggest you dress for the weather on the day of your visit.

If you're looking for a scenic ride in a full-size train, here's a place to step back in time aboard a 1920s era passenger train. 45 minute round trip train ride travels in 1920s open window coach and 1960s open air flatcar with picnic tables. The museum also offers a first-hand look at a 1950s diesel locomotive, along with a passenger car and caboose. You can even ride in the caboose with the conductor or in the cab of the locomotive with the engineer.

BELTON RAILROAD SANTA TRAIN

Belton - Belton Railroad - This event features a real train decorated in lights, complete with cookies, hot chocolate and the chance to meet Santa. The train departs the museum at 10:00am on Saturday. Admission. (first Saturday in December).

For updates & travel games visit: **www.KidsLoveTravel.com**

North West Area

BURR OAK WOODS NATURE CENTER

1401 NW Park Road (20 miles east of Kansas City) **Blue Springs** 64015

Phone: (816) 228-3766 https://nature.mdc.mo.gov/discover-nature/places/burr-oak-woods-ca

Hours: *(Trails) Daily 7:00am-6:00pm (until 8:00pm during DST). (Nature Center) Tuesday-Saturday 8:00am-5:00pm.*

Nestled in the heart of this conservation area are five hiking trails, including two paved trails, which provide easy access to most parts of the area. The area is composed of woodlands, glades, native grass and forb plantings. The Nature Center features conservation exhibits including a 3,000-gallon aquarium, a wildlife viewing room and a variety of live amphibians and reptiles. Multimedia programs allow kids to make decisions about the environment and see the results. Can you balance human wants and needs with conservation of natural resources?

FLEMING PARK & BLUE SPRINGS LAKE

22807 Woods Chapel Road (2 miles east of I-470 and Highway 291) **Blue Springs** 64015

Phone: (816) 503-4800 www.jacksongov.org

Blue Springs Lake, located in Fleming Park, offers 720 acres of water excitement. Power boating, water skiing, tubing and jet skiing are all familiar sights on this popular lake, which also features a beach. The park also has a campground, nature trails, a radio-controlled model airplane and boat area, an archery range, native hoofed animal enclosure where bison and elk roam freely, and an observation tower that lets you watch the animals from up high. Tours of the animal enclosures on a hay-filled truck are available for a small fee on Saturdays. Bring apples or pears to feed the animals.

DOGTOBER FEST

Blue Springs - Fleming Park, ***www.jacksongov.org/dogtober/*** Kemper Outdoor Education Center. A day of dog shows, competitions and fun. Many dog breed clubs and vendors are featured. Special demonstrations by Jackson County Sheriff's K9 Unit; search and rescue; and dock diving dogs. There is a special Tails for Trails dog walk. FREE. (third Sunday in October)

WALLACE STATE PARK

10621 NE Hwy. 121 **Cameron** 64429

Phone: (816) 632-3745 https://mostateparks.com/park/wallace-state-park
Admission: The Missouri state park system does not charge entrance fees. However, there are fees associated with camping, lodging, tours, museums and special events.

Close to Kansas City, this park is a destination for bird-watchers, nature lovers and anyone seeking tranquility away from the city. Hiking trails meander through the wooded hills and a campground and small lake are other features.

BIG LAKE STATE PARK

204 Lake Shore Drive (just off I-29) **Craig** 64437

Phone: (660) 442-3770 or (660) 442-5432 (Lodging)
https://mostateparks.com/park/big-lake-state-park
Admission: The Missouri state park system does not charge entrance fees.

The 625-acre, natural oxbow Big Lake borders the park, which lies along a major migratory flyway. The park features fishing, a motel, snack bar, store, camping, a pool and cabins for a fee.

TRUMAN FARM NATIONAL HISTORIC SITE

12301 Blue Ridge Blvd **Grandview** 64030

Phone: (816) 254-9929 www.nps.gov/hstr/learn/historyculture/truman-farm-home-photo-tour.htm
Hours: Grounds are open year-round for free self-guided tours. Audio tours available. Farmhouse is currently not open for tours.
Educators: Your family can take a cell phone tour of all the properties: **www.nps.gov/hstr/photosmultimedia/cell-phone-tour.htm**.

Located in the center of what was once an expansive 600-acre farm, this quiet prairie home was the stomping grounds for a young Harry S. Truman, who worked the farm into his late teens. Harry Truman's story is one of hope and frustration, choice and chance. As President, he took the US from its traditional isolationism into the age of international involvement.

J. C. PENNEY MUSEUM & BOYHOOD HOME

312 North Davis Street **Hamilton** 64644

Phone: (816) 583-2168
www.cityofhamiltonmo.com/jcpenney/index.html
Hours: Monday-Friday 9:00am-Noon, 1:00pm-5:00pm, Saturday 9:00am-Noon. Hours subject to change, please call to verify.
Admission: FREE.

The J.C. Penney Museum presents the life and career of the famous store chain entrepreneur. Penney grew up here and owned farmland here. The Museum tour includes a 20-minute video. Penney's home is restored to its late 19th century appearance. Parents like the fact that, weaved through most every quote or directive J.C. Penney gave, are hints of the Golden Rule.

CONFEDERATE MEMORIAL ST HISTORIC SITE
211 West First Street **Higginsville** 64037

Phone: (660) 584-2853 **www.mostateparks.com/confedmem.htm**
*Admission: The Missouri state park system does not charge entrance fees. However, there are fees associated with camping, lodging, tours, museums and special events.
Tours: Interpreters conduct free guided tours of portions of Historic Site. Each tour takes approximately 45 minutes and includes the chapel and cemetery.*

The home was used to house dependent Confederate veterans and their families. Foot soldiers, artillery and cavalrymen, marines, guerilla fighters and even spies found a place of rest here in their old age. The very last of these former rebel soldiers, John T. Graves, died at the home in 1950 at the age of 108. The grounds include the century-old chapel and cottage, a farmhouse, and the 1920s-era hospital building. Interpretive exhibits tell the story of the home and other historic buildings. There are picnic sites in the shade of fine old trees and fishing in one of the many lakes in the park.

1859 JAIL, MARSHAL'S HOME AND MUSEUM
217 North Main Street **Independence** 64050

Phone: (816) 252-1892 **www.jchs.org/1859-old-jail/**
*Hours: Monday-Saturday 10:00am-4:00pm, Sunday 1:00-4:00pm (April-October).
Admission: $6.00 adult, $5 senior (55+), $3.00 youth (6-16).
Note: Guided tours by Pioneer Trails offer covered wagon rides from the square featuring discussion of Independence's historic sites and Civil War history. Educators: a teacher's guide is available here:* **www.jchs.org/education/guide.html.**

Massive walls, barred windows that once housed Frank James give an authentic look at frontier justice and mid-1800s home life. In 1907, a brick jail was added to the back of the limestone jail to house chain gangs. Chain gangs were used to build roads, sewers and other tasks assigned them. They left six days a week at sunrise and returned at sunset. One inmate spent a year on the chain gang for stealing a cow. Four feet away is a federalist style house that was home for county marshal until 1920s. Everything is set up as it was at the time of the Civil War. Take a self-guided tour of the jail and museum for a first hand look at frontier justice. Tour the beautifully decorated home where the wife and children of the marshal lived.

ADVENTURE OASIS WATER PARK

2100 South Hub Drive (Just off 23rd Street, just west of the Rte. 291 intersection) **Independence** 64050

Phone: (816) 325-7843
www.ci.independence.mo.us/parksandrec/AdvenOasis.aspx
Hours: Call or see website (Memorial Day-Labor Day)
Admission: $9 adult, $6 youth/senior (12 under, over 65), $25 family.

This exciting aquatic area is a state-of-the-art facility featuring a 900-foot long continuous lazy river ride with waterfall, 6,000-square-foot interactive family play pool with zero-depth entry, six-lane 25-yard lap pool with diving area, and three water slides: 210-foot open flume slide, 197-foot enclosed tube slide and 308-foot raft slide. It also contains a 30,000 square foot sun deck, modern bathhouse and full-service concessions.

CHICAGO & ALTON TRAIN DEPOT

318 West Pacific Avenue (3 blocks South of the Independence Square) **Independence** 64050

Phone: (816) 325-7955 www.chicagoaltondepot1879.org
Hours: Monday, Wednesday, Thursday, Friday & Saturday 9:30am-4:30pm, Sunday 12:30-4:30pm. (April-October)

Independence is also home to The Chicago & Alton Train Depot - a stunning two-story depot that depicts a 1890s-era depot. As you walk through the door, you'll see the waiting room where passengers purchased tickets and an original bell from a Santa Fe train. There's also a baggage room, living quarters and an extensive display of railroad artifacts. In celebration of the holiday season, the depot hosts "A Visit from St. Nicholas" on Dec Saturdays.

NATIONAL FRONTIER TRAILS CENTER

318 West Pacific Avenue **Independence** 64050

Phone: (816) 325-7575 www.ci.independence.mo.us/nftm/
Hours: Monday-Saturday 9:00am-4:30pm, Sunday 12:30pm-4:30pm.
Admission: $6.00 adult, $5.00 senior (62+), $3.00 youth (6-17).
*Educators: Teacher Resource Packets on trails topics in history is found here: **www.ci.independence.mo.us/nftm/TeacherResources.aspx***

Learn what it would be like to be a 19th century pioneer family. Hear tales of those who headed west from Independence along the Santa Fe, Oregon and California Trails in covered wagons. Learn about mountain man John Coulter, who went west and why, hop aboard a covered wagon for a narrated tour of historic sites, and learn how wagon trains prepared for their trips west.

For updates & travel games visit: **www.KidsLoveTravel.com**

North West Area

Begin your visit by viewing the museum's award winning film, "West." This 17-minute film gives an overview of America's westward expansion. Look for two authentic pioneer wagons (large, hard to miss) and learn about the trades and businesses that prepared emigrants for the journey. Interactive exhibits test your knowledge of the trails and allow you to see some of the supplies that explorers and pioneers brought through this region. Do you know what brought the overland wagon trails to an end?

Outside: Evidence of the migration can still be seen today in the form of swales, or wagon ruts, left in the field directly across the street from the museum campus. A 1/4-mile long asphalt pathway circles around the swales. Interpretive signs. Handicapped accessible.

PIONEER TRAILS ADVENTURES

533 S. Pleasant Street (Historic Independence Square)
Independence 64050

Phone: (816) 254-2466 or (816) 456-4991
www.pioneertrailsadventures.com
Hours: Daily 9:30am-4:30pm (April-October). Reservation only (Nov-March).
Admission: $7.00 child-$25.00adult depending on tour option selected.
Tours: During April-October reservations are not required but helpful. Various tour options are available from a 30-minute Town Square Tour, up to a 45-minute Full City Tour.

See Independence as a pioneer would, by mule-drawn covered wagon (or sleigh in the snow). Visit the city where the journey to the Wild West began. The Historic Independence square was the host of two Civil War battles, William Quantrill and his raiders, General Sterling Price, Wild Bill Hickok, and notorious outlaws such as the James brothers. Pass by the home where one President began his march to the White House or the place where young Harry had his first job. On your wagon tour find out why: Frank James' jail cell door was never shut, why Order number 11 made Harry S. Truman emphatic about the Marshal Plan, how the painting of order number 11 destroyed a mighty General, why Missouri is the Show-Me-State and so much more. Pioneer history is explored with specific attention to the preparation for the journey west and the responsibility of each member on the wagon train, even the children. What would you pack for the journey? Your family should start with this tour and then determine which historical sites you may still want to visit for a tour. Often, the young ones opt out of (or take naps) stuffy old buildings but really enjoy the covered wagon tour!

TRUMAN HOME, MUSEUM AND INFORMATION CENTER

223 N Main St. (Take I-70 W to Noland Road. Exit and travel north about five miles to U.S. Highway 24 E) **Independence** 64050

Phone: (816) 254-4491 **www.nps.gov/hstr** or **www.trumanlibrary.org**
Hours: Visitors Center open Tuesday-Saturday 8:30am-5:00pm.
Tours: Thirty minute guided tours. Admission to the Truman Farm Home is by guided tour only. Each tour is limited to 6 people. Tickets on first-come first-served basis. Tour Fee: $7.00 (age 16+).
Educators: Lesson Plans on Harry Truman, the Presidency and Independence, MO are on the FOR TEACHERS>Lesson Plans

Travelers to Independence can still experience Truman's town and follow in his footsteps on a neighborhood walking tour. Start at visitor center to view a 12 minute intro slide program and buy tickets or join group tours of Truman's home and farm.

The Harry S. Truman Library & Museum recounts the life of America's 33rd president, Harry S. Truman. The museum's two permanent exhibits chronicle the Missourian's private life and political career — with exhibits depicting his most difficult decisions. As you enter, an impressive 495-square-foot mural named "Independence and the Opening of the West" depicts three decades of Independence's history in the mid-1800s. Want to see what a president was like as a kid? The "Life & Times" section chronicles Truman's boyhood, family life and his role as "Mr. Citizen." While the younger set may not "get it," the Decision Theatres offer two interactive auditoriums that put the audience into the President's shoes to make important Oval Office decisions. Kids can help their parents vote how they would respond to Truman-era issues such as 1948 election pressures and Cold War spies. Another spot that all kids recognize - the Oval Office replica.

The <u>HARRY S. TRUMAN WALKING TRAIL</u> on Truman Road is a 2.7 mile sidewalk trail that was Truman's favorite route in Independence. The 43 plaques embedded in sidewalks along the route focus on Truman and his hometown. Brochures are available at key points.

The <u>TRUMAN HOME</u>, 219 Delaware, showcases the simple life Truman and his beloved Bess enjoyed in Independence before and after his presidency. The National Park Service offers tours every 15 minutes. Also in Independence, the Truman Depot (111 W. Pacific) served as the final stop for Truman's 1948 Whistlestop Campaign. Now a working Amtrak station, more than 8,500 admirers greeted Truman and Bess there when the pair returned to town following his second term. Don't forget to stop by Clinton's Soda Fountain,

100 W. Maple, where 14-year-old Harry earned $3 a week at his first job. You can still order ice cream treats at the counter. (closed Sundays)

DID YOU KNOW? The sayings: "Monday morning quarterback" and "The buck stops here" are both expressions popularized by Truman.

PUPPETRY ARTS INSTITUTE
11025 East Winner Road **Independence** 64052

Phone: (816) 833-9724 **www.hazelle.org**
Hours: Tuesday-Saturday 10am-4pm. Visit website for most current schedule.
Admission: $5.00+/person includes program and museum. $3.00 for just exhibits.

This building is home to marionettes created by renowned manufacturer Hazelle Rollins. Institute is magical with fabulous puppets from around the world. Tour the puppet museum, paint a puppet head, dress it in a costume and perform an impromptu show. Everyone gets one Free finger puppet or make-your-own puppet head. Like many other puppet factories, most are amazed at how professional and entertaining real puppetry art is.

COOL CREST FAMILY FUN CENTER
10735 E. US Highway 40 **Independence** 64055

Phone: (816) 358-0088 https://**coolcrest.com**
Hours: Vary by season and attraction. Call or check website for current schedule.
Admission: Pricing is flexible with options ranging from individual game tokens, per ride prices, or Unlimited Fun Passes are priced per hour.

This large facility features video games and redemption games for the whole family; four 18-hole mini golf courses; an eatery featuring pizza, ice cream and such; batting cages; go-karts; and an indoor playground.

STRAWBERRY FESTIVAL AT VAILE MANSION
Independence - 1500 N Liberty. Enjoy a day of free music and entertainment, crafts, antiques, flea markets, flowering baskets, all kinds of strawberry treats, children's activities, antique cars, carriage rides, home tours by costumed guides, and concessions. Admissions to grounds is free; extra charge for home tours or carriage rides. (first Saturday in June).

AMISH COMMUNITY OF JAMESPORT
Jamesport 64648

Phone: (660) 684-6704 or (660) 684-6146 www.jamesport.net
Hours: Most stores are open 8:00am-5:00pm. All stores are closed on Sundays, and most of the Amish businesses are closed on Thursdays as well.
Tours: Various tour options from guided to self (w/CD) are available. www.stepbackintimetours.net.
Note: All stores accept cash and check. Many stores in town accept Visa and Mastercard, but most Amish stores do not.

Missouri's largest Amish Community offers Amish furniture and other handcrafted items as well as baked goods and horse-churned ice cream. Spend the afternoon browsing "English" shops downtown or Amish shops in the outskirts (a map of locations is available at City Hall). Feed Jersey calves a bottle and take a break from cell phones (no service in town), credit cards, internet and movies. The Amish are welcoming and friendly but live simple lives and do not want to be interviewed or have photos taken of them. As you Following is a list of Amish & Brethren businesses you'll probably want to visit to get the full experience:

- **H & M COUNTRY STORE, COUNTRYSIDE BAKERY** - 21910 St. Hwy 190, (660) 684-6848. They sell eight varieties of bread, dinner rolls, homemade noodles, cinnamon rolls, cookies, and pies. At H & M, you'll see an Amish grocery with bulk spices, mixes, homemade noodles, jams, butters, farm fresh eggs, dried fruit, and snacks.

- **HOMESTEAD CREAMERY** - 2059 Liv 506, (660) 684-6970. The Flory's, a Brethren family, operate this local dairy and creamery. They raise Jersey cows and make natural rinded Farmstead cheese on site. On Tuesdays, you can watch cheese making. On Saturday, we saw cheese packaging. They provide free samples of the cheeses in their shop. Often, a family member will take the kids out to the barn and teach them to bottle feed calves.

- **OAKRIDGE FURNITURE & CRAFTS** - 799 SW 80th St, (660) 684-6802. The highlight of this stop was the Horse Churned Ice Cream (available seasonally on Saturdays)! Kids are absolutely intrigued to see a horse making ice cream! At Oakridge, they sell handcrafted furniture, wooden toys, and clocks. The quilt shop features quilts and Amish Dolls. They also sell Christian books & Amish Cookbooks.

North West Area

DINING

- **GINGERICH DUTCH PANTRY**: Intersection of Auberry Grove and Broadway, (660) 684-6212. Homemade soups, noodles, sandwiches and baked goods.
- **COUNTRY CUPBOARD**: Old Hwy 6, (660) 684-6597. Home cookin' style menu.
- **JAMESPORT TAVERN & GRILL**: 209 S Locust, (660) 684-9906. Traditional grill menu. The unique feature here? The restaurant is also a retailer of shotguns, black powder supplies, antique guns and restoration.

ARTHUR BRYANT'S BARBECUE

Kansas City - *http://arthurbryants.com/*. Author Calvin Trillin once declared Arthur Bryant's "the single best restaurant in the world." Kansas City's world famous barbecue is available at more than 100 area restaurants. It's a barbecue mecca where presidents, poets and paupers have dined. Some complain that Arthur Bryant's rests on old laurels; others insist that such steadfastness is a virtue. Judge for yourself. And don't forget to wipe your chin. The sauce is like nothing you can get anywhere else. It is so unique that you might not even like it so don't plan on taking finicky kids here for BBQ (order sides for them).

FIORELLA'S JACK STACK RESTAURANTS

Kansas City - *www.jackstackbbq.com*. Experience a 50-year tradition of remarkable barbecue. Each restaurant reflects its unique neighborhood: the romance of the Country Club Plaza, the history of the Downtown Freight House (Union Station area), the energy of Overland Park, and the warm welcome waiting for you at Martin City. While Gates sauce is spicy, we liked Fiorella's Jack Stack for families. Most moms will appreciate how their kid's menu doubles as an activity sheet and they offer seven different items including Sliced Meat (just like the grown-ups), ribs, chicken, grilled cheese or hot dogs. All meals are $4.95 and include milk, juice or soft drink. Adult entrees run $10.00-$25.00 and feature beef, pork, chicken, turkey and lamb slow-smoked to perfection in an authentic brick oven. They even serve the burnt ends as a specialty! And, the dry seasoning rub – served on the table – is good enough to make you want to buy some to take home.

AMERICAN ROYAL MUSEUM & VISITOR CENTER

1701 American Royal Court, Downtown/Conv. Center area (From downtown Kansas City: Take 12th Street west to Genessee) **Kansas City** 64102

Phone: (816) 221-9800 www.americanroyal.com
Hours: Open during specific events during the American Royal season or by request. Most events are in the fall.
Admission: Contact the Visitors Center or go online for details of event fees.

Started as a livestock show in 1899, the American Royal aims to educate the public about agriculture and celebrates Kansas City's heritage of equestrian sports, rodeo and livestock shows. In the Visitors Center children can sit on an English or Western saddle, weigh themselves on a livestock scale, play with farm items, see a film about the annual rodeo or train themselves to be an American Royal judge. Exhibits explain role agribusiness plays in our lives.

AMERICAN ROYAL LIVESTOCK, HORSE SHOW & RODEO

Kansas City - One of Top 20 pro rodeos in the nation. Commercial trade show, a petting area, and a full schedule of livestock shows, competitions, rodeos, and big name entertainers. Event begins with city's largest parade and a barbecue contest. Admission. (early Oct to mid-Nov)

ARABIA STEAMBOAT MUSEUM

400 Grand Blvd. (located next to the City Market complex) **Kansas City** 64106

Phone: (816) 471-1856 www.1856.com
Hours: Monday - Saturday first tour begins at 10:00am and last tour begins at 3:30pm (new tours start every 30 minutes). Sunday first tour is Noon and last tour begins at 3:30pm. Slightly reduced hours each winter.
Admission: $14.50 adult, $13.50 senior (60+), $5.50 child (4-14).
Educators: PDFs (grade appropriate) with lessons, games and quizzes are found >Plan Your Visit>Field Trips>. These sheets are nice to fill out as the students explore the showcases and dioramas looking for clues to answer the questions.

The story of the shipwrecked *Arabia* and its excavation is a modern day tale of adventure, captivating all who visit the museum – especially any explorers in the family. Buried more than 132 years, the ship's cargo is on display at the museum and the "inventory" collected is often referred to as a Wal-Mart of the 1800s. Discover what the phrase "high flutant" comes from and why did parts of the boat have to have a shower 2-3 times a day. Can you identify the mystery items? If you have even an inkling of desire to treasure hunt and dig in the dirt – this place will wow you. They cleverly build the tour to peak your interest, show a film about the recovery and then hit you with the actual findings. This is unbelievable, especially the great conditions of the materials.

For updates & travel games visit: **www.KidsLoveTravel.com**

North West Area

CITY HALL OBSERVATION

414 E 12th Street (Downtown / Convention Center Area) **Kansas City** 64106

Phone: (816) 513-2778 http://kcmo.gov/city-hall-observation-deck/
Hours: Open 9:00am-3:00pm Monday-Friday. Closed during high winds.
Admission: FREE. Security guards need to take you up so be patient as this is an extra job for them.

View the city from the 30th floor of City Hall. City Hall is the third tallest building in the city. It measures 443 feet from the sidewalk at the north door to the top of the building. Since it's on a hill, it dominates the downtown skyline. When it was first built, it was the tallest building in the state. It remains one of the tallest city halls in the country.

CITY MARKET

20 E. 5th Street (Just a few blocks north of Downtown in the River Market district) **Kansas City** 64106

Phone: (816) 842-1271 www.thecitymarket.org
Hours: The Saturday Farmers' Market features more than 140 local vendors offering farm-fresh produce, plants, poultry & meats, baked goods, prepared foods, handmade crafts and much more. 6:00am-3:00pm. Sundays offer a more leisurely alternative 8:00am-3:00pm.
Admission: Admission to the farmers' market is free. Concerts and special events, plus any meals you purchase from vendors or restaurants on the perimeter are subject to admission, parking fees or dining prices listed.

Kansas City's oldest continuously operating business, The City Market is home to an eclectic mix of restaurants and merchants as well as the region's largest farmers' market – many with samplings of their fresh product to try before you buy. The smells and colors of the produce are so sensory. More than 30 permanent merchants offer fresh produce, specialty groceries, meats & seafood, pastries, desserts, floral, house wares and gifts that are open seven days a week, year-round, many of which are family owned and operated.

Although kids really do love a farmers market, you can really give them a taste of many cultures in one place by trying different ethnic foods at restaurants surrounding the market booths. Venture out for a crispy falafel or a handy Shawarma sandwich at Habashi House Middle Eastern Café or perhaps a flavorful stew at the Blue Nile. Try one of nearly 100 Vietnamese entrees at Hien Vuong or Indian and Pakistani cuisine at Tikka House. Try a gourmet pizza at Minsky's Pizza Café or a grilled Panini at City Market Coffee Shop. Bo Lings features a wide range of Mandarin and Cantonese cuisine as well as one of the largest Dim Sum menus in the area. Burrito Bros. offers flavorful Mexican food.

COLLEGE BASKETBALL EXPERIENCE

1401 Grand Blvd. (downtown/convention center area) **Kansas City** 64106
Phone: (816) 949-7500 www.collegebasketballexperience.com
Hours: Wednesday-Saturday 10:00am-6:00pm, Sunday 11:00am-6:00pm. Open daily each summer.
Admission: $15.00 adult, $12.00 child (4-17), $11.00 senior (65+) & military.

Further cementing the area's reputation as a hoops hotbed, Kansas City is now home to the state-of-the-art College Basketball Experience (CBE). Connected to the new Sprint Center via a common lobby, the 41,500-square-foot entertainment facility contains hands-on, interactive basketball exhibits and houses the National Collegiate Basketball Hall of Fame. Beginning with a last-minute pep talk inside the entrance elevator, a coach's voice accompanies fans throughout the facility, guiding them through several dribble, pass and shoot stations to hone their skills. SportsCenter fans will feel right at home behind the ESPNU anchor desk, where they can call the play-by-play of college's most memorable games. We soon realized our amateur skills weren't scholarship material but boy did we have fun trying to jump high and produce free-throws at a fast pace to beat the buzzer! Sweating is almost inevitable as CBE's high-energy exhibits recreate the intensity of college basketball game-from foul-line hecklers to a last-second buzzer beater.

CHIPS CHOCOLATE FACTORY

2450 Grand Blvd., Crown Center, Level 2 **Kansas City** 64108
Phone: (816) 421-0012 www.kcfudge.com

The aroma of Chocolate tickles your nose, as sweet creations of caramel apples or smooth fudge are prepared before your eyes. Call ahead for a group tour when the action is bubbling with whirlpools of chocolate. See Chip's helpers turn 20 lbs. of secret ingredients into a loaf of creamy fudge. You'll learn how every drop of chocolate starts with Cocoa Beans and you'll see their transformation from harvest through various stages of production.

COTERIE THEATRE

2450 Grand Blvd., Crown Center Shops, level 1, Ste. 144
Kansas City 64108
Phone: (814) 474-6552 www.coterietheatre.org
Hours: Matinees 5-6 days/week plus Friday evening performance.
Admission: $11.00-$17.00 per show (shows run 60-90 minutes- just right amount of time before attention wanes).

For updates & travel games visit: **www.KidsLoveTravel.com**

North West Area

Educators: Curriculum and theme Resource Guide is prepared for each production with concepts outlined and follow up activities.

This KC venue of live theatre for all ages presents plays that have short stories with "touchpoints" for all ages – witty, fun, emotional. Cute lines are followed by laughter and clapping – sometimes as much from the adults as the kids. We liked the use of puppets, too.

CRAYOLA CAFÉ

Kansas City - 2450 Grand Street, Crown Center, Level 2 64108. Phone: (816) 398-4820. *www.crayolacafe.com*. A café so colorful, you can't pass by without resisting a peak at what each table ordered. Their regular menu has some really nice sandwich plates all around $8-9.00 but the kid's menu is all the rage ($5.00). Guess what we tried? Peanut Butter and Banana Wrap (served warm on a whole wheat tortilla) and The Beach Pail - ice cream, Nilla wafers, chocolate sauce, whipped cream and a cherry on a sandy "beach" in a take-home sand pail. All kids entrees are served with beverage in kids souvenir cup and choice of French fries, tater tots, potato chips, carrot sticks or fruit salad. Every plate, placemat, decoration is super bright colors and everyone we saw was having so much fun eating! Next-door is the Crayola Store.

CROWN CENTER

2450 Grand Blvd. **Kansas City** 64108
www.crowncenter.com

Located in the heart of downtown Kansas City, Crown Center is often called a city within a city. Three levels of great shopping and dining complement two of the city's most friendly hotels. If you're staying at the Hyatt or Westin Crown Center, you are already in the center of walkable spots especially popular with families. The company's fun and creative spirit is evident throughout the entertainment complex – from the hands-on art, greeting card factory tours, water shows, play fountains, theaters, funky themed restaurants, numerous festivals and a winter ice terrace. The fountains flow year-round, but a show set to music plays spring through fall. You'll see listings for many unique restaurants, theatres and shops in the Crown Center throughout this chapter.

KANSAS CITY CHALK & WALK FESTIVAL

Kansas City - Crown Center - Artists start with empty squares of asphalt and by the end of the weekend, the squares will be transformed into magnificent pieces of artwork. FREE. (third weekend in June)

KIDS LOVE MISSOURI

FREE FRIDAY NIGHT FLICKS

Kansas City - Crown Center - Bring your blanket and lawn chairs, sit under the stars and take in a classic movie on a huge outdoor screen every Friday night. Concessions will be available. FREE (July and August)

FIESTA KANSAS CITY

Kansas City - Crown Center - Celebrate Cinco de Mayo at this tenth annual event, which features great music, food, dancing and exhibits. Sponsored by the Hispanic Chamber of Commerce of Greater Kansas City. FREE (second weekend in May).

JIGGLE JAM FAMILY FEST

Kansas City - Crown Center - featuring national and local entertainers and many kids activities. Admission. (Memorial Day weekend)

FRITZ'S RAILROAD RESTAURANT

Kansas City - *2450 Grand Blvd. Suite 214, Crown Center 64108. Phone: (816) 474-4004. www.fritzskc.com*. OK, train lovers and the families that love them – THIS IS your place to be. Fritz's inventor skills lead him to the development of a food delivery system. The "train" system runs below a moving train around the entire restaurant. Instead of having a server bring your order, the kitchen prepares the order and sends it along a track until it meets a STOP at your table. The train conveyor then gently releases your food down to arms length reach and you grab your selections. Kids get a conductors hat with their meals and the selection of food offerings is definitely kid-style = old fashioned hamburgers plain or with crazy toppings like hash browns, homemade chili, BBQ sauce, hot sauce or grilled onions. Add a milkshake on the side. Lil'engineers items are all $5.99 and include entrée, fries, and drink. Toot-toot. _____ 🍽

HALLMARK VISITOR CENTER

2450 Grand Blvd., Crown Center Complex (one mile south of downtown)
Kansas City 64108

Phone: (816) 274-3613 www.hallmarkvisitorscenter.com
Hours: Monday-Saturday 9:30am-4:00pm.
Admission: FREE. Free parking with validation.

Visit the place that creates ways for people to express themselves and celebrate life's seasons. Where do Hallmark artists, writers, and photographers go for inspiration? Begin a behind-the-scenes journey with a short movie viewing. Now that you're oriented, grab an Artifact Search. Have fun looking for each object. Enjoy a virtual visit with hoops&yoyo, Asteroid Andy and other colorful Hallmark characters. Step inside computer kiosks that provide a high tech way to learn more about the company. Kids will be very pleasantly surprised to find out Crayola is part of Hallmark (you can even watch a video to see crayons, markers & Silly Putty being made). Or, that greeting cards are made in more than 30 languages.

Crafting Area: Watch a tech make engraving dies – the metal plates that raise the 3-dimensional designs on paper or cutting dies, which work like steel cookie cutters. Try your hand at crafting yourself at one station where you make a souvenir bow to take home. Everyone leaves this center with a huge, endearing smile on his or her face! This place is really that warm & fuzzy fun!

KALEIDOSCOPE

2500 Grand Street, Crown Center Complex (right next to Hallmark Visitors Center) **Kansas City** 64108

Phone: (816) 274-8300 www.hallmarkkaleidoscope.com
Hours: Children and their adults create art together at 50-minute Creative Art Sessions. Closed holidays and Sundays. 9:30am-3:30pm (timed FREE tickets). Best ages 5-12. Admission: FREE. Call for tickets.

Be prepared to be wowed! Put your creative juices in full throttle as you walk through the dark tunnel hallway into the most colorful whimsy land any kid could imagine. Parents, stand back and watch as children use their imagination to make art with paper, ribbon, melted crayons and tons of bright, shiny, wiggly, sparkly, fluffy, puffy stuff. Your sense of touch, sight and hearing are peaked. You may start at a crazy country house, then to an under-the-sea world and on to far out outer space. Kids use Crayola art supplies and recycled materials to make take home projects such as puzzles, hats or books. It's like walking into a storybook where you get to create the props!

KC RAIL EXPERIENCE

30 West Pershing Rd **Kansas City** 64108

Phone: (816) 460-2020 www.unionstation.org/railexperience.html
Admission: now part of Science City admission

This is a hands-on journey through the exciting history of the American railroad. "Talking characters" speak to you around every corner. Climb aboard several trains including one giant "moving train" with sound and motion. Sit at the controls, blow the whistle or pull the train out of the station and speed through tunnels. This is probably our favorite indoor train museum because of the multiple interactive stations. Amazing wows from your "little conductor".

NATIONAL WWI MUSEUM AT LIBERTY MEMORIAL

100 W. 26th Street (across the street from Union Station)
Kansas City 64108

Phone: (816) 784-1918 **www.theworldwar.org**
Hours: Tuesday-Sunday from 10:00am-5:00pm. The exhibits and tower close at 4:30pm. Open summer Mondays.
Admission: $16.00 adult, $14.00 senior (65+), $10.00 youth (6-18). Military discounts. Wylie Gallery and the Liberty Memorial Tower are additional fee. Tickets may be used on two consecutive days. If purchased Sunday, the second day is Tuesday.
Note: "Over There" Café with menu items named for people and places of the Great War. Songs of the era can be heard throughout the dining area.
Educators: you can order a Free Lessons of Liberty CD on their website under>Education>For Teachers>Lessons of Liberty.

President Calvin Coolidge dedicated the Liberty Memorial to World War I veterans in 1926. The new National World War I Museum opened beneath the monument in 2006. It is the only museum in the country dedicated to WWI. Walk up to the huge tower and statues. Why do you walk over a battlefield of poppies at the entrance? You'll need to begin with the 12-minute video to engage the kids in the time period. Now, explore. Look through the clever peep-holes. Would you like to be in those trenches? What did the soldiers carry in their pockets? (cards and Bibles). The various audio stations react with conversation once you enter. The audio and viewing holes are at different levels so every size kid can participate without being held or needing a stool. Other discovery stations allow you to "play" at interactive tables using light pointers. Now go outside and travel to the top of the 217-foot tower for a bird's eye view of the city. Because the theme of the museum is war, kids who have studied some American War History engage the most and really interact with the discovery station technology.

NEGRO LEAGUES BASEBALL MUSEUM

1616 E.18th Street (In the Historic 18th & Vine Jazz District, I-70 Paseo exit)
Kansas City 64108

Phone: (816) 221-1920 **www.nlbm.com**
Hours: Tuesday-Saturday 9:00am-6:00pm, Sunday Noon-6:00pm.
Admission: $10.00 adult, $6.00 for children under 12. Free for children under 5. Discount tickets with the Jazz Museum.
Note: if you want to grab a KC authentic lunch, the original Arthur Bryant's Barbecue (1727 Brooklyn Ave.) is a few blocks to the east.

The museum is laid out as a timeline of the Negro Leagues and American history. Exhibits include hundreds of photographs, historical artifacts and several interactive computer stations. A documentary film narrated by actor

North West Area

James Earl Jones tells the story of the leagues with vintage film footage. Baseball fans will love the many baseball facts and computer trivia kiosks and parents will be touched by the stories of injustice during the 60s. At the end of all that reading and listening, you come upon the dynamic Field of Legends. 10 statues are positioned on the Field of Legends, a mock baseball diamond, where this mythical all-star team looks to be engaged in an epic battle. Visitor's are welcomed to walk onto the field. Bring kids along who are in to the history of baseball and its legends. Otherwise, children may be bored until the sculpture field at the end.

SCIENCE CITY

Union Station 30 West Pershing Rd **Kansas City** 64108

Phone: (816) 460-2020 www.sciencecity.com
Hours: Tuesday - Saturday 10:00am-5:00pm, Sunday Noon-5:00pm. Extended hours during some school breaks and holidays.
Admission: Tickets for Science City are $13.50 adults, $11.50 (age 3-12). Visit more than one attraction and SAVE! Purchase a ticket to Science City and visit the Extreme Screen, Rail Experience or Planetarium for just $5.00!

Science City is the city's first science center and features dozens of hands-on exhibits. Parents and kids can solve a crime (like a murder mystery), dig up fossils and defy gravity on a bike that's 30 feet in the air! Then, they can publish a newspaper; go into Echo Cave or watch paleontologists working in the Dino Lab. The "city" is set up like a real city with "shops", a train depot, hotels and even unique areas like Make your Own Slime in the Test Kitchens. While it's very busy and noisy in the main "city" scape, the parents stand on the perimeters while the kids totally immerse themselves in the science playground.

UNION STATION COMPLEX

30 W Pershing Road **Kansas City** 64108

Phone: (816) 460-2020 www.unionstation.org

The nation's second-largest train station, Union Station was restored to its original grandeur. The complex is filled with restaurants, shops, theaters, traveling exhibits, special events, a science center called SCIENCE CITY, and a permanent exhibit on railroads called the KC RAIL EXPERIENCE. Once the home of the historic Fred Harvey Restaurant and Lunchroom, The Harvey House Diner serves up a full breakfast menu all day long, as well as Blue Plate lunch specials, burgers, sandwiches, hand-dipped shakes and malts and fresh-baked pies seven days a week. Union Station's Theater District has a giant-screen 2D and 3D movie theater, a domed planetarium and a live-stage theater. The building features a 95-foot ceiling in the Grand Hall, three 3,500-pound chandeliers and a six-foot-wide clock hanging in the Station's central arch. Millions of people went through Union Station and there are old pictures placed around the hallways to depict that. Admission to the Union Station building is FREE, but there is a charge for the attractions.

THE NATIONAL ARCHIVES AT KANSAS CITY is adjacent at 400 W. Pershing Road. Some of the most important documents in the country now have a new home in KC. The new, state-of-the-art facility adjacent to Union Station houses more than 60 million pages of historical records-including photos, maps, letters and other items dating back to 1815. Visitors can research family trees, replicate famous signatures or view rare documents from around the region, such as the original complaint from Brown V. Board of Education, the court case which ended school segregation. Admission is free. (Open 8:00am-5:00pm. closed Sunday, Monday and Federal holidays).

KEMPER MUSEUM OF CONTEMPORARY ART

4420 Warwick Blvd., (At 45th Street and Warwick Boulevard, just north of the Country Club Plaza) **Kansas City** 64111

Phone: (816) 753-5784 www.kemperart.org
Hours: Tuesday-Thursday 10:00am-4:00pm, Friday-Saturday 10:00am-9:00pm and Sunday 11:00am-5:00pm. Admission: FREE.

The Kemper's permanent collection is virtually a Who's Who among contemporary artists — including works by Jackson Pollock, Andy Warhol, Chihuly glass, and Georgia O'Keeffe. Offered throughout the year, the museum's free Family Days feature hands-on activities, Scavenger Hunt Saturdays, live music, storytelling, docent-led tours, gallery games and dance and theatrical performances. Each exhibition has gallery games to engage kids and adults into the art form. Have lunch at Café Sebastienne. It's hard to miss the café's colorful walls where 110 paintings called the History of Art fit together like a puzzle. Don't forget to snap a photo of the Kemper outdoor sculptures - the 1600 pound bronze Spider on the front lawn or the "baby" spider crawling up the outside of the museum building.

For updates & travel games visit: **www.KidsLoveTravel.com**

North West Area 105

NELSON-ATKINS MUSEUM OF ART

4525 Oak Street (Take I-35 to Hwy 71 South. Exit at Emanuel Cleaver II Boulevard) **Kansas City** 64111

Phone: (816) 751-ART www.nelson-atkins.org
Hours: Wednesday 10:00am-5:00pm, Thursday-Friday 10:00am-9:00pm, Saturday 10:00am-5:00pm and Sunday Noon-5:00pm.
Admission: FREE. There is charge for special exhibitions. Parking $10.00.
Note: Rozzelle Court Restaurant is an open-air Italian courtyard and offers buffet-style service. On select Fridays, enjoy live jazz music.

Imagine a 67-story office building lying on its side, and you'll get an idea of how large Kansas City's premier art museum is. But what really draws the kids in are the sculptures: no one can miss the main building lawn as four giant badminton shuttlecocks are positioned on the front lawn or, even the parking garage is topped by a sculpture in a large reflecting pool that allows light to filter through the water into the garage area below. Once inside the museum, a series of galleries connect by stairs and ramps and five stunning, translucent and transparent glass "lens" emerge from the space beneath. With a permanent collection that contains more than 34,500 works of art, the Nelson-Atkins is best known for its Asian art, European paintings and modern sculpture. Kids remember the knight in full parade dress, an authentic Chinese temple and many of the sculpture pieces most.

THOMAS HART BENTON HOME AND STUDIO STATE HISTORIC SITE

3616 Belleview (I-35 to Southwest Trafficway or Rainbow Blvd. Exit. Follow signs) **Kansas City** 64111

Phone: (816) 931-5722 https://mostateparks.com/park/thomas-hart-benton-home-and-studio-state-historic-site
Hours: Monday and Thursday-Saturday 10:00am-4:00pm, and Sunday 11:00am-4:00pm. (November-March). Monday and Wednesday-Saturday 10:00am-4:00pm, and Sunday Noon-5:00pm. (April-October).
Admission: The Missouri state park system does not charge entrance fees. However, there are fees associated with camping, lodging, tours, museums and special events. $3.50-$5.00 admission for house tour (ages 6+).
Educators: you will find Teacher's Guides covering pre-and-post visit activities, vocabulary and more background on Benton on their Teacher's Guide page.

Missouri's most noted 20th century artist lived in this late Victorian style house from 1939 until his death in 1975. He had been working on a mural for the Country Music Hall of Fame, called The Sources of Country Music, which was nearly complete. The house and the carriage house, which Benton converted into an art studio, contain many of his personal belongings.

TOY AND MINIATURE MUSEUM

5235 Oak Street (just a few blocks from Country Club Plaza - University of Missouri-Kansas City) **Kansas City** 64112

Phone: (816) 333-2055 or (816) 333-9328 **www.toyandminiaturemuseum.org**
Hours: Wednesday-Monday 10:00am-4:00pm.

Admission: $5.00 general (age 5+). Additional fees for special events.

The Toy & Miniature Museum is the largest collection of nostalgic toys in the Midwest. Near the beginning of the tour a mechanical man explains the difference between toys we play with and miniatures we place on shelves. The collection features tiny versions of decorative artifacts adorning exquisite homes and palaces from various eras – past and present. Examples of intricate miniature pieces are the Noah's Ark and the Palace of Versailles. One million marbles are in the Marble Games Gallery. Visitors can try their hand at the game in a real marble ring, or become mesmerized by colorful marbles looping and winding through the intricate marble maze stationed in the middle of the room. In an another area, kids will rave over the play food and kitchen utensils. Some French pastries look good enough to eat.

DID YOU KNOW ? The museum's oldest doll is Georgiana, an English wooden doll circa 1750. Georgiana stands just over 26 inches tall and has a wig made from human hair.

JOHN WORNALL HOUSE

6115 Wornall Road **Kansas City** 64113

Phone: (816) 444-1858 **www.wornallmajors.org/the-john-wornall-house**
Hours: Wednesday-Saturday, First tour begins at 10:00am - last tour begins at 3:00pm. Sunday: First tour begins at 1:00pm - last tour begins at 3:00 p.m.
Admission: $8.00 adult (13-60), $6.00 senior (60+) & $5.00 child (5-12).
Tours: All tours of the Museum are guided and last approximately 1 hour. Reservations are welcome but not necessary.
Note: Easter Egg Hunt on the Lawn weekend before Easter. Small admission.

In 1858, Kentuckian John B. Wornall built this elegant home in the Greek Revival style. Accurately restored to the period, its interior spaces and authentic furnishings demonstrate why the house was called the most pretentious house in the section. The house was used as a hospital during the Civil War and has lots of stories. Staff provides group tours, ghost tours, living history, hands-on workshops and other activities.

- OPEN HEARTH COOKING DEMONSTRATIONS - The Wornall House offers open hearth cooking demonstrations on some Saturdays of each month. Come see how Mrs. Wornall prepared meals during the 1850s.

For updates & travel games visit: **www.KidsLoveTravel.com**

KANSAS CITY CHIEFS - ARROWHEAD STADIUM

One Arrowhead Drive (East on Interstate 70. Exit at Blue Ridge and Arrowhead Stadium will be located on the right) **Kansas City** 64129

Phone: (816) 920-9300 **www.kcchiefs.com**

Arrowhead Stadium is home to the Kansas City Chiefs. The new state-of-the-art sports and entertainment destination received many fan improvements, including a new stadium club, an expanded memorabilia store and a Hall of Honor which commemorates more than 45 years of Chiefs memories. Nowhere does football quite like Kansas City, home to one of the NFL's loudest stadiums. They have a very active Kids Club, too.

KANSAS CITY ROYALS - KAUFFMAN STADIUM

One Royal Way **Kansas City** 64129

Phone: (816) 921-8000 **www.royals.com**

Tours: Kauffman Stadium tours to the public run April thru October. Tickets for the Classic 90-minute tour (recommended tour for kids-note: lots of walking) run $17.00(ages 4+). Tours are not available on game days. Can be scheduled by going online: http://kansascity.royals.mlb.com/kc/ballpark/tours/index.jsp

Educators: Educational Tours: The $10.00 student fee includes a ballpark tour and 3, 20-minute units of instruction dealing with Science, Math, Social Studies, Language Arts, Character Education, History and Health & Physical Education.

The Kansas City Royals' Kauffman Stadium has reestablished its place as one of the best ballparks in Major League Baseball. In addition to wider concourses, more restrooms and added concession stands, other new amenities include a 9,500-seat, open-air pavilion; 1,500 fountain view seats; a new Fan Walk; a sports bar-restaurant; a Royals Hall of Fame; Interactive Kids Area; and there are special events and promotions planned all summer long including Fireworks Fridays and Fun Runs on Sundays (when all fans can run the bases following the game). And, of course, many vendors selling barbeque. The Kansas City Royals play more than 80 home games each year at Kauffman Stadium. Tickets as low as $15.00 each.

TOURS: Kauffman Stadium's unique features include 104' high video board and a 322-foot wide water spectacular. A tour of this "Crown Jewel" of baseball stadiums will take you to areas of the ballpark not normally open to the public including the Royals Dugout, Press Box, Royals interview room, and Visitor's locker room. Tickets for all public tours can be purchased in advance or on the day of your tour at the main ticket office located behind home plate at Kauffman Stadium.

KANSAS CITY ZOO

6800 Zoo Drive (I-70 W, merge onto I-435 S via Exit 8A. Then take Exit 66, Blue Parkway/MO-350 E. Take the 63rd Street ramp towards Raytown) **Kansas City** 64132

Phone: (816) 513-5700 www.kansascityzoo.org
Hours: Daily 8:00am-4:00pm. Until 5pm weekends. The Zoo is closed only on Thanksgiving, Christmas and New Year's Day.
Admission: $16.00 adult, $15.00 senior, $13.00 child (3-11). FREE parking.
Note: IMAX Theater. Five transportation options to explore the Zoo. Golf cart and Segway tours, as well as boat, train and tram rides are available to the public seasonally. Located throughout the park, the zoo's three restaurants and six snack bars offer everything from cotton candy and Dip-N-Dots to meals. Picnic areas are also available. FREEBIES: Downloadable Word Search and games: **www.kansascityzoo.org/education/classroom-activities** Also on that page: themed self-guided Scavenger Hunts.

The Kansas City Zoo features an impressive collection of animals in naturalistic settings-all stretched across 200 acres in Swope Park. The Zoo's exhibits are organized by continent with major sections for Africa and Australia. Check out the North American river otter exhibit just inside the zoo's entrance. The zoo is home to critically endangered Sumatran tigers, Langka and Manis. Look for the polar bears and penguins. If you love monkeys, this zoo has one of the largest chimpanzee environs in North America. In the Tropics area are adorable, yes really, porcupines. Children can get up-close with lemurs, meerkats and squirrel monkeys in the indoor Discovery Barn. A free, year-round activity lets Zoo visitors feed and interact with small lorikeet birds.

LAKESIDE NATURE CENTER

4701 E. Gregory Blvd., Swope Park **Kansas City** 64132

Phone: (816) 513-8960 www.lakesidenaturecenter.org
Hours: Tuesday through Saturday, 9:00am-4:00pm.
Admission: FREE.
FREEBIES: a Scavenger Hunt is available here:
www.lakesidenaturecenter.org/Edu_Scavanger%20Hunt.pdf

Wildlife education programs for all ages with live animals. The Nature Center is free, has a hiking trail, picnic pavilion and native Missouri wildlife exhibit. The nature center is one of Missouri's largest wildlife rehab facilities and typically houses about 75 animals including two bald eagles, two turkey vultures, three barred owls, and many hawks and falcons. The Center even has a box turtle named "Wilma" that is thought to be about 76 years old. The Mother Nature Reads storytime and crafttime is free but there is a small fee for events like Breakfast with the Beasts.

MAGIC WOODS

Kansas City - Lakeside Nature Center. Watch the forest come alive at Lakeside Nature Center's annual Magic Woods for a safe, family-friendly event. Admission is $5; children 3 and under are free. Activities include face painting, tattoos, games, crafts and live animal presentations, actors from Coterie Theatre and Eco Elvis. (second weekend in October)

CAVE SPRING HISTORIC SITE AND NATURE CENTER

8701 E Gregory Blvd. **Kansas City** 64133

Phone: (816) 358-CAVE (2283)   **www.cavespring.org**
Hours: (Park & Trails) Trails are open daily, year round. 8:00am-dusk. (Nature Center) Tuesday-Friday 10:00am-4:00pm. Admission: $2.50 adult, $1.50 child.

The easily traveled hiking trails combined with the natural features of a cave and wildlife habitat pond allow many opportunities to pursue ecological studies. Visit the interpretive center with its history and nature exhibits. Learn why Cave Spring was an important part of the westward movement. Take a nature hike to learn which plants and trees were important to Pioneers and how they used them. See the cave and spring just like the Pioneers did in the mid-1800's. Come and enjoy the beauty of the natural surroundings while taking a trip along the Sante Fe Trail. Cave Spring provides trail directions, and scavenger hunt booklets for each student, if you ask.

COCO KEY WATER RESORT

9103 East 39th Street (Holiday Inn Kansas City Sports Complex-across the street from Arrowhead & Kauffman Stadiums) **Kansas City** 64133

Phone: (816) 737-0200   **www.cocokeykansascity.com**
Hours: Thursday-Saturday 10:00am-9:00pm and Sunday 10:00am-6:00pm. Admission: Splash Packages start at $139 (includes waterpark passes and room). Day Pass only - $17.99-$19.99 per person, per day. Online and local coupons are available.

The year-round CoCo Key Water Resort features body slides, tube slides - including the Barracuda Blast two-person raft slide - an adventure river, and the Palm Grotto indoor/outdoor spa. It also offers Parrot's Perch interactive play island with a 300-gallon tipping bucket. Younger children love the Dip-In Theatre, a shallow pool with a constant display of movies and cartoons. Dry off and head on over to Key Quest Arcade, their interactive game room filled with state-of-the-art video games.

The hotel's 374 guest rooms were recently renovated. The Tradewinds Restaurant is inside the property and a Pizza Hut express / A&W service counter is too.

LONGVIEW LAKE PARK

11100 View High Drive (Take the Raytown Road Exit #4 off I-470 and turn south. Go 1 mile) **Kansas City** 64149
Phone: (816) 503-4800 **www.jacksongov.org**

The centerpiece is Longview Lake - good for powerboating, waterskiing, jet-skiing, or pontoon boating (with full service marina and fishing). Lake has a sand beach, playground, picnic, a 6 mile asphalt lakeside bike path and another 4-mile nature trail, plus a campground with tent and RV sites (spring thru September).

CHRISTMAS IN THE PARK

Kansas City - Longview Lake Park. The park campgrounds host an elaborate drive-through lighted display with more than 225,000 lights and 175 animated scenes. Donations requested. (Thanksgiving thru December)

SHOAL CREEK LIVING HISTORY MUSEUM

Hodge Park, 7000 NE Barry Road (I-435, take Highway 152 east. Go 1/2 mile, then turn north onto Shoal Creek Parkway) **Kansas City** 64156
Phone: (816) 792-2655 **www.shoalcreeklivinghistorymuseum.com**
Hours: Daily, dawn to dusk
Admission: FREE to just walk around property. Most events are $5.00 per person (age 6+).

Shoal Creek Living History Museum is a village of more than 20 authentic 19th century buildings. The buildings date from 1807-1885 and include log cabin and clapboard structures to an antebellum brick mansion home. You can take a self-guided tour of the park but honestly the best time to come for kids is during special events (ex. Reenactments) to get more insights from costumed interpreters showing you the ways of 1800s people and lifestyles.

HARVEST FESTIVAL

Kansas City - Shoal Creek Living History Museum. Join them for an old fashioned County Fair. Bring your baked goods, sewing, handcrafts for judging or participate in the buffalo chip throwing or sack races! (second Saturday in October)

A VISIT WITH ST. NICHOLAS

Kansas City - Shoal Creek Living History Museum. Experience Christmas in the 19th century. Visit log cabins of 1825 and 1835, a school, church, mercantile and then St. Nicholas, resplendent in green velvet robes. Ride the horse drawn sleigh and take the walking tour through 17 historic buildings. (first Saturday in December)

OCEANS OF FUN

4545 Worlds of Fun Avenue (10 minutes northeast of downtown Kansas City on I-435 exit 54) **Kansas City** 64161

Phone: (816) 454-4545   www.worldsoffun.com
Hours: Oceans of Fun is open seasonally from May through September. Daily operating hours vary; call or visit the Web site for more details.
Admission: Regular (ages 3+) is ~$39.99 & includes Worlds of Fun. Parking $10.00.
Note: With several different food locations has everything from hometown barbecue to traditional pizza.

The waterpark's attractions include a million-gallon wave pool, an 800-foot lazy river and a family kayaking/canoeing area. Paradise Falls is the Midwest's largest family water playhouse with several interactive areas to explore. A gigantic bucket sits atop the playhouse, dumping 1,000 gallons of water onto its guests every five minutes. The newest of the waterpark's 18 water slides is Hurricane Falls, a family raft ride boasting a 680-foot flume. "Superpool" Coconut Cove features 20,000 square feet of fun, including floating characters, water obstacles and other challenging activities. Young guests will love Crocodile Isle, a "sprayground" just for small children and their parents. Those who prefer pure relaxation can float along the Caribbean Cooler, an 800-foot gently flowing lazy river. Worlds of Fun is next door. For easy access, use the Ride & Slide Gate that links the two parks.

WORLDS OF FUN

4545 Worlds of Fun Avenue (10 minutes northeast of downtown Kansas City on I-435 exit 54) **Kansas City** 64161

Phone: (816) 454-4545   www.worldsoffun.com
Hours: Worlds of Fun is open seasonally from April through October. Daily operating hours vary; call or visit the Web site for more details.
Admission: Regular (age 3+) is around $39.99. Parking $10.00.
Note: The Worlds of Fun Village resort features 20 cottages, 22 log cabins and 82 deluxe RV sites. Park visitors can choose from more than 40 different food locations including three dine-in restaurants: All Stars Grill, Coasters Drive-In and Zarda Bar-B-Q. Concession options range from light snacks to meal-sized entrees. Annual Festivals are held in the park.

Worlds of Fun offers more than 170 acres of wild rides, unique food and live entertainment in five themed continent areas: Americana, Africa, Europa, the Orient and Scandinavia. The wooden Prowler zig-zags its way through the deep woods of the theme park's Africa section. The smooth, "bobsled-like" ride has an initial drop of 85 feet and peaks at a speed of 51 mph. Another mammoth thrill ride is the Patriot. Camp Snoopy at Worlds of Fun offers kids the chance to meet Peanuts characters and ride "kid-sized" rides similar to the big thrill rides. Peanuts Playhouse is a three-story interactive funhouse with more than 5,000 foam balls plus slides, geysers, catapults and blasters. Visitors can use the Ride & Slide Gate to access the adjacent waterpark.

FEDERAL RESERVE BANK OF KANSAS CITY

1 Memorial Drive (Crown Center Area, adjacent to the Liberty Memorial) **Kansas City** 64198

Phone: (816) 881-2683 **www.KansasCityFed.org/MoneyMuseum**
Hours: Open Monday - Friday 9:30am-4:00pm excluding bank holidays.
Admission: FREE.
Educators: lesson plans grade 5-12: www.kansascityfed.org/moneymuseum/includes/educators.cfm

Visit the Federal Reserve Bank of Kansas City's Money Museum – a billion dollar experience! Free and open to the public, the Money Museum offers guests the opportunity to watch millions of dollars in currency be processed in a giant vault, lift a gold bar worth nearly $400,000 and enjoy fun, interactive exhibits while learning about the economy. Compare real and counterfeit money or learn to use an automated teller machine that spits out real receipts. At the end of your self-guided tour (only takes one-half hour), each guest receives a free souvenir bag of real money - shredded - sorry! Still, a wonderful free souvenir that kids can show-and-tell to friends when they get home.

SCHLITTERBAHN VACATION VILLAGE WATERPARK

9400 State Avenue west loop of I-435 at Exit 13. just east of Kansas Speedway and Village West) **Kansas City** 66112

Phone: (913) 312-3110 **www.schlitterbahn.com/kc/**
Hours: Starting weekends mid-May and daily all summer, hours are generally 11:00am-6:00pm with later closing times mid-summer.
Admission: $31.99-$41.99 per person (ages 3+). Online and two-day discounts. Many hotels in the area offer discount ticket overnight packages.
FREEBIES: FREE parking, use of inner tubes, use of life jackets and guests are permitted to bring their own food and beverages INSIDE THE PARK!

North West Area

Schlitterbahn Vacation Village is one of the world's largest tubing parks with miles of interconnected rivers plus the current signature attractions--Torrent River and the Master Blaster, a six-story uphill water coaster. The outdoor waterpark features a thrilling uphill water coaster, two mammoth tubing rivers including the world's longest tidal wave river, three huge slides, a white water tube chute, 13 mini slides for kids, three relaxing beach areas and a giant hot tub with swim-up refreshment bar.

The park's entertainment venues are connected by a state-of-the-art Transportainment River System. A fusion of transportation, sport and entertainment, man-made rivers carry guests between lodging units and attractions.

FESTA ITALIANA

Kansas City - Zona Rosa. *www.zonarosa.com*. One of Kansas City's favorite festivals, Festa Italiana, the unique celebration of Italian traditions and Italian-American culture, will be hosted once again at Zona Rosa this year! This longtime local ethnic festival draws visitors from across metropolitan Kansas City and beyond. This popular family event has free admission and showcases Italian food booths, live Italian music, dancers, a kids play area, firework display and more. FREE. (first weekend in June)

KCRIVERFEST

Kansas City - Riverfront Park, 5th St. and Grand Blvd. KCRiverFest is Kansas City's Premier Independence Day Festival. The annual KCRiverFest features the largest fireworks display in Downtown Kansas City, great bands, crafts, a Children's Zone with rides and entertainment, river boardwalk, a variety of foods, exhibits and more. Discount advance tickets available:*www.KCRiverFest.com*. Adm. (July 4th weekend)

FAULKNER'S PUMPKIN FARM & RANCH

Kansas City - *10600 Raytown Rd. (Conveniently located just 1/4 mile South of I-470 on West side of Raytown Rd). Phone: (816) 763-4644 www.faulknerspumpkinfarm.com*. Take home the perfect pumpkin, bump along on the hayride and meet the barnyard friends in the petting farm at their farm and ranch located right by Longview Lake! Try the new Pumpkin Cannon - target shooting with pumpkins. Farm train rides. Wild West playground. Duck races and pony rides. Field maze, pedal karts and moonwalks. Croquet games with brooms or ranglin' on steel horses. Admission. (entire month of October)

KANSAS CITY BALLET PRESENTS "THE NUTCRACKER"

Kansas City - *Music Hall, 301 W 13th Street.* www.kcballet.org. Kansas City Ballet's enchanting presentation of "The Nutcracker" with the music of Tchaikovsky accompanied by live orchestra. Featuring elaborate scenery, stunning choreography and vibrant costumes, Clara's magical adventure captures the imaginations of all ages. KCB's "The Nutcracker" is the largest production in an eight state region and lasts approximately two hours. Admission. (two weeks leading up to Christmas)

BATTLE OF WESTPORT

6601 Swope Parkway **Kansas City (Westport)** 64111

Phone: (913) 345-2000
www.battleofwestport.org/pdf/Battle%20of%20Westport%20Self-Guided%20Auto%20Tour%20Map.pdf.

The most important Civil War battle in the Kansas City area was the Battle of Westport, known as the "Gettysburg of the West." On Oct. 23, 1864, the ragtag brigades of Gen. Price's Confederate army met Union armies that outnumbered him two to one. Westport was a Union victory, but Price was spared a total disaster when Brig. Gen. "JO" Shelby's Iron Brigade made a last stand on the site of present-day Forest Hill Cemetery, where Shelby was buried long after the war.

GREAT WOLF LODGE

10401 Cabela Drive (I-435 exit 13) **Kansas City, KS** 66111

Phone: (913) 299-7001 www.greatwolf.com/kansascity/waterpark
Admission: Lodge room suites include 4-6 waterpark passes. Rooms vary from $169-$499 per night but off-peak and seasonal specials are always being updated online. Note: all suites: family, KidCabin (log cabin in room with bunk beds) have a microwave and small refrigerator. Check out the wonderful holiday theme packages they offer for Easter, Fall Harvest, Thanksgiving and Christmastime.

Serving as Kansas' Year-Round Family Resort, Great Wolf Lodge provides a comprehensive package of destination lodging amenities, including 281 family-sized suites; featuring a grand scale waterpark; arcade with ticket redemption; children's craft and activity room; Aveda® Concept Spa; fitness room; northwoods-themed restaurant; confectionery café; spacious outdoor pool; gift emporium and a performing Great Clock Tower. It's always a balmy 84 degrees inside the resort's huge, 38,000 square-foot indoor waterpark. Bear Track Landing puts the emphasis on fun with 8 waterslides, three pools and a four-story treehouse waterfort. Two areas for the 10 and under crowd are the nightly Storytime by the lobby fireplace (come in your pajamas) or the craft room, Cubs Cabin. This "safe" waterpark and dry activity environment is probably the key factor for recommendation to young families - especially with kids age 10 and under.

RENAISSANCE FESTIVAL

Kansas City, KS - Adjacent to Sandstone Amphitheater. **www.kcrenfest.com**. Come explore the 16th century village as it comes to life for seven spectacular autumn weekends. The Festival provides an enchanting escape within nearly 16 acres of shaded lanes. Experience the joust, where knights in armor duel on horseback to win the Queen's honor. Interact with over 500 costumed characters and listen to the soothing music of the dulcimer, mandolin and harp. If you prefer, catch exhilarating shows like fire eating and zany comedy on one of 13 stages. Feast on food fit for a king such as giant turkey legs, roasted corn on the cob, Scotch eggs and chocolate covered cheesecake on a stick. For the perfect day, join them for the Feaste of Fooles! In addition, there are over 162 shops to explore jewelry, glass, leather goods, and more. Explore unique games and rides like the Crows Nest and Slay the Dragon. Kids will also enjoy their Children's Realm filled with games, shows and crafts and Knightings by the King each day in the Children's Realm! Admission. (weekends starting Labor Day thru Columbus Day in October)

JESSE JAMES FARM & MUSEUM

21216 James Farm Road **Kearney** 64060

Phone: (816) 736-8500 www.jessejames.org
Hours: Daily 9:00am-4:00pm (May-September), Monday-Saturday 9:00am-4:00pm, Sunday Noon-4:00pm (October-April).
Admission: $8.50 adult (16+), $7.50 senior (62+), $5.00 child (8-15).

In Kearney, tour the Jesse James Farm and Museum, the birthplace and family home of Jesse James. The museum offers displays relating to the famous Missouri outlaw and his brother, Frank, and the role the Civil War played in their lives. On display are Jesse James and James family artifacts including three of Jesse's guns, the boots he was wearing when he was killed, a pair of boot spurs, and the family Bible, with inscriptions written in Zerelda's own hand. Even the picture Jesse was straightening on the wall when he was shot is on display. Inside the log cabin home, you'll see the bedroom Jesse was born in and the bedroom where Frank died of a stroke. Most every object in the home is original and of 1875 era vintage. Was his gang member a coward or a hero for ending Jesse's life? Each Jesse James historical attraction may have a different viewpoint.

POWELL GARDENS

1609 NW US Hwy 50 (30 miles east of KC) **Kingsville** 64061

Phone: (816) 697-2600 www.powellgardens.org
Hours: Daily, 9:00am-5:00pm (until 6:00pm April-October).
Admission: $10.00 adult, $9.00 senior, $8.00 military, $4.00 child (5-12) (April-October). Discounted rates November-March. Rates for special events vary.
Note: Powell Gardens' Café Thyme offers a wide variety of menu options for brunch, lunch and snacks.

Kansas City's botanical garden features 915 acres of beautiful, ever-changing gardens, nature trails, and year-round events. The 3.25-mile Nature & Hiking Trail leads visitors past frog-filled ponds, through woods of honey locust and into a field of meadow flowers. There's also lakeside gardens, the secluded Island Garden and a 600-foot "living" rock wall, the largest of its kind in North America.

Powell Gardens has unveiled what may be the first garden of its kind in the country. The 100-percent-edible, 12-acre Heartland Harvest Garden shows the path of food from seed to plate. The area includes a demonstration kitchen, education garden and four acres of intricate quilt gardens that visitors can view from the top of a 45-foot silo. The view from high in the silo vs. ground level is worth the trip. In the Seed to Plate Greenhouse, sprouting seeds illustrate the beginning of the botanical miracle that ultimately leads to the foods on our dinner plates. Down the path, the Apple Celebration Court showcases Missouri's finest apple varieties. Last but not least is the youth education garden and Fun Foods Farm, where children can dig in for hands-on learning about plant science, water conservation and nutrition using curriculum tied to Missouri and Kansas education standards. The children's garden features a tutti-fruitti maze, a fun garden that explores the origin of candy flavors (yum), sculptures for climbing and a pioneer day sod house.

FESTIVAL OF BUTTERFLIES

Kingsville - Powell Gardens. Get up close and personal with hundreds of live butterflies in our free-flight conservatory exhibit. Enter through our butterfly breezeway where native species abound, then take a turn through the conservatory to view the Blue Morpho, Gulf Frittilary, Mexican Bluewing and other special exotics. Children can catch and release butterflies and enjoy butterfly-related arts and crafts; all ages can learn how to grow a butterfly garden, buy butterfly-attracting plants and much more. Admission. (first two weekends in August)

GEN. JOHN J PERSHING BOYHOOD HOME STATE HISTORIC SITE
1100 Pershing Drive **Laclede** 64651

Phone: (660) 963-2525 **https://mostateparks.com/park/gen-john-j-pershing-boyhood-home-state-historic-site**
Admission: The Missouri state park system does not charge entrance fees. However, there are fees associated with camping, lodging, tours, museums and special events. Tours: Monday-Saturday 10:00am-4:00pm and Sundays Noon-6:00pm (April-September). Tuesday-Saturday 10:00am-4:00pm (October-March). $4.00 adult (13+), $3.00 child (6-17).

General John J. Pershing, one of the highest-ranking military officers in U.S history, grew up in Laclede. Tour his boyhood home and Prairie Mound School, with exhibits of the many obstacles he walked through during his boyhood and military career. Walking tours originate at the visitor contact point and depart for the boyhood home, which is located nearby. Visitors will be taken inside the two-story house that has been furnished to reflect its appearance when Pershing was growing up here from 1866 to 1882. What was the famous General like as a kid? The Prairie Mound School Museum is open to the public for self-guided tours at no charge. John Pershing taught in this one-room school before departing Missouri for West Point in 1882. Themes in the museum reflect the doorways that Gen. Pershing passed through in his lifetime. From the doorway of the Prairie Mound School as a young adult, to the doorway of Walter Reed Hospital in Washington D.C., where he passed away on July 15, 1948 at age 87.

PERSHING STATE PARK
29277 Hwy. 130 **Laclede** 64651

Phone: (660) 963-2299 **https://mostateparks.com/park/pershing-state-park**
Admission: The Missouri state park system does not charge entrance fees. However, there are fees associated with camping, lodging, tours, museums and certain special events.

This park is an example of a pre-European settlement landscape of northern Missouri. A hike down the 1.5-mile boardwalk or 6.5-mile Riparian Trail allows visitors to glimpse a slice of pre-settlement Missouri. Along Locust Creek are forested bottomlands, shrub swamps, marshes and a wet prairie. The park also offers small fishing lakes, hiking trails and campsites.

WATKINS MILL STATE PARK & HISTORIC SITE

26600 Park Road North **Lawson** 64062

Phone: (816) 580-3387 https://mostateparks.com/park/watkins-mill-state-park
Hours: (Visitor Center, Museum Exhibits, Grounds) Monday-Saturday 9:30am-5:00pm, Sunday 10:30am-5:00pm. (Tours of Watkins Woolen Mill and the Watkins House - See admission fee below) Monday-Saturday 10:00am-4:00pm, Sunday 11:00am-4:00pm. Mill tours are given on the even hours (10:00am, Noon, 2:00pm, 4:00pm) and house tours are on the odd hours (11:00am, 1:00pm, 3:00pm). Visitors must be with a tour guide to enter the house or mill.
Admission: Entrance to the park, historic site and visitor center is free. There are fees for guided tours of the historic buildings, camping and reservation of the shelter house and church.
Tours: Admission $3.00-$4.00. Tours are one hour and focus on the house and mill properties.
Note: The mill and house are not heated or air-conditioned. Educators: if you send them an email, they have Teachers Guides they can send you.

WATKINS WOOLEN MILL STATE HISTORIC SITE - The Visitor's center focuses on life in the region in the 1870s. Tours of the house and mill are offered. This site interprets the landholdings of Waltus Locket Watkins. Tour his house and woolen mill, the only 19th century American woolen mill with its original machinery still intact. You'll see original machinery, Watkins home, a church, a school, and several smaller buildings. Tours of the home include the first two floors of the home, the dairy cellar, summer kitchen, icehouse, smokehouse, fruit dryhouse, garden and poultry coops.

In addition to tours, the site offers a 25-minute orientation film that is recommended for all ages. The park also has a lake for fishing, swimming and boating; camping, hiking and equestrian trails; and a paved bicycle trail.

CHRISTMAS OPEN HOUSE

Lawson - Watkins Mill. Plantation decorated for the season and costumed re-enactors perform the music, crafts, and another activities as well as serve refreshments that were popular in the 1870s. (mid-December)

MISSOURI TOWN 1855

8010 E. Park Road (located in Fleming Park) **Lee's Summit** 64064

Phone: (816) 503-4860 www.jacksongov.org/historicsites
Hours: Tuesday-Sunday 9:00am-4:30pm (March - mid-November). Weekends only 9:00am-4:30pm (mid-November - February).
Admission: $7.00 adult, $4.00 senior (62+) and child (5-13).
Educators: a thorough and easy to follow Teachers Guides is available off the main page under "Teachers Guides."

For updates & travel games visit: **www.KidsLoveTravel.com**

Missouri Town 1855 is composed of more than 25 buildings dating from 1820 to 1860. This living history museum uses original structures, furnishings and equipment. Also depicting the 19th-century lifestyles are interpreters in period attire, authentic field and garden crops, and rare livestock breeds. Find out what clothing from the 1850s was like, see and touch lye soap or pet one of the Missouri Town 1855 oxen. With the 1800s demonstrations going on (especially events and weekends), kids feel like they're walking around the "Little House" set.

CHILDREN'S DAY AND NATIONAL TRAILS DAY

Lee's Summit - Missouri Town 1855. Time honored games, such as sack races, tug-of-war and pie eating contests are just a few activities. National Trails Day. Admission. (first Saturday in June)

INDEPENDENCE DAY

Lee's Summit - Missouri Town. Experience hearth cooking, enjoy period music and engage in special speeches which made commemorating the anniversary of independence. Guests invited to join in a parade through Missouri Town 1855, a recreated antebellum community. Admission. (July 4th)

CHRISTMAS CELEBRATION

Lee's Summit - At Missouri Town 1855, experience how our ancestors prepared for Christmas in the 1850s. Interpreters share the customs of French, English and German settlers. Carolers, hot cider. As day turns into night, lanterns and luminaries light your way as you reflect on a Christmas of simpler times. Admission. (second Saturday in December)

PARADISE PARK FAMILY ENTERTAINMENT CENTER

1021 NE Colbern Road **Lee's Summit** 64086

Phone: (816) 246-5224 **www.paradise-park.com**
Admission: Priced per area or attraction ($4-$8). From $0.25 for gameroom tokens to Unlimited Indoor/Outdoor attractions for $32.99/person.

Paradise Park has three activity areas - The Family Entertainment Center, The Children's Edutainment Center, and indoor meeting/party rooms, in addition to an outdoor picnic pavilion. The park is a clean environment and the staff like to work here. The Family Entertainment Center offers a mix of indoor and outdoor attractions for all ages, including go karts, miniature golf, batting cages, bumper cars, rock climbing, a game room, and the foam factory. The Children's Edutainment Center caters to younger children.

BATTLE OF LEXINGTON STATE HISTORIC SITE

1101 Delaware Street (I-70 exit Hwy 13 north for 19 miles) **Lexington** 64067
Phone: (660) 259-4654 https://mostateparks.com/park/battle-lexington-state-historic-site
Admission: The Missouri state park system does not charge entrance fees. However, there are fees associated with camping, lodging, tours, museums and special events.
Tours: Interpreters conduct guided tours of the historic house and battleground on the hour. Cost is $3.00-$5.00 per person (age 6+). Tours run Wednesday - Saturday 10:00am-4:00pm and Sunday Noon -5:00pm.
Educators: Comprehensive Lesson Plans: https://.mostateparks.com/page/55022/

lesson-plans

Explore the 100-acre battlefield preserved in Lexington walking a one half mile self-guided trail around the battlefield. A visitor center explains why the "Battle of the Hemp Bales" lifted Southern spirits and further dampened Northern hopes of an easy victory in the struggle for Missouri. They have exhibits and an audio-visual program. Tour the Anderson-Davis House, used by both sides as a field hospital. The house changed hands three times, and soldiers met their death in the downstairs hallway. Probably the most interesting part of the tour for kids are the bullet holes in the walls and the story of the cannon ball shot through the attic.

JESSE JAMES BANK MUSEUM

103 North Water Street (Located on the northeast corner of the historic Liberty Square) **Liberty** 64068
Phone: (816) 736-8510
www.claycountymo.gov/Historic_Sites/Jesse_James_Bank_Museum
Hours: Monday-Saturday 10:00am-4:00pm.
Admission: $6.00 adult (16+), $5.50 senior (62+), $3.50 child (8-15).

This bank in Liberty was the site of the first daylight bank robbery during peacetime, which was attributed to the James gang. The original safe (where the money was taken from) is still there to see. The rest of the museum is set up to look as the bank did back then and it is furnished with period pieces of furniture. It gives you a feel of a boom town's quaint feeling and images of bandits demanding money are easily recalled from movies you may have watched. If you are planning on visiting his farm/house in Kearney this is on the way. It's about a 25-minute ride from both Kansas City & Independence.

For updates & travel games visit: **www.KidsLoveTravel.com**

MARTHA LAFITE THOMPSON NATURE SANCTUARY
407 North La Frenz Road **Liberty** 64068

Phone: (816) 781-8598 www.naturesanctuary.com
Hours: (Nature Center) Monday-Saturday 8:00am-5:00pm. Same hours for trails except the trails are also open Sunday.
Admission: FREE.

The 100-acre nonprofit nature sanctuary offers four miles of trails, while the center features several exhibits and has live animals and a gift shop. See the live animals, view the fossil display or sit and relax at the bird feeding station. Other exhibits are designed for touch and feel (animal pelts game, leaf identification). Most of the trails are less than a mile in length.

CAROLYN'S COUNTRY COUSINS FARM PUMPKIN PATCH

Liberty - *17607 N.E. 52nd Street (just 15 minutes from downtown Kansas City). Phone: (816) 781-9196* **www.carolynscountrycousins.com.** *Hours: Daily, 10:00am-7:00pm. Admission: $8.00/person. Additional fees apply.* Open seasonally, everyday activity options include making a scarecrow, touring the animal barn, peddling along the trike path, romping in the play yard and riding Little Bud's Railroad. On weekends, Uncle Lester's pig races, the Antique Pedal Tractor Carousel and Uncle Earl's Mining Camp add to the fun. Take a hayride to the pumpkin patch. Dig around in the Colossal Fossil House or grab a bite to eat at Aunt Kate's Kitchen. (begins mid-September thru October)

WALT DISNEY HOMETOWN MUSEUM
120 East Santa Fe Avenue **Marceline** 64658

Phone: (660) 376-3343 www.WaltDisneyMuseum.org
Hours: Tuesday-Saturday 10:00am-4:00pm, Sunday 1:00pm-4:00pm. Closed Monday. (April-October)
Admission: $5.00 adult (11+), $2.50 child (6-10).

One city where pop culture and history meet is Marceline, the childhood home of Walt Disney. By his own account, Walt's happiest childhood memories were of his time in this town. Disney spent part of his youth in this railroad town, which retains its ties to the animation pioneer through the WALT DISNEY DREAMING TREE AND BARN, located on the old family farm, and the Walt Disney Hometown Museum.

The Walt Disney Hometown museum is the recipient of a unique collection of family effects, never seen anywhere else in the world. Housed in the restored train depot, the Hometown Museum will excite young train buffs when they hear the real, live trains whizzing by the museum (more than 70 trains pass through town daily). The museum contains letters written by Disney. Museum guests will be thrilled to find a Midget Autopia car still in its original condition. Walt Disney retired the ride in Disneyland and sent it to his hometown Marceline in 1966. Because Walt Disney premiered the Midwest showing of the Great Locomotive Chase in Marceline's Uptown Theatre in 1956, the museum now houses a display of memorabilia from the movie. And don't worry, the museum gift shop is well stocked with Disney items.

MOZINGO LAKE AND RECREATION AREA

32348 East 245th Street (4 miles east of Maryville on Hwy. 136 then 1 mile north on Liberty Road) **Maryville** 64468

Phone: (660) 562-8001 www.mozingolake.com
Admission: FREE.

This facility includes 26 miles of shoreline around a 1,006 acre lake and offers fishing, swimming, walking trails, a beach, cabins, a 70-site RV park, primitive campsites and five boat docks.

FOUNTAIN GROVE CONSERVATION AREA

32988 Blackhorn Drive **Meadville** 64659

Phone: (660) 938-4124
Hours: Daily 8:00am-10:00pm.

Fountain Grove Conservation area sits in the floodplain of the Grand River and serves as an important migration stop for a variety of wildlife. It also plays an important role as a wintering habitat for Canada geese. Here you'll find diverse wetland habitats including marshes, bottomland forests, grain fields, oxbow lakes and sloughs. Bald eagles are commonly seen in the area throughout the winter. Things to Do: Fishing, camping, hiking, wildlife viewing, picnicking and, the kids favorite - frogging.

DID YOU KNOW ? Nearby Chillicothe is the Home of Sliced Bread. (the Grand River Historical Society Museum & the Murals of Chillicothe, downtown, tell the story)

For updates & travel games visit: **www.KidsLoveTravel.com**

North West Area   123

VAN METER STATE PARK
32146 N. Hwy. 122 **Miami** 65344

Phone: (660) 886-7537 https://mostateparks.com/park/van-meter-state-park
Admission: The Missouri state park system does not charge entrance fees. However, there are fees associated with camping, lodging, tours, museums and special events. Hours: Cultural Center-10am-4pm Saturdays and Noon-4pm Sundays. Summer hours extra days.

The state of Missouri and its principal river were both named after a tribe of Native Americans, known by the French explorers as the "Oumessourit" or Missouri Indians, that once lived in the area of Van Meter State Park. Today, the park provides outdoor recreational opportunities and interprets the area landscape and the Native Americans who found it to be bountiful. A hand-dug earthwork, known as the Old Fort, and several burial mounds lie within park boundaries.

This park features Missouri's American Indian Cultural Center, which interprets the history of nine tribes that once inhabited Missouri. Many of the artifacts on display were found on the property. The large wall mural gives you a real sense of the ancient Indian landscape. Beneath black walnut and oak trees, visitors can find a campground, picnic area, hiking trails and a fishing lake.

SQUAW CREEK NATIONAL WILDLIFE REFUGE
(just off of Interstate 29. Take exit 79, & drive 3 miles west on Highway 159) **Mound City** 64470

Phone: (660) 442-3187 www.fws.gov/midwest/SquawCreek/
Hours: (Refuge Headquarters) Monday-Friday 7:30am-4:00pm, (Visitor Contact Station) Monday - Friday 7:30am-4:00pm (year-round) and 10:00am-4:00pm weekends (Mid-March to early May) and (Mid-October to early December). (Wildlife Drive/Outdoor Facilities) - Open daily, dawn to dusk (year-round). Admission: FREE.

Located in northwest Missouri and in the Missouri River flood plain, this large refuge was established as a resting, feeding and breeding ground for migratory birds and other wildlife.

EAGLE DAYS

Mound City - Squaw Creek National Wildlife Refuge. During this time you can view 100s of bald eagles and learn about the comeback of our national symbol. Guided eagle tours, a movie about eagles, captive eagles on display. (December or January)

CHAPPELL'S RESTAURANT & SPORTS MUSEUM

323 Armour Road **North Kansas City** 64116

Phone: (816) 421-0002 **www.chappellsrestaurant.com**
Hours: Monday-Thursday 11:00am-10:00pm, Friday-Saturday til 11pm.

Filled floor to ceiling with sports items from the present to nearly 100 years ago, Chappell's is home to the nation's largest collection of sports memorabilia displayed in a restaurant. Can you count all 1,000 football helmets or find the dozens of autographed Hall of Fame baseballs? They offer typical American fare at moderate prices. Try Chappell's Cheese Fries (topped with zesty cheese queso or blue cheese sauce?), championship steaks (even steak soup), huge sandwiches or low carb and lite items.

SHATTO MILK COMPANY

9406 N. HWY. 33 **Osborn** 64474

Phone: (816) 930-3862 **https://shattomilk.com/**
Hours: Visitors can stop by the farm to look around on their own and visit the country store 365 days a year (during business hours).
Tours: Tours of the dairy, bottling facility and farm are available by appointment, Tuesday through Saturday throughout the year. Tours typically last one and a half hours from start to finish. There is a modest $6 charge per person, and children ages two and under are free.
Note: The farm has an annual Easter Egg Hunt and Family Day at the Farm in June.

Shatto Milk Company is a small family owned dairy farm just north of Kansas City that makes milk more fun than ever. The Shatto Family offers tours of their farm year-round. It starts with the cows. Get a first-hand look at where 120 cows live, what they eat, and how they are milked. Try milking a live cow or bottle feeding baby calves. Next, learn how their milk is bottled in the processing plant. Your visit includes a tour of the processing plant and viewing the actual process, along with a description of each step their milk goes through before it ends up on your table. Things get really interesting when flavors are mixed in. The choices? Banana, orange, strawberry, chocolate, root beer and eggnog - each in glass bottles. Watch the bottle wash station and then the filling station. At the end of your tour, sample many of Shatto Milk Company's tasty products.

DID YOU KNOW ? Shatto raises Holstein Cows for milking as they tend to produce more milk than cream.

North West Area

PUMPKINS ETC.

Platte City - 10701 Farmer Lane. Phone: (816) 858-5758 **www.pumpkins-etc.com**. Visitors play in the mazes, jump on the haystacks and steer wheelbarrows toward their favorite pumpkins. FREE. KARBAUMER FARM HAYRIDES is also in town offering wagon rides through the countryside. Call for rates. (mid-September thru October, Friday-Sunday, 10am-6pm)

LEWIS AND CLARK STATE PARK

801 Lake Crest Blvd. **Rushville** 64484

Phone: (816) 579-5564 https://mostateparks.com/park/lewis-and-clark-state-park
Admission: The Missouri state park system does not charge entrance fees. However, there are fees associated with camping, lodging, tours, museums and certain special events.

This park is dedicated to explorers Meriwether Lewis and William Clark, who visited the area July 4, 1804, on their westward journey. On the border of the Lake, the park offers picnic sites, camping, fishing, and a beach.

FORT OSAGE NATIONAL HISTORIC LANDMARK

107 Osage Street **Sibley** 64088

Phone: (816) 650-3278 **www.fortosagenhs.com**
Hours: Tuesday-Sunday 9:00am-4:30pm (March - mid-November). Weekends Only 9:00am-4:30pm (mid-November - February).
Admission: $8.00 adult, $4.00 youth, senior, Under 5 free.

The Fort Osage National Historic Landmark was built in 1808 under the direction of William Clark, co-leader of the Lewis & Clark expedition. The site was deemed an excellent place for camp. Clark came back in 1808 and built the fort. Overlooking the Missouri River, the Fort served as both a military garrison and trade center. This historic site has been reconstructed to portray Fort Osage as it was in 1812. Today, you can tour the blockhouses, officers' quarters and soldiers' barracks that frequently come to life in living history programs of the period. Authentically attired interpreters provide living-history insights into the daily life of both the military and civilian populations.

COALITION OF HISTORIC TREKKERS NATIONAL GATHERING AT FORT OSAGE

Sibley - Fort Osage. Experience the lifestyles of the early 1800s as re-enactors from across the country converge on Fort Osage for their national gathering. A variety of activities engage the visitors, offering a better understanding of how early explorers manage daily life. Special guided hikes introduce guests to the flora and fauna of the region. (mid-April weekend)

INDEPENDENCE DAY AT FORT OSAGE

Sibley - Fort Osage. The year is 1812. The soldiers and residents of Fort Osage are commemorating the anniversary of their independence against rumors of another impending war w/ Great Britain. Toasts are made and speeches are given. Don't miss the firing of the cannons & muskets along w/ military drills. Admission. (July 4th)

GRAND FESTIVAL OF CHEZ CANSES

Sibley - Fort Osage. Volunteers demonstrate the lifestyles of our colonial ancestors. From period appropriate clothing to arts and crafts, you will share this rich segment of our heritage. Special displays of everyday objects appropriate to Colonial America will help you better understand life of the period. Admission. (second full long weekend in September)

FIRST STREET TROLLEY

702 S. 5th Street **St. Joseph** 64501

Phone: (816) 233-6700
Hours: Season runs May-October. Admission: $1.75+

Getting around St. Joseph is easy aboard the popular First Street Trolleys. These reproductions of turn-of-the-century streetcars wind their way through the city with frequent stops at some of St. Joseph's most popular and historically significant attractions.

ROBIDOUX ROW MUSEUM

3rd & Poulin **St. Joseph** 64501

Phone: (816) 232-5861 **www.robidouxrowmuseum.org**
Hours: Tuesday-Friday 10:00am-4:00pm, Saturday/Sunday 1:00pm-4:00pm
Admission: $2.50 adult, $2.00 senior, $1.00 student, 12 and under free.

The city served as a starting point for wagon trails filled with pioneers heading west. Commercial growth included meat packing companies, drug companies, wholesalers and bankers. As the pioneers headed west, they occasionally stopped a while to reload and repair their wagons. This museum consists of living units (lined in a row) built in the 1840s by city founder Joseph Robidoux. How much better do you think these small dwellings were for pioneer families? Were they spoiled, maybe not wanting to go on?

North West Area 127

JESSE JAMES HOME MUSEUM
1202 Penn Street St. Joseph 64503

Phone: (816) 232-8206
www.ponyexpressjessejames.com/index.php?pid=jesse
Hours: Monday-Saturday 9:00am-4:00pm, Sunday Noon-4:00pm. (April-October).
Weekends only (November-March).
Admission: $4.00 adult, $3.00 senior, $2.00 student.

Of all the worlds' legendary characters, few have attracted world-wide fascination like the outlaw, Jesse James. Some call him America's Robin Hood, while others see him as a cold-blooded killer. Perhaps he was all of these things. See the house where Outlaw Jesse James was shot in the back and killed by a friend for reward money. The place doesn't exaggerate his lifestyle nor do you want to glorify it to your kids, but this was a significant time in "Wild West" history. If you'd rather, focus on the science of DNA testing that occurred in 1995 when they exhumed the body to determine if it was truly THE Jesse James and not a fake. The DNA testing results showed a 99.7% certainty that it really was Jesse James in the grave and this is where it happened.

PATEE HOUSE MUSEUM
1202 Penn Street St. Joseph 64503

Phone: (816) 232-8206 www.ponyexpressjessejames.com
Hours: Monday-Saturday 9:00am-4:00pm, Sunday Noon-5:00pm (April-October).
Weekends Only (November-March)
Admission: $6.00 adult, $5.00 senior, $4.00 student. Kids 5 and under are admitted FREE.

The town's focal point is the Patee House. This National Historic Landmark was a pioneer hotel and headquarters for the Pony Express in 1860. Visit the "Streets of Old St. Jo," enjoy western art, antique toys, telephones and cars. Climb aboard an 1860 train, ride a vintage carousel and stroll the streets of 1860s St. Joseph to visit a general store, a dentist's office or a jail. In the Buffalo "Saloon" volunteers occasionally serve soft drinks and popcorn. The BEST part about is you can get UP CLOSE to almost all of the objects. The museum is not only housed in the restored Pony Express headquarters office but it was also home to where the Union Army held war trails. It is one block away from the home of infamous outlaw Jesse James, where he was shot and killed by Bob Ford. After his death, the James family stayed and were interviewed in the hotel.

PONY EXPRESS MUSEUM

914 Penn Street **St. Joseph** 64503

Phone: (816) 279-5059 or (800) 530-5930 **www.ponyexpress.org**
Hours: Monday-Saturday 9:00am-5:00pm, Sunday 11:00am-4:00pm.
Admission: $6.00 adult, $5.00 senior (60+), $3.00 student (7-17).
Educators: Ask the front desk (or call ahead) for the scavenger hunt and several worksheets the attraction has developed for school groups.

On April 3, 1860, a young man named Johnny Fry took off from St. Joseph on horseback, the first of a relay of riders on a new mail service to California. The museum is located on the site of the original stables and opens with a diorama of Fry on his horse, eager for the stable door to open so he can begin his ride into history. The route ran from St. Joseph through Kansas, Nebraska, Colorado, Wyoming, Utah and Nevada to Sacramento, California…almost 2,000 miles in 2 weeks…by horseback. Buffalo Bill Cody was one famous rider. Rider's horses were changed every 10 to 15 miles, and new riders mounted every 75 to 100 miles. The delivery service was set up because folks on the West Coast were eager for news from back East, where a new president was about to be elected and the country was edging toward civil war. You can imagine the quickest run ever was the delivery of President Abraham Lincoln's inaugural address (took seven days and 17 hours to complete).

Begin your tour watching a 15-minute Pony Express video. Next, move around the museum but plan to spend the most time in the interactives areas such as the "Family Life on the Frontier," where kids are able to dress up as a pioneer and experience life in the 1800s. Pump water from the same well that was used to water the horses. Ride a wooden sawhorse equipped with a saddle. Do you feel cavalier? Did you know saddlebags (that carried the mail) were called mochilas? Walk inside a desert air, mountain cold, and experience some of the smells encountered along the riders' trips between Missouri and California. Do you know how to choose horses that can endure the elements and the fast pace? Finally, tap out messages on a telegraph - the invention that put the Pony Express operation out of business.

PUMPKINFEST

St. Joseph - Pony Express Museum. The spirit of the fall harvest is celebrated here with family arts festival featuring live entertainment, a children's costume parade, festival rides, pumpkin games, food, and the lighting of the Great Pumpkin. The Great Pumpkin Mountain - part of the annual PumpkinFest, is giant racks and tiers of decorated pumpkins lined to form a "tree". FREE. (second weekend in October)

REMINGTON NATURE CENTER

1502 MacArthur Drive (I-29 to I-229, exit on Highland Avenue (Exit 7). Go west on Highland Avenue. Right on MacArthur Drive) **St. Joseph** 64505

Phone: (816) 271-5499 www.stjoenaturecenter.info
Hours: Monday-Saturday 10:00am-5:00pm, Sunday 1:00-5:00pm.
Admission: $1.00-$3.00 per person (age 4+)
Note: Gift shop and snack shop. Friday Fish Feeding at 10:30am. FREEBIES: the website "JUST FOR KIDS" page has a Scavenger Hunt sheet, coloring pages and links to national wildlife sites for kids.

Upon entering the Nature Center guests are greeted by a life-sized Mammoth and calf along with the only mammoth bones excavated in Missouri, which happen to have been found in Buchanan County. As you walk down the hallway, you will have the opportunity to observe native Missouri River fishes in a 7,000 gallon aquarium. Stand shoulder to shoulder with a bison, see a black bear weighing over 600lbs (an average bear weighs 200 lbs.) and get closer to a wolf than you every thought you would as you take in the vast collection of taxidermy animals that are found throughout the Center. Kids can explore a beaver dam, watch a functioning beehive, and gaze out the expansive windows to the Missouri River and the wildlife found there. Watch as several Missouri animals make tracks in the sand right before your eyes. You can then go outside to see the Mighty MO up close or walk down the riverwalk and view the bluffs.

The historical part of the museum takes you back to BC to the turn of the 20th century. Walk along the city streets of the 1800s, learn unique farming techniques Indians used to produce food, and go back further to the Woodlands Period and the pottery native women produced. Camp in the fur trapper tent and shop for goods in the trader cabin. Stop by the theater to watch a film about Westward Migration, the California Gold Rush, Oregon Trail and ancient Indian tales.

You can tell this attraction is newer as the developers created fresh, interactive spaces spattered with ancient artifacts. In other words, the kids are engaging in learning without really knowing it.

SCHWEIZER ORCHARDS

5455 SE State Route FF Highway (exit 44, the Hwy 169 South exit, off I-29 and head east) **St. Joseph** 64507

Phone: (816) 232-3999 www.schweizerorchards.com
Hours: (Market) Monday-Saturday 9:00am-5:30pm, Sunday 1:00-5:00pm.
Tours: Fall field trips cost $1.50 per student and include story, walking tour of orchard and a special treat. Add a little more for pumpkins.

Peeking out from the bluffs overlooking the Missouri River is an orchard that has grown apples for more than four generations. Schweizer Orchards boasts a variety of apples and offer pick-your-own strawberries in the spring and several types of both yellow and white peaches in the summer. Each season offers a new fruit. A fall field trip extends your visit with the playground area and a stroll through the hay maze. Have you tried their apple and cherry cider slushies?

TRAILS WEST FESTIVAL

St. Joseph - Civic Center Park, downtown. Phone: (800) 216-7080. Festival has musical entertainment, melodramas, rousing historical reenactments, food booths, and children's activities, including an art tent with hands-on art projects and performances by jugglers and magicians. Admission. (third weekend in August)

SWAN LAKE NATIONAL WILDLIFE REFUGE

16194 Swan Lake Avenue **Sumner** 64681
Phone: (660) 856-3323 http://midwest.fws.gov/SwanLake/

The primary purpose of the refuge is to provide nesting, resting, and feeding areas for waterfowl, primarily ducks. An important secondary purpose was to preserve a remnant flock of prairie chickens. Unfortunately, adequate grassland habitat to maintain a viable population of the birds was not available. So, now they expanded efforts to include Canada geese each winter. This refuge still has one of the largest concentrations of Canada geese in North America and is now the primary wintering area for the Eastern Prairie Population. Folks say you'll see more deer and geese here than you would have imagined.

CROWDER STATE PARK

76 NE State Highway North **Trenton** 64683

Phone: (660) 359-6473 **https://mostateparks.com/park/crowder-state-park**
Admission: The Missouri state park system does not charge entrance fees.

The rolling hills of northern Missouri serve as a memorial to Maj. Gen. Enoch H. Crowder, a Missourian who founded the Selective Service System. The park offers a lake, a beach, camping and hiking, mountain biking and equestrian trails. A couple of the trails run along the Thompson River.

SNOW CREEK SKI AREA

1 Snow Creek Drive **Weston** 64098

Phone: (816) 640-2200 **www.skisnowcreek.com**

Snow Creek Ski Resort has 12 ski trails, served by 6 lifts. Trails: 30% beginner, 60% intermediate, 5% advanced. Snow Creek Ski Resort is located in Weston, MO, about 40 minutes from Kansas City, MO, and St. Joseph, MO. They have a SnowMonsters clubhouse and mascot for kids. Snowboarding.

WESTON BEND STATE PARK

16600 Hwy. 45 N **Weston** 64098

Phone: (816) 640-5443 **www.mostateparks.com/westonbend.htm**
Admission: The Missouri state park system does not charge entrance fees.

Near Kansas City, this park features picnic tables and shelter houses, a campground, a three-mile paved bicycle trail and hiking trails. A scenic overlook, accessible to persons with disabilities, provides visitors with a view of the Missouri River, Fort Leavenworth and beyond. A hiking trail meanders through the woods and along the edge of the bluff provides great views.

WESTON RED BARN FARM

16300 Wilkerson Road **Weston** 99909

Phone: (816) 386-5437 **www.westonredbarnfarm.com**

This educational farm showcases baby animals in the spring and has a peach harvest from July to August. You can pick pumpkins, apples and blackberries (when in season), go through the corn maze, shop in the country store or take a wagon ride.

South East Area   133

Chapter 4
South East (SE)

QUICK LOOK...

Old Mills & Mines

Natural Caves & Caverns

Civil War Forts

Ancient Rocks

State Parks & Getaway Cabins

Black
- Koinania Cottages & Cabins

Bonne Terre
- Bonne Terre Mine

Burfordville
- Bollinger Mill State Historic Site

Cape Girardeau
- Cape Girardeau Conservation Nature Center
- John Wesley Powell's Fort D
- Lazy L Safari Park
- My Daddy's Cheesecake
- Port Cape Girardeau Restaurant
- Red House Interpretive Center
- Cape Girardeau Air Festival

Chester, IL
- Popeye Statue And Park

Davisville
- Dillard Mill State Historic Site

Doniphan
- Civil War Days

East Prairie
- Big Oak Tree State Park
- Towosahgy State Historic Site

Ellis Grove, IL
- Fort Kaskaskia & Kaskaskia Bell State Historic Site

Eminence
- Alley Spring Grist Mill Historic Site
- Crystal Creek Ranch

Graniteville
- Elephant Rocks State Park

Jackson
- St. Louis Iron Mountain & Southern Railway
- Trail Of Tears State Park

Leasburg
- Onondaga Cave State Park

Malden
- Bootheel Youth Museum

Marble Hill
- Bollinger County Museum Of Natural History

Middlebrook
- Taum Sauk Mountain State Park
- Johnson's Shut-Ins State Park

New Madrid
- New Madrid Historical Museum

Park Hills
- Missouri Mines State Historic Site
- St. Joe State Park

Patterson
- Sam A. Baker State Park

Pilot Knob
- Fort Davidson State Historic Site

Poplar Bluff
- Dunlap Pumpkin Farm

Potosi
- Sayersbrook Bison Ranch

Prairie Du Rocher, IL
- Fort De Chartres Historic Site

Puxico
- Mingo National Wildlife Refuge

Rolla
- Mineral Museum

For updates & travel games visit: www.KidsLoveTravel.com

South East Area

Salem
- Bo's Hollow
- Montauk State Park
- Ozark Natural & Cultural Resource Center

Sikeston
- Lambert's Café: Home Of The Throwed Rolls
- Beggs Family Farm

St. James
- Maramec Spring Park

Stanton
- Jesse James Wax Museum
- Meramec Caverns

Ste. Genevieve
- Bolduc House Museum Complex
- Felix Valle State Historic Site
- Great River Road Interpretive Center
- Hawn State Park
- Ste. Genevieve Museum

Sullivan
- Jour De Fete
- ASL Pewter Foundry

Sullivan
- Meramec State Park

Thayer
- Grand Gulf State Park

Van Buren
- Ozark National Scenic Riverways Headquarters

West Plains
- West Plains Motor Speedway

Wickliffe, KY
- Wickliffe Mounds

Williamsville
- Lake Wappapello State Park

Winona
- Heritage Day At Twin Pines

Sites and attractions are listed in order by City, Zip Code, and Name. Symbols indicated represent: 🍽 Restaurants 🛏 Lodging

RIVER FERRIES OVER THE MISSISSIPPI RIVER
www.greatriverroad.com/SecondaryPages/ferries.htm

Early American ferries consisted of rafts, rowboats and horse boats that could cross rivers where demand for transportation existed but where there weren't any easy crossings. The advent of railroads and bridges put most ferries out of business and motorized vessels replaced the earlier forms of transportation of those that survived. For modern travelers, the remaining ferries in operation can save time as well as providing scenic river views.

- **STE. GENEVIEVE-MODOC FERRY** - N. Main Street. Follow N. Main Street about 1 1/2 miles from the Historic District of Ste. Genevieve to the Little Rock Landing on the Mississippi River. The Modoc Landing is accessible from IL-3 and IL-155 in Randolph County on the Illinois side. The ferry runs during daylight hours approximately every fifteen minutes and a fee is charged. This is the easiest way to get to the French colonial sites on the Illinois side of the river. (ex. Pierre Menard Home, Fort Kaskaskia Historic Site, and Fort de Chartes State Historic Site - the huge, partially restored stone fort kids can climb around. **http://stegenmodocferry.com**. Cash only. Roundtrip = $25.00.

KOINANIA COTTAGES & CABINS

1231 County Road 66 (I-55 exit 174B -Rte. 67 south to 32 west. For rest of directions, refer to website) **Black** 63625

Phone: (573) 269-4544 **www.koinaniacottage.com**
Admission: Three units-Lodging fees start at $145.00 per night up to $225.00 per night with discounted weekly & off season stays. The units available: Cottage 3 BR-2B, Ranch House Duplex 6 BR-3B-2 kitchens-2 living rooms, Cabin on Lake-sleeps 4. Full kitchens-includes linens-deck furnishings-grills.

Just 2 hours southwest of St. Louis, on 110 private acres in the beautiful Arcadia Valley in the Ozarks surrounded by Mark Twain National Forest, the folks at Koinania offer cottages and cabin lodging near the Black River. The 1/2 mile of private river frontage is a child's paradise of nature discovery an swimming fun . This isn't just a place to overnight, this is a property designed for days and days of wholesome family fun and adventures around their stocked fishing lake, hiking trails, enjoying a campfire at night, or playing in the rustic playhouse next to a small stream. This country destination has a "*Little House On The Prairie*". The owners have equipped closets with dress up clothes, toys, games, books, DVDs and the family friendly dogs and lovable cats top off the joy of your stay. Can you imagine catching little lizards, tree frogs, and turtles and making them your pets for a week and then letting them return to the forest? Or, early evening playing board and card games together and then watching movies, eating popcorn and staying up late?

While you could just stay on the property and explore for days, many families go horseback riding at a nearby stable, swim and play on the rocks at Johnson Shut Ins State Park or hike the trails and climb the rocks at Elephant Rocks State Park. Many families enjoy a visit to the Civil War State Historic Site at Fort Davidson and top it all off with ice cream at Pilot Knob or Caledonia.

BONNE TERRE MINE

185 Park Avenue (Hwy 47 & Allen Street) **Bonne Terre** 63628
Phone: (573) 358-2148 **www.bonneterremine.com**
Hours: Daily (Boat Tours - includes walking tour), 9:30am- 3:30pm (hourly).
Admission: Boat tour (includes walking tour) $27 adult, $20 child (under 11).

A cool way to learn more about Missouri's mine heritage takes place 80 feet below the earth's surface in Bonne Terre Mine, formerly the world's largest lead mine. One day the miners walked out and the mine began to fill with water, forming the Billion Gallon Lake and 17 miles of remote shoreline. The fact the mine is man-made makes it even more amazing, especially when you see the tools used by the men who created it. The Lake is illuminated with 500,000 watts of lighting. A total of 24 dive trails have been laid out for divers to explore (you must be a certified diver to go underwater).

- WALKING TOUR - Take a one hour guided walking tour through the first and second levels of the mine along the "Old Mule Trail". Along this tour, you will see Huge Pillar Rooms, Grand Canyon, Billion Gallon Lake, Trout Pond, Underground Flower Gardens, Beautiful Calcite Falls, and ancient Abandoned Mining Tools and Rail Systems.

- BOAT TOUR - See the No. 1 Elevator, Submerged Ore Carts, Wrapped Pillars, and Ancient Abandoned Overhead Wooden Cat Walks suspended 50-100 feet above the lake.

It's a little spooky down there but you'll have tons of other tourists and a knowledgeable guide to comfort you and lead the way through an unusual tour of Missouri history.

BOLLINGER MILL STATE HISTORIC SITE

113 Bollinger Mill Road (off Hwy 34) **Burfordville** 63739

Phone: (573) 243-4591 https://mostateparks.com/park/bollinger-mill-state-historic-site
Hours: grounds open daily from dawn to 10:00pm.
Admission: The Missouri state park system does not charge entrance fees.
Tours: Typically Monday-Saturday 10:00am-4:00pm, Sunday Noon-4:00pm. Call ahead during off season to confirm. Tours run $4.00-$5.00 per person.

Bollinger Mill State Historic Site is unusual in featuring both a working mill and a covered bridge, side by side. The present mill, dating back to the Civil War period, is a massive four-story stone and brick building where visitors can still observe corn being ground into meal by water power. The Burfordville Covered Bridge standing alongside stretches its 140-foot span across the Whitewater River, which power the mill. Begun in 1858, it is the oldest of only four remaining covered bridges in Missouri. You can tour the mill and view exhibits about how the process of milling has changed over the years. The 43-acre site also has a tree-shaded picnic area, and a quarter-mile of stream bank. Great lazy afternoon activity.

CAPE GIRARDEAU CONSERVATION NATURE CTR

North County Park, 2289 County Park Drive **Cape Girardeau** 63701

Phone: (573) 290-5218 www.mdc.mo.gov/areas/cnc/cape/
Hours: Tuesday-Saturday 8:00am-5:00pm. Admission: FREE

The Nature Center features a 160-seat auditorium, nature gift shop, classrooms, hands-on exhibits for all ages, a scientific research laboratory, freshwater aquariums, and an indoor wildlife viewing area. View Native American primitive tools used to harvest plants and animals hundreds of years ago. Interactive exhibits encourage exploration of the forest, marsh, swamp, and big river habitats of Southeast Missouri by crawling through a beaver dam or watching local fish. Outside, help a child learn how to fish at the "Kids Only" fishing pond near the nature center's entrance. Or, view sinkholes and explore ravines during a two-mile hike through White Oak Trace trail. The trails also connect to Wood Duck Swamp and Maple Hollow Trail. Kids think it's pretty cool to walk alongside a swamp. Native plants featured in the nature center's landscape provide habitat for hummingbirds, butterflies and other wildlife species.

For updates & travel games visit: **www.KidsLoveTravel.com**

JOHN WESLEY POWELL'S FORT D

(4 blocks south of SR 74 & Sprigg Street, just west of the Miss. River Bridge) **Cape Girardeau** 63701

In the summer of 1861 at the beginning of the Civil War, four forts were built around the strategic city of Cape Girardeau. The forts were built by soldiers, Engineers and local militia under the direction of Illinois Lt. John Wesley Powell. Powell, who would later gain fame as the explorer of the Grand Canyon, was detached from his regiment by a newly appointed general... Ulysses S. Grant, in order to raise a local company to man the forts. This Powell did, and his new Battery F served the forts until leaving for the Battle of Shiloh. Fort D featured as many as five cannons, the largest of which could fire a 32-pound cannon ball. The fort was manned throughout the Civil War. The fort grounds, featuring interpretive signs, are open free to the public dawn to dusk. **http://cityofcapegirardeau.org**.

LAZY L SAFARI PARK

2763 County Road 618 **Cape Girardeau** 63701

Phone: (573) 243-7862 **www.lazylsafari.com**
Hours: Daily 10:00am-6:00pm (Memorial Day-Labor Day), Weekends (April, May, & September, October). Admission Gate closes at 6:00pm but Zoo closes at 7:00pm. Open wkends November-March 10am-4pm.
Admission: $7.00 per person (ages 2+).

The park features exotic animals from around the world in a comfortable and natural setting. Take a stroll along the creek while gazing into the fields to watch zebras or antelope graze. Go on "safari" and feed the pygmy goats, watch baby animals, peer into the reptile aquariums, or check out the emu eggs in their incubator. You'll find several benches for quiet reflection or animal watching, a gift shop, a picnic shelter, and a snack shack. Be sure to visit the Petting Zoo area where you can pet and feed the animals and you won't want to miss viewing baby animals in the Animal Nursery.

MY DADDY'S CHEESECAKE

Cape Girardeau - 63701. **www.mydaddyscheesecake.com**. Mississippi Mud and Turtle are among the most popular cheesecake served but kids gravitate to the Gooey Louie cookie wedge - chocolate, pecans and graham crackers, or the frozen cheesecake on a stick - covered in chocolate. Start your day off right with breakfast at My Daddy's! For lunch or dinner enjoy the "best" wraps, sandwiches and salads.

PORT CAPE GIRARDEAU RESTAURANT

Cape Girardeau - *19 North Water Street 63701. Phone: (573) 334-0954. www.portcape.com*. During the civil war, this historic 1830s building on the riverfront housed general Ulysses s. Grant's headquarters. The building is one of the oldest standing structures west of the Mississippi River. Lunch or dinner with menu offering great BBQ, catfish, pork and a kids menu. Price Range: $7.00-$25.00.

RED HOUSE INTERPRETIVE CENTER

128 S. Main Street **Cape Girardeau** 63701

Phone: (573) 334-0757 or (573) 335-1631.
www.orgsites.com/mo/redhouseinterpretivecenter/
Hours: Saturday 10:00am-4:00pm (May-October). Open additional days in summer. Call or visit website for current schedule.

Admission: $3.00 adult, $1.00 child.
Educators: there are clever Scavenger Hunt Questions at the bottom of this Teachers Page: **www.orgsites.com/mo/redhouseinterpretivecenter/_pgg2.php3**.

The Red House Interpretive Center commemorates the visit of Meriwether Lewis and William Clark in November 1803. Louis Lorimier, Cape Girardeau's founder, welcomed the expedition members at his home, the Red House. The Interpretive Center houses an early 1800's exhibit that reflects the lives of the early settlers of the "Old Cape Girardeau District." In addition, a rendering of the Louis Lorimier Trading Post displays authentic items that would have been sold during the early 1800's. The trading post was Cape's main business at the time when Lewis and Clark arrived. What would you trade for some new skins?

CAPE GIRARDEAU AIR FESTIVAL

Cape Girardeau - Cape Girardeau Regional Airport. www.capegirardeauairfestival.com Military and civilian aircraft are on display and take part in aerobatics. Food booths. Admission. Additional fee for airplane, helicopter and simulator rides. (late June or mid-July weekend)

POPEYE STATUE AND PARK

(off IL 3, Great River Road) **Chester, IL** 62233

Phone: (618) 826-2326

The towering Popeye Statue in the Elzie C. Segar Memorial Park is found by crossing the Mississippi River, the Chester Bridge. The monument honors

Elzie Segar, creator of Popeye who was born in Chester. There's more Popeye than spinach at Spinach Can Collectibles inside Chester's historic 1875 Opera House building. Popeye merchandise and a mini-Popeye museum fill the space and headquarters of the Popeye Fan Club.

DILLARD MILL STATE HISTORIC SITE

142 Dillard Mill Road **Davisville** 65456

Phone: (573) 244-3120   http://mostateparks.com/park/dillard-mill-state-historic-site

Admission: The Missouri state park system does not charge entrance fees.
Tours: Daily 10:00am-4:00pm with the last tour beginning at 3:00pm. The last tour of the day starts at 3:00pm. (May-October). Wednesday -Sunday only (November-April). $4.00-$5.00 per person to tour the mill. The mill is not heated. Please be sure to bring a jacket during cooler weather.

One of Missouri's best-preserved water-powered gristmills is tucked between Ozark hills and pine-topped bluffs next to the Huzzah Creek. Today, most of the original machinery is still intact and operational. Visitors can see the remaining machinery come to life during a tour of the mill. With the turn of a wheel, the mill begins to operate as it did years ago, grinding grain into flour. The sound of the water gushing over the dam outside the mill is replaced with the sounds of the belts and rollers turning. Tour the mill (built in 1900), have a picnic lunch and take a hike in this picturesque setting.

CIVIL WAR DAYS

Doniphan - Heritage Homestead, 201 Franklin Street. Phone: (573) 996-5298 **www.doniphanmissouri.org/civil_war_days**   Craft demonstrations, music, food, fun with a strong dose of living history. Spring of 1861. Men have answered Governor Jackson's call to join the Missouri State Guard and repel the invading Federal forces. The men have gathered at Camp Burrows in Ripley County to organize and drill. The men are poorly equipped and trained; much of the time around camp is spent drilling. The novelty of war has yet to be replaced by the horror that will follow. The men are excited and looking forward to the opportunity to quickly whip their foe and return home with stories to tell their families. Women and children have gathered around the camp to watch the activities. Merchants and settlers appear, trying to capitalize on the needs of the men and spectators. FREE. (last full weekend in April)

BIG OAK TREE STATE PARK

13640 South Hwy. 102 **East Prairie** 63845

Phone: (573) 649-3149 http://mostateparks.com/park/big-oak-tree-state-park
Admission: The Missouri state park system does not charge entrance fees. .

A boardwalk gives a close-up view of the swamp forest that once covered Missouri's Bootheel. Large, stately oaks and stands of giant cane give way to enormous cypress trees in the swamp. The boardwalk is accessible to people with disabilities. A nature center, picnic area and small lake are available. The center features the history of the logging and drainage of Missouri's bootheel; changes in the Mississippi River floodplain; and the New Madrid earthquake. Other displays focus on the park's champion trees, wildlife and unique plants (open Tuesday-Saturday 10:00am-4:00pm, April thru September). After a nature hike through the forest, visitors can enjoy a picnic lunch under the open shelter or at one of many picnic tables nestled beneath the lofty trees.

TOWOSAHGY STATE HISTORIC SITE

County Road 502 (East Prairie/Matthews exit off I-55 (Exit 58), east on Hwy. 80, south on Hwy. 77, 1 mile west on County Road 502, Mississippi County) **East Prairie** 63845

Phone: (573) 748-5340 http://mostateparks.com/park/towosahgy-state-historic-site
Admission: The Missouri state park system does not charge entrance fees.

This site preserves the remains of a once fortified Indian village, which was an important ceremonial center. Indians of the Mississippian Culture lived here between AD 1000 and AD 1400. The name, Towosahgy, was borrowed from the Osage Indians and means "old town." Visitors to the 64-acre tract of land can see remnants of past activities in the form of earthen mounds constructed for ceremonial, residential and religious purposes. Visitors can envision the lifestyle of a people who lived in a far distant time in Missouri pre-settlement history. A kiosk with exhibits interprets the history.

FORT KASKASKIA & STATE HISTORIC SITE

4372 Park Road (take MO 51 Bridge over to IL. Take IL 3 north & follow signs to Fort) **Ellis Grove, IL** 62241

Phone: (618) 859-3741
www2.illinois.gov/dnrhistoric/sites/experience/
Hours: Daily 8:00am-4:00pm. Admission: FREE

Fort Kaskaskia State Historic Site preserves what's left of the old fort-one of the first built on the Mississippi River. The fort was built to protect Kaskaskia from British attack during the American Revolution. Lewis and Clark's boats landed here, establishing a recruitment base and post office. All that remains today are the earth works around the perimeter. A scenic overlook offers views of the Mississippi and Kaskaskia Rivers and of Old Kaskaskia.

ALLEY MILL HISTORIC SITE

State Highway 106 (6 miles west of Eminence) **Eminence** 65466

Phone: (573) 226-3945
www.nps.gov/ozar/learn/historyculture/alley-mill.htm
Hours: Daily 9:00am-4:00pm (Memorial Day - Labor Day).
Admission: FREE (donations accepted).
Note: still on Hwy 106, see the vivid blue water at one of the state's prettiest springs, BLUE SPRING. It's a half-mile walk from the parking area. The steep approach ride is not recommended for large vehicles like buses. (www.nps.gov/ozar). Several canoe, raft and tube rental providers are in town. Many offer lodging or camping, too.

In 1894, this roller mill and one-room schoolhouse was the focal point of the Alley Spring community. Visit the historic 1894 Alley Mill to learn about life in those days. Park rangers in period costume show you how the mill worked, and how school was taught in the one-room schoolhouse. They offer a variety of historic programs.

CRYSTAL CREEK RANCH

County Road 414 (HCR 3 Box 55) **Eminence** 65466

Phone: (573) 226-2222 **www.crystalcreekranch.com**
Hours: Overlook deck, self-guided ranch tours, walking trails, labyrinth, outside primitives, and horse drawn equipment open Daily until dusk (April-October).

Turn off the pavement onto the one mile gravel road to the Ranch, and travel thru an Ozark forest, down the rolling hills and past the creek to the Ranch Headquarters. This ranch has lodging, free self-guided ranch tours, four-level look-out deck, a small animal area, walking trails, labyrinth and farm primitives museum. (April -October). FREE just to stop by.

ELEPHANT ROCKS STATE PARK

Route 21 (4.2 miles from 21 and "221" via 21 North) **Graniteville** 63656
Phone: (573) 546-3454 http://**mostateparks.com/park/elephant-rocks-state-park**
Admission: The Missouri state park system does not charge entrance fees.

A train of circus elephants dance trunk-to-tail. This is the appeal of Elephant Rocks State Park, named for a train of gigantic pink granite boulders perched atop a hill, just like circus elephants! There is no record of the actual number of "elephants" inhabiting the park. Old ones erode away and new elephants wait beneath the cracks and joints of the granite hillside. The park's pink patriarch, Dumbo, is 27 feet tall, 35 feet long and 17 feet wide, weighing in at a colossal 680 tons! The park's one mile circular interpretive trail was the first state park trail in Missouri designed for visitors with physical and visual handicaps. Known as the Braille Trail, signs written in Braille and regular text, guide visitors along a paved, handicap-accessible trail which allows visitors to see the huge rocks and seven acres of the park's over 131 acres. Camping is not allowed in the park, but thirty picnic sites and a playground area provide families with the opportunity to explore the park.

ST. LOUIS IRON MOUNTAIN & SOUTHERN RAILWAY

(Intersection of Highway 61 & 25) **Jackson** 63755
Phone: (573) 243-1688 **www.slimrr.com**
Hours: Saturday Tour @ 1:00pm (May-December). Jackson to Gordonville and back (10 miles - 2 hours).
Admission: $17.00 adult (13+), $10.00 child (2-12).
NOTE: The steam engine is not currently available for service. The diesel engine will be running on all trips.

Hear the stories of a Jesse James Gang robbery, learn how hobos traveled the rails and see first-hand what a real diesel locomotive looks like at the St. Louis, Iron Mountain and Southern Railway. Known as the state's only full-sized passenger train, it will take you back to the 1950s and the era of passenger rail transportation. Watch out, while on your ride you may experience a James Gang robbery, magic show and Bonnie and Clyde.

ST. LOUIS RAILWAY SANTA EXPRESS

Jackson - St. Louis Railway. Passengers can enjoy the magic of the season on December themed rides. While onboard, children can hear the story of "The Polar Express" and enjoy a visit from Santa. Admission. (December weekends)

For updates & travel games visit: **www.KidsLoveTravel.com**

TRAIL OF TEARS STATE PARK

429 Moccasin Springs Road **Jackson** 63755

Phone: (573) 290-5268   https://mostateparks.com/park/trail-tears-state-park
Hours: the Visitors Center is generally open 9:00am-5:00pm weekdays and 10:00am-4:00pm weekends.
Admission: The Missouri state park system does not charge entrance fees. However, there are fees associated with camping, lodging, tours, museums and special events.

Walk through 3,000 acres of what serves as a memorial to the Cherokee Indians. A portion of this wooded park was part of the Trail Of Tears. Camping, a lake, a beach, fishing, a visitor center, an overlook, and hiking and equestrian trails are offered. An overlook provides a view of the Mississippi River. The park's visitor center features exhibits that interpret the forced relocation, as well as the park's many natural features. Dioramas show a peaceful people who were forced to abandon homes and lands preparing for the journey.

ONONDAGA CAVE STATE PARK

7556 Hwy. H **Leasburg** 65535

Phone: (573) 245-6576 or (573) 245-6600 (Cave Tours)
https://mostateparks.com/park/onondaga-cave-state-park
Admission: The Missouri state park system does not charge entrance fees.
Admission for Onondaga Cave Tours: $15.00 adult (13+), $9.00 child (6-12).
Admission for Cathedral Cave Tours: $10.00 adult (13+), $8.00 teen (13-17), $6.00 child (6-12).
Tours: Onondaga Cave - Tours leave from the visitor center and are available from March-October. Tours offered at the minimum every 2 hours from 10:00am-4:00pm. They are walking tours, just less than one mile long, and last about one hour and 15 minutes. The cave's temperature is 57°F (13°C) year-round, so, bring a jacket and comfortable shoes. Cathedral Cave - Tour every Saturday at 10:00am-1:00pm and Sunday at 10:00am (Memorial Day-Labor Day). Tours are given on Saturdays at 1:00pm and Sundays at 10:00am (April, May, September & October). It is a lantern tour that lasts approximately two hours. The tour begins at the campground showerhouse and includes a short one-third mile walk up Deer Run Trail to the cave's entrance. The cave tour itself lasts about 90 minutes.
Note: across the river from the park is the OZARK OUTDOORS RIVERFRONT RESORT offering canoe, raft, tube rentals to float the rivers or camping/RV sites, a swimming pool, sport courts and a restaurant on site. (*www.ozarkoutdoors.net*)

Bordering the Meramec River, the park offers fishing, a visitor center, a store, picnicking, camping, a boat ramp, a lake and scenic hiking trails.

- **ONONDAGA CAVE** - Features some of the nation's best cave formations including towering columns and intricately woven draperies of rock. Learn about geologic wonders such as the King's Canopy, the Twins and other unusual speleothems. Guided tours point out massive stalagmites that rise like peaks from the floor of the Big Room, said to be large enough to hold a football stadium. This cave even has a river flowing through it.

Vilander Bluff Natural Area provides visitors with a panoramic view of the Meramec River. Come and take a hike through the Meramec River valley, canoe or fish in the Meramec River or enjoy a picnic lunch. Learn about the park's natural resources above and below the earth's surface through exhibits inside the visitor center. The park's campground offers both basic and electric/water campsites, many of which are reservable.

BOOTHEEL YOUTH MUSEUM

700 North Douglass Street **Malden** 63863

Phone: (573) 276-3600 www.bootheelyouthmuseum.org
Hours: Tuesday-Saturday 10:00am-4:00pm, Sunday 1:00pm-4:00pm.
Admission: $4.00 adult (18+), $6.00 child (3-17).

A hands-on discovery museum with large spaces focused on science, math, human relations, natural resources and the arts. Includes Children's Village, This Island Mars, Lewis and Clark, and a children's theater. Some workshop areas deal with gooey or acidic messes. Simple Machines is a large area where students can actually use a lever, pulleys, wheels and gears. What ratios do you need to make work easier?

BOLLINGER COUNTY MUSEUM OF NATURAL HISTORY

207 Mayfield Drive **Marble Hill** 63764

Phone: (573) 238-1174 www.bcmnh.org
Hours: Thursday-Saturday Noon-4:30pm.
Admission: $2.00 adult, $1.00 child (18 and under).
FREEBIES: Dino coloring pages & games found on website's KIDS PAGE.

Home of the Missouri dinosaur, this museum also showcases Civil War artifacts, American Indian exhibits, natural history specimens from around the world and regional historic exhibits. What grabs the kids is the story of how the bones were found by a farming family by accident. Dinosaur Dan was the first scientist to investigate. A new breed of dinosaur was named Parrosaurus missouriensis, and described as probably being a sauropod - a large plant eating dinosaur with a massive body, long tail, long neck and small

For updates & travel games visit: **www.KidsLoveTravel.com**

South East Area

head - such as Brontosaurus (Apatosaurus) or Diplodocus. To this day, the Chronister farm site continues to yield significant fossils of dinosaurs, turtles, amphibians and fish.

Besides the dino exhibit, there is also one on the Wreck of the Montana, the largest stern wheel steamboat that ever traveled the Missouri River. Fossil lovers will enjoy the Ozark Fossils exhibit and adventuresome kids will love the displays of real items Lewis & Clark took on the Voyage of Discovery.

DID YOU KNOW? That the birds in your back yard are related to dinosaurs and that Velociraptors were covered with feathers?

TAUM SAUK MOUNTAIN STATE PARK

(Highway 21 to Highway "CC") **Middlebrook** 63656

Phone: (573) 546-2450 **https://mostateparks.com/park/taum-sauk-mountain-state-park**

Admission: The Missouri state park system does not charge entrance fees. However, there are fees associated with camping, lodging, tours, museums and special events.

Want to hike to the top of a mountain? Just park in the lot of Taum Sauk Mountain State Park and walk a mere 1,000 feet on a paved path to Missouri's highest point. Here, an elevation marker sits, guiding visitors to the mountain's 1,772 foot summit. If that's not enough, the hike to Mina Sauk Falls will take your breath away. Nearby, a small camping area offers 12 basic campsites ($9 per night) and a picnic area which gives visitors a chance to enjoy a relaxing picnic under the trees.

JOHNSON'S SHUT-INS STATE PARK

148 Taum Sauk Trail (Highway 21 to Highway "N") **Middlebrook** 63658

Phone: (573) 546-2450 **https://mostateparks.com/park/johnsons-shut-ins-state-park**

Admission: The Missouri state park system does not charge entrance fees.

Years ago, violently explosive volcanoes hurled hot gasses and ash. The ashes and gas fell and cooled, forming rhyolite rock. Many years later, shallow inland seas swallowed the ancient, worn-down mountains, burying the igneous rock under thousands of feet of sedimentary rock such as limestone, sandstone, shale and dolomite. The result is a grand mixture of beautiful multi-colored pools, unique rock formations and even giant holes in the middle of huge rocks. Visitors can access the East Fork of the Black River at various locations throughout the park for swimming, wading or fishing. At the north picnic area, there is easy access to the river and a gravel bar.

The campground includes basic, electric, sewer/electric/water, equestrian and walk-in campsites plus camper cabins. The visitors center has kid-friendly interactive displays. A new boardwalk provides easy access to the shut-ins for viewing or swimming.

DID YOU KNOW? Why the park name, Shut-ins? The swift Black River runs around huge exposed boulders to create gorges, or "shut-ins".

NEW MADRID HISTORICAL MUSEUM

1 Main Street **New Madrid** 63869

Phone: (573) 748-5944
http://mo-newmadrid.civicplus.com/index.aspx?NID=133
Hours: Monday-Saturday 9:00am-5:00pm, Sunday Noon-5:00pm (April-November). Monday-Saturday 10:00am-4:00pm, Sunday 1:00-4:00pm (December-March). Schoolhouse only open summertime.
Admission: $1.00-$2.00 per person for each museum.
Note: Christmas Candlelight Tours (second weekend evenings in December)

Located on the Mississippi River in a former saloon at the foot of Main Street, the New Madrid Historical Museum reflects the history of this river town from the Mississippian period up through the early 20th century. You'll see some ancient Indian artifacts and a home set up in early 1900s. The real draw to this town is the tragic quakes of 1811 and 1812. The epicenter of New Madrid Seismic Zone is a web of earthquake faults that reach into five states. The 1811 quake is the strongest earthquake ever recorded in North America. Shocks occurred over eight weeks, crevasses swallowed buildings, enormous trees were uprooted and the Mississippi river even ran backward for a short time. The seismograph on the premises gives evidence of continuing activity along the New Madrid fault.

Just down the street is the **HIGGERSON ONE ROOM SCHOOLHOUSE**. This one-room schoolhouse displays rural American education practices. Experience the typical school day of youngsters attending all eight grades in one room with one teacher.

MISSOURI MINES STATE HISTORIC SITE

Hwy. 32 (south side of Hwy. 32 at Flat River Drive overpass, 1.5 miles west of US Hwy. 67) **Park Hills** 63601

Phone: (573) 431-6226 https://mostateparks.com/park/missouri-mines-state-historic-site
Admission: The Missouri state park system does not charge entrance fees. However, there are fees associated with camping, lodging, tours, museums and special events.
Tours: $3.00-$4.00 (age 6+) Hours: Monday-Saturday 10am-4pm, Sunday Noon-5pm.

For updates & travel games visit: www.KidsLoveTravel.com

Weekends only each winter.

You'll feel small next to the St. Joe shovel at Missouri State Mines Historic Site. Located in Federal Mill No. 3, the largest mill in the old Lead Belt, the museum presents Missouri's mining history and contains mining machinery, a film on lead mining and the milling process, and an expansive mineral collection. Step outside and you'll notice the ghost town quality of the site. Photographers will appreciate the opportunity to capture weathered mine buildings on a stark landscape.

ST. JOE STATE PARK

2800 Pimville Road **Park Hills** 63601

Phone: (573) 431-1069 **https://mostateparks.com/park/st-joe-state-park**
Admission: The Missouri state park system does not charge entrance fees. However, there are fees associated with camping, lodging, tours, museums and certain special events. Note: Be sure to call or visit website for complete list of rules that apply to all off-road vehicles and riders using this area.

St. Joe State Park offers more than 8,000 acres for recreational purposes including at least 2,000 acres designated as the state's premier off-road vehicle riding area. The heart of the "Old Lead Belt" now pulses with several modes of transport, from ATVs to hooves to hiking boots.

SAM A. BAKER STATE PARK

Hwy. 143 (4 miles north of Patterson) **Patterson** 63956

Phone: (573) 856-4411 **https://mostateparks.com/park/sam-baker-state-park**
Admission: The Missouri state park system does not charge entrance fees. However, there are fees associated with camping, lodging, tours, museums and certain special events.

Set in the unspoiled wilderness of the scenic St. Francois Mountains, this park has a nature center, campsites (including equestrian), trails, cabins, float trips, dining and a clear stream for splashing. Several miles of hiking, backpacking and equestrian trails provide glimpses of the area as the early settlers found it. To explore the natural and cultural history of the park, visit the park's visitor/nature center. Visitors can spend the night in either the rustic cabins or one of two large campgrounds. The shaded picnic area is equipped with a playground, covered shelters and picnic tables. If guests prefer to eat indoors, the dining lodge overlooking Big Creek features excellent country cooking.

BATTLE OF PILOT KNOB STATE HISTORIC SITE

(Hwy 221 to Pilot Knob/Ironton/Arcadia. Just before you reach Hwy 21)
Pilot Knob 63663

Phone: (573) 546-3454 https://mostateparks.com/park/battle-pilot-knob-state-historic-site
Admission: FREE tours are offered.
Hours: Tuesday-Sunday 10am-4pm. Open summer mondays.

In September 1864, an army of Confederate soldiers 12,000 strong marched into Missouri from Arkansas, led by Major General Sterling Price. Headed north toward St. Louis, this massive cavalry soon arrived at the southern terminus of the St. Louis and Iron Mountain Railroad in Pilot Knob. There, a federal fort, Fort Davidson, stood, garrisoned by only 1,500 Union soldiers led by Brigadier General Thomas Ewing Jr. Re enactments are held every 3 years.

The earthworks of the fort are mostly intact and visitors can explore this aspect of the battle as well as a portion of the original battlefield. Maps for this self-guided tour are available at the Visitor's Center and Museum that are also on the site. This free interpretive center provides detailed information about the battle, offering visitors an opportunity to see artifacts found just outside the museum's walls as well as from the war in general. It seeks to interpret the battle and Major General Price's raid with a diorama of the battle. Visitors also have a chance to view a 27 minute film or a 15 minute fiber optic show that demonstrates the troop movements during battle. Do you know who retreated? Who evacuated? On site picnic and playground area.

DUNLAP PUMPKIN FARM

Poplar Bluff - 1189 Township Line Road. Phone: (573) 686-4375. Shop the patch of pumpkins already gathered from the field, take a train ride, run through a bale maze, and see a variety of farm animals. (October)

SAYERSBROOK BISON RANCH

11820 Sayersbrook Road **Potosi** 63664

Phone: (573) 438-4449 or (888) 472-9377 www.sayersbrook.com
Tours: Open tours are conducted most Saturdays at 10:00am (April-November). It includes the video, Q&A, the herd tour and a visit to the country store. Reserved group tours cost $12.50 adult, $6.50 child and include a wagon tour and feeding of a bison herd.
Note: Looking for campsites nearby? COUNCIL BLUFF RECREATION AREA: Route 8. Camping, swimming, a beach, fishing and hiking ops. Also several federal recreation areas with scenic hiking trails are around town.

You can tour the ranch, view a video about bison and the history of the ranch, watch Skip feed the herd from the tour wagon, enjoy fishing, boating and hiking. The ranch's country store has souvenirs and more than 70 bison products.

DID YOU KNOW ? **HUGHES MOUNTAIN NATURAL AREA**: Cedar Creek Road in town is an amazing stop for anyone interested in geology: The Precambrian rock outcrops on the mountain are among the oldest exposed rocks in the United States. FREE. www.mdc.mo.gov.

FORT DE CHARTRES HISTORIC SITE

1350 State Route 155 (at Ste. Genevieve, take the toll ferry over the River. Follow signs north) **Prairie Du Rocher, IL** 62277

Phone: (618) 284-7230 **www.fortdechartres.us**
Hours: Wednesday-Sunday 9:00am-5:00pm.
Admission: FREE. Donations suggested $4 adult, $2 child, $10 family.

This great stone fort, formerly one of the strongest forts in North America, was built in 1753 as the seat of government for the French colony in America. Fort de Chartres' limestone gateway, guardhouse, and some of the outer walls have been rebuilt atop original stone foundations. The chapel, priest's room, commander's office and ammunition storage room (complete with cannon balls and weaponry) have been restored. The storehouse is home to the Piethman Museum, which uses discovered artifacts to interpret life in Illinois during the colonial period. What your kids like best? Climbing around the fort walls.

FORT DE CHARTRES TRAPPERS AND TRADERS RENDEZVOUS

Prairie Du Rocher, IL - Fort De Chartres. Hundreds of military and civilian re-enactors set up camp and present authentic cooking, crafts, dancing, and other activities from the French Colonial period. (first wkend in June)

MINGO NATIONAL WILDLIFE REFUGE

24279 State Highway 51 **Puxico** 63960

Hours: Monday-Saturday 8:30am-4pm. Closed winter Saturdays.
Phone: (573) 222-3589 **www.fws.gov/refuge/mingo**

The largest remaining tract of bottomland hardwood forest in southeast Missouri features the Mingo Swamp and adjacent hills, which are nestled in a basin of the Mississippi River. A Visitors Center has exhibits and access to trails.

- **DUCK CREEK WILDLIFE AREA** - Route 51. This area contains 2,400 acres of wetland in addition to forest and some cropland. Facilities include four boat ramps, boat rentals, boat dock, primitive camping, six fishing jetties and an 1,800 acre lake. FREE admission.

MINERAL MUSEUM

111 Fairgrounds Road (I-44 exit 184) **Rolla** 65402

Phone: (573) 341-4616 http://dnr.mo.gov/geology/edclarkmuseum.htm
Hours: Monday-Friday closed school holidays. 8:00am-5:00pm.
Admission: FREE.
Tours: The mine is open to the general public for guided tours by special arrangement with two weeks notice by calling (573) 341-6406 or contact the Department at (573) 341-4753.
Note: A half-scale replica of Stonehenge was created at Missouri University of Science and Technology using water-jet technology. (14th Street and Bishop Ave)

On Rolla's main campus, look for the world's largest university mineral collection (approximately 3,500 specimens) at McNutt Hall in the Minerals Museum www.mst.edu. Many of the minerals exhibited at the World's Fair in St. Louis from 1904 lie encased here including gold, diamonds and meteorites.

At the Experimental Mine, students, staff and faculty of Missouri University of Science and Technology work underground in a mine founded in 1921, one of the only working mines on a university campus in the world. Students also compete in international events for mine rescue and mucking teams.

BO'S HOLLOW

22516 Bo's Hollow Lane (2 miles south of Montauk State Park)
Salem 65560

Phone: (573) 548-2429 **www.bohollow.com**
Hours: Friday & Saturday 10:00am-4:00pm (April-May & September-October), Thursday, Friday & Saturday 10:00am-4:00pm (June-August) plus Memorial Day & Labor Day Weekends.
Admission: To visit Bo's Hollow you need a $5.00 Wooden Nickel. You can get your Wooden Nickel & trade your wooden token for a Model A Ride, BBQ Lunch or Jerky.

Travel the last mile to this place on a gravel road. It gets you in the mood to explore this 1930s style village with a fully functional service station, a feed and hardware store, a post office and a restoration barn. Sneak a peak inside the buildings and look around. Then, take a ride in a Model A and have a picnic lunch near Ashley Creek. Their BBQ meal is one of the $5.00 options. Jerky is another.

MONTAUK STATE PARK

RR 5, Box 279 (located at the headwaters of the Current River)
Salem 65560

Phone: (573) 548-2201 or (573) 548-2434 (Lodging)
https://mostateparks.com/park/montauk-state-park
Admission: The Missouri state park system does not charge entrance fees. However, there are fees associated with camping, lodging, tours, museums and certain special events.

Offering some of the finest trout fishing in the Midwest, Montauk State Park is located at the headwaters of the famed Current River. The park's springs combine with tiny Pigeon Creek to supply 43 million gallons of water to the river each day. The cool, clear stream is an ideal home for rainbow trout, and the scenic valley is the perfect setting for camping, hiking and other outdoor pursuits. When traveling by river on the upper Currently, you can see Cave Spring, where you can paddle inside the cave for approx.100 feet; Welch Spring and ruins of a 19th century hospital; and historic Akers Ferry, which takes visitors across the river. Other features include an old gristmill, camping, lodging, dining, trails and a store.

OZARK NATURAL & CULTURAL RESOURCE CENTER

202 South Main (Hwy 19) **Salem** 65560

Phone: (573) 729-0029 www.oncrc.org
Hours: Monday-Friday 9:00am-5:00pm.
Admission: Most exhibits FREE. Donations appreciated.
Note: Several Canoe and Campground companies dot the area. Their brochures and contact info are available on the center's website and by visiting the info center in person.

A complete center for information on the nature and culture of the area with local and touring exhibits featured. During your visit, you might find musicians playing or an artist creating. People in the Missouri Ozarks developed certain life skills as a way of survival which still blends in modern practices. Some still practiced in the original manner are blacksmithing, spinning, weaving, quilting, traditional soap making, pottery making, beekeeping, cooking sorghum molasses, and home canning. Many hand crafted and one-of-a-kind Ozark Gifts, as well as educational and entertaining books, audio CDs, and video DVDs are available for sale at the ONCRC.

LAMBERT'S CAFÉ: HOME OF THE THROWED ROLLS

Sikeston - *2305 E. Malone 63801. Phone: (573) 471-4261 www.throwedrolls.com.* Hours: Daily, 10:30am-9:00pm. Good food and tableside entertainment. During your meal, fresh-baked rolls are thrown to you and you can choose from "pass-around" side dishes that change daily and are FREE of charge when you purchase an entrée. Sample sides include onion fried potatoes, fried okra, macaroni & tomatoes, and black-eyed peas. These are brought around constantly and are free with any meal. But look out, you can get hooked on those fried potatoes. Large portions. No Credit Cards, but Checks are welcome. Lunch and dinner daily.

BEGGS FAMILY FARM - FALL HARVEST CELEBRATION

Sikeston *2319 State Highway U. www.beggsfamilyfarm.com/. Phone: (573) 471-3879* Activities include a corn maze, moonlight barnyard golf, pig races, a Express train, the Twister vortex, the maze with a real gemstone mining sluice, and a wooden play fort. There's also a rope maze, a corn cannon, wagon rides, bonfires, a milking cow, pick-your-own pumpkins, monster slide, straw jump and plenty of farm animals. Admission $10-$11. (October)

MARAMEC SPRING PARK

21880 Maramec Spring Drive (6 miles East of St. James) **St. James** 65559

Phone: (573) 265-7287 **www.maramecspringpark.com**
Hours: Dawn to Dusk. Call or visit website for exact seasonal times.
Admission: $5.00 per car.

Two museums, one featuring old tools used in agriculture and a second that explains the history of the Meramec Ironworks. Encompassing almost 2000 acres, the park includes a café, general store, camping, wildlife viewing, picnicking, shelters and trout fishing. Maramec Spring is Missouri's fifth-largest spring. Privately owned. The Missouri Department of Conservation raises thousands of trout in the fish rearing pools located near the head of the Spring. Small fish are hatched at other state hatcheries, transported to Maramec Spring and placed into the rearing pools. The fish are fed 3 times each day. Even if you aren't a fishermen you will enjoy tossing feed to the fish and watching them come to the surface. Fish feeders have been placed along the rearing pools for your convenience.

The **PICK AND SHOVEL CAFE** is located at the entrance to Maramec Spring Park. Breakfast and lunch are served Wednesday through Sunday during the Catch and Keep fishing season.

South East Area   155

JESSE JAMES WAX MUSEUM
2432 Route W (I-44 - Exit 230) **Stanton** 63079

Phone: (573) 927-5233 www.jessejameswaxmuseum.com
Hours: Daily 9:00am-6:00pm (June-August). Saturday & Sunday only 9:00am-5:00pm (April-May) & (September-October). Closed November-March.
Admission: $6.00 adult (12+), $2.50 (5-11).

The museum is based on the testimony of Rudy Turilli, who says that Jesse James was not shot by Robert Ford. In fact it was all a ruse, and Jesse lived to be 102. There is a video that you watch when you first enter the exhibit, with live video of Jesse James along with a WAX figure of the 102 year old. Besides the somewhat believable story, touring the museum you'll find amusement viewing the life-like wax figures set in dioramas depicting Jesse's home, the Civil War, robberies and more. It's an old style museum, nothing fancy, but the stories they unfold make it a fun tourist trap.

MERAMEC CAVERNS
Highway W (I-44 west, exit 230) **Stanton** 63079

Phone: (573) 468-CAVE (3166) www.americascave.com
Admission: (Cave Tour) $20.00 adult, $10.00 child (5-11). Additional fees for various other activities like campgrounds.
Tours: (Cave Tours - 1 hour) 9:00am-7:00pm+ (Summer). Closes at 4:00 or 5:00pm rest of year. Tours depart every 25 minutes throughout the day.

The oldest tourist attraction on the Mother Road is Meramec Caverns in Stanton. Opened in 1935 by Lester Dill, the "creator" of the bumper sticker, wanderers take a fascinating underground look at the region's history and geology. Fans of bank robber Jesse James can retrace his legendary steps though Missouri and hide out in the same cave he did over 130 years ago. In the early 1870s, Jesse James and his band returned to Meramec Cavern on numerous occasions because it afforded a complete hideout for men and horses after train and bank robberies. Guided tours by rangers along handicapped-accessible lighted passageways offer views of some of the rarest and largest cave formations in the world, including a limestone wine table and a seven-story mansion.

- CAVEMAN ZIP LINE ADVENTURE - Soar through the tree tops and across the Meramec River on a hour long adventure of a lifetime. Open May-October. Rates: $49.00 Adults, $39.00 Children. Try it, it's worth it.
-
-

- RIVERBOAT RIDES - Enjoy a relaxing, history filled, half hour long excursion on the Meramec River aboard a canopy-topped riverboat. Boats run April through September, dependant upon weather and river conditions. Additional $6.00-$9.00.

- CANOE FLOATS - Take a six or eleven mile float on the scenic Meramec River. A shuttle bus will take you up river and you can float back to your car, here at the caverns. Reservations are required, please call (573) 468-6463. Only available when weather permits. Rental fees apply.

- PAN FOR GOLD - While parents shop at the Mine Store for beautiful rock gifts or at Granny's Candy Store for home-made fudge, children can pan for fool's gold, fossils, and other gemstones in a 19th century setting. The Meramec Mining Company and Granny's is open during the summer months only. Additional fee for panning. ($7.00-$10.00).

ASL PEWTER FOUNDRY

183 South Third Street Ste. Genevieve 63670

Phone: (573) 754-3435 www.aslpewter.com
Gallery Hours: Daily 10:00am-5:00pm. Occasionally closed on Mondays.
Tours: just a look during gallery hours is fine but educational tours are pre-arranged by groups. Call ahead.
Educators: If you have a home school or other school related group, they can work with your history, business or arts curriculum. Just give them an outline of the information you want to have covered, as it relates to pewter, owning and operating a small business and/or Early America.

Pewter is one of the oldest known alloys, dating back to the Bronze Age. Since they make all of the pewter pieces in their studio in Louisiana, MO, the studio is always open. Visit them as they create a "new antique" or a piece destined to become a family heirloom. See how the crafters spin metal and cast in antique molds. Other works are turned - pushing a flat piece of pewter into shape over a wooden form using wooden tools. Afterwards the pewter pieces are assembled or altered, including soldering, cutting, pressing, polishing, and finishing - all done by hand. Learn about what pewter is made of (90% tin plus scarce amounts of silver, copper, bismuth, and antimony)

While in town, look for the 24 murals commemorating historical events from Louisiana and the United States. Visit this website beforehand (www.louisiana-mo.com) or pick up a map at the Chamber of Commerce just up the street from the pewter shop.

CENTRE FOR FRENCH COLONIAL LIFE &BOLDUC HOUSE MUSEUM COMPLEX

198 Market St (corner of Market & Second Sts) **Ste. Genevieve** 63670
Phone: (573) 883-3105 **www.frenchcoloniallife.org**
Hours: Friday-Saturday 10am-5pm, Sunday Noon-5pm.
Admission: $10.00 adult, $5.00 child for guided tours.

The Bolduc House is regarded as the first most authentically restored Creole house in the nation. Watch the sign outside the Linden House for the daily schedule of kids' activities including colonial games, a salt making relay race, crafts, and other activities that will connect you to what life in 18th century Ste. Genevieve was like. Touch and explore everything in the Hands-On History Room (located in the Bolduc-LeMeilleur House) at your own pace. There are felt boards, guessing games, matching games, a playable dollhouse, and learn to speak a few French words as you play colonial games like dominoes or continental checkers.

FELIX VALLE STATE HISTORIC SITE

198 Merchant Street **Ste. Genevieve** 63670
Phone: (573) 883-7102 **www.mostateparks.com/felixvalle.htm**
Hours: Monday-Saturday 10:00am-4:00pm, Sunday Noon-5:00pm (April-October).
Thursday-Saturday 10:00am-4:00pm, Sunday Noon-5:00pm (November-March).
Tours are available during these times.
Admission: $4.00-$6.00 for tours.

Built in 1818, it was the home of Felix & Odile Pratte Valle; they were from one of Ste. Genevieve's premier colonial families. Many elements of Ste. Genevieve's 18th century streetscape have been preserved in its historic district. Its narrow streets, historic buildings and fenced gardens offer a glimpse of a time when Missouri was part of a vast colonial empire in North America held by France and Spain. The site offers visitors a rare glimpse of Missouri's French colonial past. It has been restored to its original configuration and thus has two doors, one for the mercantile store of the historic trading firm of Menard and Valle. This side has been authentically restocked. The second door was for the family's living quarters.

Just across the street is the Dr. Benjamin Shaw House. The earliest portion of this white frame building was constructed in 1819 by Jean Baptiste Bossier as a storehouse for his mercantile business. Today, the house provides interpretive space for the site.

GREAT RIVER ROAD INTERPRETIVE CENTER

(corner of Market and Main Streets) **Ste. Genevieve** 63670

Phone: (573) 883-7097 **www.ste-genevieve.com/tourism.htm**
Hours: Most days 9:00am-4:00pm.

The Gallery is a permanent exhibit and displays a great number of original sketches of Ste. Genevieve. The main gallery has changing exhibits, many showing the movement of the Mississippi River over the last 500 hundred years. The Center has a walking tour video, gift shop, public rest rooms and brochures on the surrounding area. Good stop before you explore the area.

HAWN STATE PARK

12096 Park Drive (Hwy. 144) **Ste. Genevieve** 63670

Phone: (573) 883-3603 https://mostateparks.com/park/hawn-state-park
Admission: The Missouri state park system does not charge entrance fees. However, there are fees associated with camping, lodging, tours, museums and certain special events.

One of Missouri's most unspoiled landscapes, this park features Pickle Creek - one of the few places in the state where visitors can see such a wide variety of rock types exposed at the surface. It offers a campground, trails and picnic sites under the pine trees. Hawn State Park is the perfect setting for visitors eager to explore the unspoiled natural beauty of the Show-Me-State. Several trails are less than one mile in length and easy to navigate for families.

STE. GENEVIEVE MUSEUM

306 Merchant St. (DuBourg and Merchant Streets-Court House Square)
Ste. Genevieve 63670

Phone: (573) 883-3461 **www.sgmlc.org**
Hours: 9:00am-11:00am & Noon-4:00pm (April-October), Noon-4:00pm (November-March). Admission: $2.00 adult, $1.00 student

The museum contains many items of interest relating to the town's history such as artifacts from the salt works at Saline Spring (photo right,) the town's first industry, can be seen. Other items include weapons, prehistoric and historical Native American relics, old documents, and memorabilia of the mid-1800s. The scale model of the Mississippi River Railroad Transfer Boat is neat. Dinosaurs and vikings, too.

JOUR DE FETE

Ste. Genevieve - Downtown. ***www.greatriverroad.com/stegen/sgattract/ jourfetehome.htm***. Parades, folk dancing, live entertainment, and large craft fair. Actors dressed as early French settlers also reenact frontier life. (mid-August week)

MERAMEC STATE PARK

115 Meramec Park Drive **Sullivan** 63080

Phone: (573) 468-6072   https://mostateparks.com/park/meramec-state-park
Admission: The Missouri state park system does not charge entrance fees. However, there are fees associated with camping, lodging, tours, museums and certain special events.
Tours: 90-minute guided tours thru Fisher Cave with handheld lights are available April - mid-October. Most days @ 1:00pm & 3:00pm and in summer also at 9:30am & 11:30am. Cave Tour fee $10.00 (20+), $8.00 teen (13-17), $6.00 child (6-12).

Naturalist-led tours, offered on a seasonal basis, provide an interesting adventure at Fisher Cave, located within Meramec State Park. From low, narrow streamside passages to huge rooms filled with calcite deposits, Fisher Cave offers a vast array of intricate hellectites, massive columns, and cave wildlife. But what do the kids think is coolest? The well preserved bear claw markings on the walls. The Visitor Center includes a 3500 gallon aquarium and life size diorama. Other features are canoe rentals, lodging, trails and camping.

GRAND GULF STATE PARK

Route W (off Hwy. 19) **Thayer** 65791

Phone: (417) 264-7600   https://mostateparks.com/park/grand-gulf-state-park
Admission: The Missouri state park system does not charge entrance fees. However, there are fees associated with camping, lodging, tours, museums and certain special events.

Often called the Little Grand Canyon, Grand gulf was created when the ceiling of a giant cave collapsed. The "Grand Gulf" stretches for nearly a mile with walls almost 130 feet high, making the chasm deeper than it is wide. Boardwalks with overlooks allow visitors to descend partway into the chasm to view one of the largest natural bridges in Missouri. Also, a 118-step descent to the bottom of the gulf can be accessed from the parking lot. From a canyon to a cave to a natural bridge -- this state park has plenty to see and much to do. Picnic tables are scattered among the trees. Note, no guardrails are installed on trails to keep the pristine nature in place so grab hold of little hands if you're going out on hikes.

OZARK NATIONAL SCENIC RIVERWAYS HEADQUARTERS

404 Watercress Drive **Van Buren** 63965
Phone: (573) 323 4236 www.nps.gov/ozar
Educators: Teachers Guide www.nps.gov/ozar/forteachers/skin-deep.htm

Missouri's largest national park offers canoeing, hiking, fishing, camping and other activities along 134 miles of the Current and Jacks Fork rivers. Streams in area are classes I & II meaning they provide an easy float and are suitable for novices and families with kids. The website references several river and float trip companies, some with RV/campgrounds.

OZARK HERITAGE DAYS

Van Buren - Big Spring (Rte 103). Enjoy a peek into the Ozarks of yesteryear with traditional craftsmen demonstrating the essential skills of life in the Depression era Ozarks. There are woodworkers, fiber craftsmen, fiddle makers, period agricultural techniques, plus live music and storytelling. Friday is focused on children; Saturday is for everyone. FREE. (2nd wknd in June)

LEGIT SPEEDWAY

10603 Route 63 **West Plains** 65775
Phone: (417) 469-4749 www.legitspeedway.com

This 3/8 mile red clay, oval track features weekly racing and major national events. Super stock, hobby cars and trucks and cruiser class. $5.00-$12.00. More for special events. March-October.

WICKLIFFE MOUNDS

94 Green Street (take US 60/62 over the River and stay on US 51/62)
Wickliffe, KY 42087
Phone: (270) 335-3681 http://parks.ky.gov/parks/historicsites/wickliffe-mounds
Hours: Daily 9:00am-5:00pm (May-September). Closed Monday and Tuesday (March, April, October and November). Closed winter. Admission: $4.00-$5.00 (ages 6+).

This Research Center and Archeological Site is where they've excavated prehistoric (1100-1350 AD) Mississippian Mound culture villages. Unearthed for current viewing is a burial mound, home sites and a temple mound. The Ceremonial Mound is intact and can be accessed for a beautiful bird's eye view of the park. A Hands-On Activity Touch Table rounds out a museum tour where visitors can use prehistoric tools, and learn about Mississippian artifacts, technology and their environment.

For updates & travel games visit: www.KidsLoveTravel.com

LAKE WAPPAPELLO STATE PARK

Hwy. 172 (Hwy. 172 ends in the park) **Williamsville** 63967

Phone: (573) 297-3232 **https://mostateparks.com/park/lake-wappapello-state-park**

Admission: The Missouri state park system does not charge entrance fees. However, there are fees associated with camping, lodging, tours, museums and special events.

Nestled in the southeast region of Missouri, Lake Wappapello State Park offers a variety of recreation opportunities ranging from an exciting day on Lake Wappapello to a quiet stroll through the Ozark forest. Located on Wappapello Lake, the park's scenic coves are known for camping, fishing and picnicking spots. The park also offers cabins, camper cabins, boat ramps, a beach and hiking, backpacking, equestrian and mountain biking trails.

HERITAGE DAY AT TWIN PINES

Winona - Twin Pines Conservation Education Center. Look back at life the way it was in the 1900 Ozarks Hills as we celebrate the rich forest heritage and the pioneer spirit that made everyday life in the hills possible. See demonstrations of soap making, tie hacking, spinners, paddle makers, blacksmiths, forestry tools, and local forest products. Early logging and mill equipment on display. Fishing and archery for the kids. Shuttle service is available for overflow parking. FREE. ***www.mdc.mo.gov/areas/areas/twinpines/.*** (mid-April Saturday).

South West Area 163

Chapter 5
South West (SW)

QUICK LOOK...

Branson Amusements / Entertainment
Little Houses on Prairies
Civil War Battlegrounds
Ozark Mountain Nature
Wonders of Wildlife Parks

Ash Grove
- Nathan Boone Homestead State Historic Site

Branson
- Branson Amusements
- Branson Campgrounds
- Branson Theaters
- Adventure Helicopters
- Billy Gail's Café
- Branson Landing Cruises
- Branson Scenic Railway
- Dewey Short Visitors Center
- Dick's Oldtime 5 & 10
- Dixie Stampede
- Hollywood Wax Museum
- Imax Entertainment Complex
- Ride The Ducks
- Ripley's Believe It Or Not Museum
- Shepherd Of The Hills
- Shepherd Of The Hills Fish Hatchery And Conservation Center
- Showboat Branson Belle
- Sight & Sound Theatre
- Silver Dollar City
- Table Rock State Park
- Titanic
- Tribesman Resort
- White Water Water Park
- World's Largest Toy Museum
- Branson Fest
- Port Of Lights

Branson (Ridgedale)
- Big Cedar Lodge Resort

Branson (Walnut Shade)
- Branson Zipline & Canopy Tours

Branson West
- Talking Rocks Cavern

Carthage
- 66 Drive-In Movie Theatre
- Battle Of Carthage State Historic Site
- Civil War Museum
- Precious Moments Park

Cassville
- Mark Twain National Forest - Cassville District
- Roaring River State Park

Diamond
- George Washington Carver National Monument

Joplin
- Candy House Chocolate Factory
- Grand Falls
- Joplin Amusements
- Joplin Museum Complex
-

Joplin (Tipton Ford)
- Undercliff Grill

Lamar
- Harry S Truman Birthplace State Historic Site

Lampe
- Persimmon Hill Berry Farm

Liberal
- Prairie State Park

Mansfield
- Laura Ingalls Wilder Historic Home And Museum

Nevada
- Bushwhacker Hist'l Museum & Old Jail Historic Site

Noel
- Bluff Dwellers' Cavern & Browning Museum

Ozark
- Doennig Sport Swings & Ozark Paintball

For updates & travel games visit: www.KidsLoveTravel.com

South West Area

- Ozark Festival Of Lights

Pineville
- Jesse James Days

Point Lookout
- College Of The Ozarks

Rockbridge
- Rockbridge General Store And Restaurant

Springfield
- History Museum For Springfield & Greene County
- Air & Military Museum Of The Ozarks
- Dickerson Park Zoo
- Fantastic Caverns
- Springfield Conservation Nature Center
- Discovery Center
- Springfield Little Theatre
- Bass Pro Shops Outdoor World
- Incredible Pizza Company
- Springfield Hot Glass Studio
- Missouri Sports Hall Of Fame
- Gray / Campbell Farmstead Lifestyle Exposition
- Festival Of Lights

Springfield (Republic)
- Wilson's Creek National Battlefield

Stockton
- Stockton State Park
- Hammons Products Pantry & Visitors Center

Strafford
- Wild Animal Safari

Walker
- Osage Village State Historic Site

Sites and attractions are listed in order by City, Zip Code, and Name. Symbols indicated represent: 🍽 Restaurants   🛏 Lodging

NATHAN BOONE HOMESTEAD HISTORIC SITE

7850 N. State Hwy. V **Ash Grove** 65604

Phone: (417) 751-3266 https://mostateparks.com/park/nathan-boone-homestead-state-historic-site

Hours: *Wednesday-Saturday 10:00am-4:00pm, Sunday 1:00pm-4:00pm (April -October). Friday & Saturday 10:00am-4:00pm & Sunday 1:00pm-4:00pm. (November-March).*

Admission: *The Missouri state park system does not charge entrance fees. However, there are fees associated with camping, lodging, tours, museums and special events.*

Tours: *Guided tours are available during normal hours and last approximately one hour. $4.00 adult (18+), $2.75 youth (6-17).*

Early Missourians knew Nathan Boone as a hunter, soldier, surveyor and entrepreneur. They also knew him as his father's son. Boone, youngest child of the famous Daniel Boone, carried his family's legacy deep into the Missouri Ozarks and the American West. This log house, built in 1837, was the home of Col. Nathan Boone, the son of Daniel Boone and a military officer and early developer of Missouri. Other than time spent away on military service, he lived in the house until his death in 1856. A network of trails leads visitors through the Site's natural and cultural resources. In addition to the Boone home, visitors can explore the site's springs, woodlands, grasslands and glades. Visitors can also picnic.

BRANSON AMUSEMENTS

Branson

Admission: usually free to enter facility but each activity charges a fee.

- **BRANSON FAMILY FUN FACTORY** - 2400 Route 165. Laser tag (huge space) and glow in the dark mini-golf.
- **THE TRACK FAMILY FUN PARKS** - www.bransontracks.com. Four different locations on Route 76 for go-carting.
- **PIRATES COVE ADVENTURE GOLF** - www.piratescove.net/location/13.
- **BROOKSIDE MINI GOLF** - www.brooksideminiaturegolf.com
- **GREATEST ADVENTURES MINI GOLF** - minigolfinbranson.com

BRANSON CAMPGROUNDS
Branson

www.explorebranson.com/lodging/campgrounds-rv-parks

- <u>CITY OF BRANSON CAMPGROUND</u> - (on Lake Taneycomo). 100s of full hookups, fishing docks, boat ramps, and picnic shelters.
- Whether you're on a cross-country road trip or headed for the Ozarks, Branson and its surrounding area are the perfect place to park your tent or RV. Enjoy the waterfront beauty and water activities at Bull Shoals Lake and Table Rock Lake. Or stay in the quiet woodlands of nearby state parks. With 50-amp service and campfire rings, along with the proximity of so many great shows and attractions, it's little wonder Branson is one of America's favorite camping destinations. Many of the campgrounds provide amenities likes internet access, laundry facilities, restrooms and showers to make your stay enjoyable.

BRANSON THEATERS
Most are located on Route 76 **Branson**

www.explorebranson.com/shows

Note: most every showplace listed is known for their magical Christmastime shows.

Now, after more than 50 years, the cast of entertainers includes singers, musicians and comedians. Most of the music ranges from Country to Old Rock tunes - some oldies ballads from the masters, too. Branson, known as the Las Vegas of the Midwest, offers visitors more than 50 live-performance theaters. Many shows start around $30.00 for adults and half-price for kids. Various online and tourism sites offer discounts on admission and you save bringing a group. To assure seats, make reservations. Most theaters are open spring thru Christmas but many take off winters. Some of the most popular:

- <u>PRESLEYS' COUNTRY JUBILEE</u> - www.presleys.com.
- <u>BALDKNOBBERS HILLBILLY JAMBOREE</u> - www.baldknobbers.com.
- <u>INCREDIBLE ACROBATS OF CHINA</u> - www.acrobatsofchina.com. Very different from the rest, this show has more than 40 acrobats showcasing classic Chinese dance and physical performance art. Circus meets modern dance.

BRANSON THEATERS (cont.)

- **JIM STAFFORD SHOW** - www.jimstafford.com. Comedy.
- **AMERICANA THEATRE** featuring The Haygoods - www.hotbransonshows.com/haygoods.html
- **BRETT FAMILY SHOW** - www.brettsshow.com
- **BUCK TRENT MORNING SHOW** - www.bucktrent.com. Country.
- **CIRCLE B CHUCKWAGON & COWBOY MUSIC SHOW** - www.circlebshow.com - Chuckwagon dinner and cowboy show.
- **CLAY COOPER'S COUNTRY MUSIC EXPRESS** - www.claycooper.com - country.
- **DOUG GABRIEL SHOW** - www.douggabriel.com - morning show.
- **LEGENDS IN CONCERT** - www.bransonshowtickets.com. Elvis, Hank Williams, Mark Twain and many more.
- **GRAND OLD GOSPEL HOUR** - www.gospelhour.org - gospel, Sunday morning show.
- **HUGHES BROTHERS SHOW** - www.hughes-brothers.com.
- **NUMBER 1 HITS OF THE 60s SHOW** - www.1hitsofthe60s.com
- **PIERCE ARROW THEATER** - www.piercearrowtheater.com. Family rock-the-house gospel.
- **SIX** - www.thesixshow.com. Just six human voices with powerhouse vocals.
- **YAKOV THEATRE** - www.yakov.com - each season features different performing artist - ex. Dino (piano-Christmas), Neal McCoy (country); Yakov comedy in person and a Moscow Circus.

ADVENTURE HELICOPTER TOURS

3309 W Hwy 76 **Branson** 65615

Phone: (417) 334-6102 www.adventurehelicoptertours.com/bransontours.php
Hours: Call or visit website for current flight availability. Tours vary in length from a 5-7 minute "Sneak Peak" to a 25 minute "Branson" tour.
Admission: $29.00-$119.00/person.

The tours take passengers over Branson Landing, Hwy 76, Table Rock Dam, Lake Taneycomo, Inspiration Tower and Silver Dollar City...1000 feet above! The staff have years of experience and are comfortable, yet professional in guiding you through any concerns or anxiety.

For updates & travel games visit: **www.KidsLoveTravel.com**

South West Area

BILLY GAIL'S CAFÉ

Branson - 5291 State Highway 265 65616. Phone: (417) 338-8883. While Billy Gail's is said to serve up a mean burger, the restaurant was, in 2009, honored by a regional magazine for having the best breakfast in the entire (417) area code. The pancakes there are literally fall-off-the-plate huge. Breakfast & lunch 7am-2pm. www.facebook.com/BillyGailsCafe

BRANSON LANDING CRUISES

Branson Landing (Near Branson Landing Blvd and E Main Street) **Branson** 65616

Phone: (212) 209-3270   www.bransonlandingcruises.com
Hours: (Sightseeing) departs at 9:45am and/or 1:45pm on select dates. Other tour options available. Call or visit website for current schedule.
Admission: (Sightseeing) 33.75 adult (12+), $7.00 child (4-12).
Tours: Sightseeing tours last approximately 90 minutes with narration and lunch.

The Lake Queen is a modern paddle wheel vessel offering sightseeing, lunch and dinner cruises. Sightseeing Cruises - Enjoy daily 1.5 hour sightseeing cruises on Lake Taneycomo on the Lake Queen Paddleboat on select dates. Hear about Baldknobber's, Branson's first roller skating rink, and the Hillbilly Jamboree. Cruise past the Branson Landing waterfront and see the $7.5 million spectacular water attraction of merging water, fire and music! Pass beneath majestic Mt. Branson as you wind your way back north. View the immense diversity of Branson's wildlife, from the American Bald Eagle, Night Heron and Brown Thrasher to foxes, coyote, mink and flying squirrels.

BRANSON SCENIC RAILWAY

206 E. Main Street **Branson** 65616

Phone: (800) 2-TRAIN-2 or (417) 334-6410   www.bransontrain.com
Hours: Trains run at 9:00am, 11:30am, 2:00pm, 4:30pm (June-July). Similar schedules rest of year (minus the 4:30 train - Closed January & February). Call or visit website for current schedule.
Admission: $28.25 adult (13+), $17.75 child (3-12).

Take in the sights of the beautiful Ozark foothills on this 40-mile round trip excursion. The tour takes you through tunnels and across bridges, all while giving passengers a history lesson on the Branson area.

POLAR EXPRESS

Branson - Branson Scenic Railway. Children...hop aboard The Polar Express, an experience based on the children's book (and animated motion picture). This journey begins as the train departs from the 1906 original train depot located in Downtown Branson. Once aboard, the porter punches the passengers' tickets, and chefs hand out cups of hot chocolate, as children—dressed in their pajamas—settle down for a nighttime train adventure. The story is read aloud during the train ride, and children can relive the adventure of "The Polar Express" while the train transports them to the North Pole. Admission. (December weekends)

DEWEY SHORT VISITORS CENTER

(on State Hwy 165 at the south end of Table Rock Dam) **Branson** 65616

Phone: (417) 334-4101 (Main Office) **www.swl.usace.army.mil/Missions/Recreation/Lakes/Table-Rock-Lake/Recreation-Activities/**
Hours: Daily 9:00am-5:00pm (March-late November).
Admission: FREE.
Note: There is a courtesy dock on the Visitor Center grounds, if you'd like to visit by way of boat.

The center features exhibits detailing the natural history of the area. Exhibits show four seasons of Ozarks looped nature trail and educational tour of the powerhouse to see how the dam generates electricity. There are also three short films you can watch:

- *Taming of the Riviera Blanche* (20 minutes): an introduction to the Table Rock Lake/White River area, detailing the construction and purpose of Table Rock Dam. It also shows what the area was like back in the day.
- *Where Eagles Soar* (14 minutes): the story of how eagles were brought back from endangerment in Missouri.
- *The Expedition of Lewis and Clark, 1804-1806* (32 minutes): tells of their exploration, encounters, objectives and accomplishments.

Bring a picnic lunch, a swimsuit or a fishing pole for a leisurely afternoon on the shoreline of Table Rock Lake. The Table Rock Lakeshore Trail is adjacent to the Visitors Center, too. This is probably one of the only FREE things you can do in the area.

DICK'S OLDTIME 5 & 10

103 Main Street **Branson** 65616

Phone: (417) 334-2410 **www.dicksoldtime5and10.com**
Hours: Monday-Saturday 8:30am-9:00pm, Sunday 9:00am-9:00pm.
Admission: FREE.

Features more than 50,000 items you may view or purchase; many hard-to-find items. Displays include a collection of World War II photos, White River Arrow Head collection, baseball hall of fame. Fun stop to browse and buy a unique item or two.

DOLLY PARTON'S STAMPEDE

1525 West Highway 76 **Branson** 65616

Phone: (417) 337-9400   www.dptampede.com/branson
Hours: (Showtimes) 5:30pm and 8:00pm.
Admission: ~$50 adult (12+), ~$30 child (4-11). Children 3 years old and younger are free only if they sit in a parent's lap and eat from their plate. If you wish for your child to receive a seat or a meal, a regular children's admission will apply.
Note: Meet the horses in the show before the shows. Farm animal allergies? Be prepared with antihistamines taken before entering the show arena.

The very action-packed dinner and show features dozens of magnificent horses, beautiful costumes, gallant heroes, incredible horsemanship, and a stand-to-your-feet patriotic finale. All this excitement while enjoying a fabulous four-course feast that you have to eat with your hands! You may be asked (kids and parents) to participate in several races - don't worry, everyone laughs with you and cheers you on. You'll love the dancing horses and several other unusual animal races.

FRITZ'S ADVENTURE

1425 W. Hwy. 76 **Branson** 65616

Phone: (417) 320-6138   www.fritzsadventure.com
Hours: Monday-Saturday 10am-8pm, Sunday Noon-8pm (summer). Similar schedules rest of year. Call or visit website for current schedule.
Admission: $29.95 adult (13+), $21.95 child (4-11).

Fritz's indoor adventure space boasts more than 80,000 square feet of hands-on thrills, including climbing, tunneling, sliding, ziplining and more.

The newest addition to its facility, Fritz's vertical, outdoor wind tunnel flight experience allows visitors to enjoy the thrill and challenge of skydiving in a safe, controlled environment. Fritz's Aerodium Outdoor Flying Adventure opens as a seasonal offering, with advance reservations booked spring-fall.

Fritz's Adventure offers two- and three-flight packages, each with a 40-minute flight experience which includes a stunt demonstration, flight school, safety equipment and a formal flight lesson, and actual flight time. The vertical, open-air wind tunnel generates winds upwards of 140 miles per hour, allowing guests to fly under instructor supervision. The attraction is open to visitors ages four and up, with no previous experience required.

HOLLYWOOD WAX MUSEUM

3030 W. Hwy. 76 **Branson** 65616

Phone: (417) 337-8277 www.hollywoodwaxmuseum.com/branson/
Hours: Daily, 8:00am-Midnight (Summer). Closes earlier other times of the year. Visit website for current hours and online discounts.
Admission: $22.99 adult (12+), $12.99 child (4-11).

Inject your family vacation with a much needed dose of celebrity when you rub elbows with all of your favorite stars, from today and yesteryear. Recent stars like Gwyneth Paltrow, Johnny Depp, Jamie Foxx, and Jennifer Garner stand side by side with classic entertainers like Elvis Presley, Marilyn Monroe, Michael Jackson, and John Wayne. You'll rub elbows with the stars—caught in the act of performing the most famous scenes in entertainment history. Skip down the Yellow Brick Road, sail aboard the Titanic, encounter Frankenstein and Freddy, and lots more. Before you leave be sure to take your photo with the gargantuan 40-foot King Kong.

IMAX ENTERTAINMENT COMPLEX

3562 Shepherd of the Hills Expressway **Branson** 65616

Phone: (800) 419-4832 www.bransonimax.com
Hours: Open year-round.
Admission: Varies greatly by show selected. Many choices/themes are available. Call or visit website for current showtimes and admission fees.

What's Showing at the Branson IMAX? Come see a Branson exclusive and take a powerful journey through the rich history and heritage of the region with the GIANT-screen IMAX® adventure, "Ozarks Legacy & Legend." Or choose from other "New" IMAX® films for a special treat during your vacation!

RIDE THE DUCKS

2320 W Hwy 76 **Branson** 65616

Phone: (417) 266-7600 (office)   www.bransonducks.com
Hours: Ride The Ducks operates seven days a week during daylight hours.
Admission: $26.50 adult (12+), $25.50 senior (62+) and $14.50 child (ages 4-11). Be sure to check website for special deals and discount pkgs.
Tours: The Classic Table Rock Lake Adventure departs the duck dock on the Strip at 2320 West Highway 76 from early March - mid-December. The Lake Taneycomo Adventure departs the Branson Landing from Memorial Day-Labor Day and on select spring and fall weekends.

Splashdown to fun as you see the Ozarks on amphibious military vehicles that tour land and water. Your trusty mount for this adventure is a duck boat that travels on land and then right into the lake where you can take the reins and drive if you want. Hear tall tales, grab your shades, listen to groovy music, and discover seasonally themed looks at classic attractions. Duck tours have become our family's favorite way to first tour town and discover all there is to see. Plus, the captain sneaks in history trivia in such an amusing way, kids don't realize they're learning.

RIPLEY'S BELIEVE IT OR NOT MUSEUM

3326 West Hwy 76 **Branson** 65616

Phone: (417) 337-5300 **www.ripleysbranson.com**
Hours: Sunday-Thursday, 9:30am-8:00pm. Friday & Saturday 9:30am-9:00pm.
Admission: $19.99 adult, $12.99 child (3-11). Discounts and package deals online.
Note: If you are taking in young ones, have one adult go ahead and "scope out" the next hallway or room. Some rooms are creepy and might frighten sensitive children.

From the outside, the building looks like an earthquake split it in half. If you want to see the strange, unique, and unusual...this is the place to go. There is some interesting and useful information in there, hidden among all the 2 headed goats and drums made of human skin. There are so many unusual things here to see: brain teasers, artifacts made out of unusual things, small buildings made out of toothpicks and match sticks, a slanted room that makes you feel like you are on ship, a giant ball of string... They even have the Chitty-Chitty Bang-Bang car. We do love the mirror and there are some Branson-themed displays in this one that the others don't have.

SHEPHERD OF THE HILLS

5586 West 76 Country Boulevard (Old Mill Theatre) **Branson** 65616

Phone: (417) 334-4191 **https://theshepherdofthehills.com**
Hours: (May-October). Drama Summer Tuesday, Thursday and Saturday evenings.
Admission: Drama, $39.75 adult, $18.00 child (4-16). Combo discounts available.

An adventure park where the story of the early Ozark people is kept alive:

- INSPIRATION TOWER: You can see places the author stayed while writing the book and ride up 225 foot inspiration tower to get panoramic view of ozarks. Additional fee.
- OLD MATT'S HOMESTEAD: Trail rides (Off road ATVs). Vigilante Extreme ZipRider - riding down from the top of the observation tower across the park at speeds of more than 50 miles per hour. Highest launch point in the world. Additional fee.
- OUTDOOR DRAMA: Sit under the stars in the rustic outdoor theatre with action-packed reenactment of the famous novel, The Shepherd of the Hills, full of love and tragedy.

SHEPHERD OF THE HILLS FISH HATCHERY AND CONSERVATION CENTER

483 Hatchery Road (on Highway 165 just south of Branson, below the dam at Table Rock Lake) **Branson** 65616

Phone: (417) 334-4865   http://mdc.mo.gov/areas/hatchery/shepherd/
Hours: Daily 9:00am-5:00pm (Memorial Day-Labor Day) Tuesday-Saturday (Sept-June)
Tours: Guided tours, weekday summers at 10:00am, 11:00am & 1:00pm & 2:00pm, and introductory film provide good overview of area. During the remainder of the year, self-guided tours are available. FREE.

This site features guided and self-guided tours showing how the site raises rainbow and brown trout for release in the Missouri lakes. Trails begin at hatchery lead thru from the shoreline of the lake to high rocky bluffs overlooking the white river valley. Inside the center, several aquariums showcase Ozark fish. Did you know fish are raised in raceways? Twelve, outdoor concrete raceways are used for intermediate rearing, and final rearing is completed in twenty outdoor concrete raceways. The area has a boat ramp and several trout fishing access points along Lake Taneycomo, year-round.

SHOWBOAT BRANSON BELLE

4800 St Highway 165   **Branson** 65616

Phone: (800) 475-9370   www.showboatbransonbelle.com
Hours: All cruises run approximately two hours and 15 minutes, and begin at noon or 4:00pm and/or 8:00pm. (March-December). Visit website for current operating schedule.
Admission: Cruises start at $55.00 adult (12+), $28.00 child (4-11) and include a meal. Optional seating and menu choices available at additional cost. Visit website for combo pkgs & discounts.

Take your family on a fantastic lake cruise aboard the magnificent Showboat Branson Belle in Branson, Missouri! Journey past lush Ozark Mountains on the crystal clear waters of Table Rock Lake during your 2-hour lake cruise where you'll experience fabulous Branson dining and the best in Branson shows. Your lake cruise and Branson dinner show features Showstoppers, an exciting production starring a tremendously talented cast showcasing over 30 award-winning numbers.

SIGHT & SOUND THEATRE

1001 Shepherd of the Hills   **Branson** 65616

Phone: (417) 335-7900   www.sight-sound.com
Hours: (Showtimes), generally at 3:30pm & 7:30pm. Performances will vary depending

For updates & travel games visit: **www.KidsLoveTravel.com**

South West Area

on season. Call or visit website for current schedule.
Admission: (Show) $43.00 adult, $25.00 teen, $10.00 child. (Behind the Scenes Tour) $10.00/person.
Note: the Miracle of Christmas production captures the reason for the season.

Sight and Sound Theaters offer original musical productions that bring biblical stories to life onstage. Shows focus on familiar bible characters like Noah, Ruth or Daniel. Through inspirational productions, they seek to encourage others to be dedicated stewards of our God-given talents and resources. Amazing side stage and live isle-way entrances/exits bring Bible stories fantastically to life! Most major story scenes are mouth-droppers. Don't be afraid of the price, it's worth it. Seasonal shows each Christmas and Eastertime.

SILVER DOLLAR CITY

399 Silver Dollar City Parkway **Branson** 65616

Phone: (Tickets) (800) 475-9367 www.silverdollarcity.com/theme-park
Hours: Vary by season but most days in June and July is 9:30am-7:00pm. Opens earlier and closes later depending on date. (April-December).
Admission: $65.00 adult (12-61), $63.00 senior (62+), $54.00 child (4-11). Military and combo discounts online.

Branson's Number 1 Attraction for 50 years. Meet 100 demonstrating craftsmen, browse 60 unique shops, see 40 live shows daily, thrill to 30 rides and attractions, enjoy a dozen restaurants and six festivals. Smell the fresh-baked bread at Sullivan's Mill, try some Honey Heaven honey, grab an ice cream cone and then ride Fire in the Hole. Tom and Huck's RiverBlast - America's biggest water battle - is the newest feature ride. You look like a bunch of Huck Finn's *"fightin er out on these supped-up bumper boats"*.

Hop on the FRISCO SILVER DOLLAR LINE STEAM TRAIN in the park and enjoy a beautiful 20-minute steam train ride through Ozark country. Watch out for the zany train robbers who briefly interrupt your ride.

Located under Silver Dollar City theme park, MARVEL CAVE is one of the deepest caves in the state with tours included in park admission. To begin, you will travel 300 feet below the surface and enter the Cathedral Room. The breathtakingly beautiful Cathedral Room is the largest cave entrance room in the United States. While the stairs and walkways are strenuous at times, those who venture the 500 feet below the surface can rest on a unique cable train ride out of the cavern.

DID YOU KNOW ? The theme park was literally built around the entrance to Marvel Cave, upon the foundations of a genuine 1800s mining town - Marmaros.

WORLDFEST

Branson - Silver Dollar City. One of America's largest international festivals, bringing the world's intriguing cultures to the Ozarks. See incredible performances by Chinese Acrobats; The World's Only Flying Fiddler; Trinidad's Folk Performers; plus performers from Ecuador, Russia, Argentina and Mexico. Sample exciting cuisine from around the globe. Admission to Silver Dollar City is required. (early April thru early May)

NATIONAL HARVEST & COWBOY FESTIVAL

Branson - Silver Dollar City, the Home of American Craftsmanship, welcomes hundreds of visiting craftsmen to demonstrate and display their unique talents. The festival includes the Crafts in America Exhibit, displaying 50 of the nation's most stunning works of art; the Caricature Carvers of America Showcase; and a reunion of some of Silver Dollar City's legendary veteran craftsmen. Plus, don't miss America's Biggest Barn Dance. Admission to Silver Dollar City required. (mid-Sept thru Oct)

AN OLD TIME CHRISTMAS

Branson - Silver Dollar City. Celebrate the magic and meaning of the holidays. More than four million lights, a holiday light parade, a five-story special effects Christmas tree, fun family shows, including A Dickens' Christmas Carol, and festive food await in this dazzling winter wonderland. Admission to Silver Dollar City is required. (early November thru end of December)

WHITE WATER WATER PARK

3505 West 76 Country Blvd **Branson** 65616

Phone: (800) 475-9370 (tickets) www.silverdollarcity.com/white-water.aspx
Hours: Daily 10:00am-6:00pm+ (Memorial Day Weekend - Labor Day Weekend). Open 1+ hours longer in summer. Call or visit website for current schedule.
Admission: $44.00 adult (12-61), $32.00 senior (62+), $20.00 child (4-11). Cabana rental extra.

White Water is Branson's only outdoor water park and offers water-blasters, super-soakers, speed water slides, and a wave pool. Plus, Kalani Towers - the 6-lane Freefall and Racing thrill slide! Choose between two 75-foot freefall drop lanes or four mat racing lanes over 310-feet long. They have a few tube slides, a kid area for ages 6-12(Raintree Island w/ dumping bucket and chutes and ladders), and an area that is mostly sprinklers for the younger kids, plus a wave pool. Folks rave about the food - good, fresh choices at modest prices. The Kalani Towers slides probably give the most thrills. Lots of rides, and the park is relatively small, so you can walk from one end of the park to the other. White Water is clean and well staffed, plenty of lifeguards everywhere.

For updates & travel games visit: **www.KidsLoveTravel.com**

South West Area

TABLE ROCK STATE PARK
5272 State Hwy. 165 **Branson** 65616

Phone: (417) 334-4704 https://mostateparks.com/park/table-rock-state-park
Admission: *The Missouri state park system does not charge entrance fees. However, there are fees associated with camping, lodging, tours, museums and special events.*

Located adjacent to Table Rock Lake and near Branson, Table Rock State Park offers easy lake access and is a short drive to area attractions. This park is ideal for outdoor sports as it features a marina, parasailing equipment, a boat ramp, picnic sites, campgrounds, hiking and mountain biking trails and a paved walking and bicycle trail. The Lake is know for great fishing. Here's other amenities:

- **STATE PARK MARINA** - www.boatbranson.com. Rent water vehicles, including jet skis, pontoon boats, ski boats, canoes, paddleboats, and fishing boats. They also have para-sailing rides offered.
- **SPIRIT OF AMERICA** - www.sailbranson.com. 90 minute excursions on 49 passenger catamaran tours.
- **THE BOATHOUSE BBQ AND BURGERS CAFE** - summers.

TITANIC
3235 West 76 Country Boulevard **Branson** 65616

Phone: (417) 334-9500 www.titanicbranson.com
Hours: *Daily 10:00am-7:00pm. Open later in1summer and peak seasons.*
Admission: *$26 adult (12+), $13 child (5-11). $89 Family Pass.*
Note: *Parents and preteens interested in the storyline should purchase the audio tour, it offers more information and back story and you can hear firsthand accounts from survivors. Educators: Teachers Guide page is available here: www.titanicbranson.com/titanic_guide_home.php. Great ideas on the dynamics of wealth and the working class z+ studies about the science of the boat and the waters it sailed in.*

Towering 100 feet above street level, this ship-shaped venue holds more than 400 artifacts and historic treasures. It allows each visitor to encounter the personal, heroic and tragic stories of Titanic's passengers. Each guest is assigned a passenger or crew member to follow. The museum does a wonderful job to re-create many parts of the ship including the magnificent grand staircase and the dining room. See where each class slept for the night or try to stay afoot as the museum floor slopes down like the sinking ship. You also have the opportunity to see what 28 degrees feels like (temperature of frozen water surrounding the ship). Younger kids may be a little scared when they get to the part of the ship sinking (noises). There are staff peppered throughout in period costume who are kind and helpful. This themed exhibit is very well done and well worth admission. Btw, did your passenger survive?

TRIBESMAN RESORT
416 Cave Lane **Branson** 65616

Phone: (417) 338-2616 or (800) 447-3327 www.tribesmanresort.com

The Tribesman is located on a peninsula called Indian Point. The Tribesman Resort has seven unique sections. This resort, whether staying at the fully-equipped condos, apartments or cabins is family oriented and may remind you of an upscale summer camp. Activities include: indoor and outdoor pools, fireplaces, boat rentals, golf cart rentals, fishing dock, shuffleboard, paddle boats, scavenger hunts, and themed parties like Captain Kids Day. It isn't a luxury resort and it's a bit dated (like most other resorts in Branson) but it is very clean and well kept with everything needed for a family to have a comfortable stay at a fair price. Oh, and you'll love the close proximity of a Super Walmart (10 miles - for meal supplies) and Silver Dollar City (3 miles away). Rates range $60.00 (quiet season) to about $150 average during peak season. _____

WORLD'S LARGEST TOY MUSEUM
3609 W 76 Country Blvd **Branson** 65616

Phone: (417)-332-1499 www.worldslargesttoymuseum.com
Hours: Monday-Saturday 9:00am-8:00pm.
Admission: $16.95 adult, $12.95 child. Children 6 and under are FREE. Family Pass $49.95.

It's like Christmas morning every day here as parents and grandparents rediscover the joy of their favorite toys and reminisce about childhood heroes. You'll find toys as old as the 1800s and as new as Star Wars, tiny objects and big boy toys (like a full-size Rolls Royce). Girls may gravitate to the dollhouses and boys to the toy cars and trucks. Barbies, action figures, antique toy train sets and cap pistols, too.

On the premises: HAROLD BELL WRIGHT MUSEUM - Original hand-written manuscript of the book "The Shepherd of the Hills." Discover how tourism began in the Ozarks. Closed Sundays.

BRANSON FEST

Branson - www.explorebranson.com. 5 day sampler of everything Branson offers. Indoor and outdoor events, a parade, celebrity autograph sessions, food booths. (late March or early April)

South West Area

PORT OF LIGHTS

Branson - Off Highway 13 on a peninsula that juts into the Lake. Thousands of glittering Christmas displays light up the night on a Table Rock Lake peninsula, offering a 3 mile stretch of holiday displays. Two drive-through displays are Snowflake Tunner and Hollywreath Tunnel, while the Candy Cane forest will lead visitors past doll houses, glittering buggies, and trucks. *www.tablerocklake.org/port_of_lights*. Admission. (early Nov thru Dec evenings).

BIG CEDAR LODGE RESORT

612 Devil's Pool Road (10 miles south of Branson on Table Rock Lake)
Branson (Ridgedale) 65739
Phone: (800) 225-6343 **www.bigcedar.com**   Online pricing starts ~$200/night.

Have kids and want to get away for a few days to a private cabin on the lake? This resort meets your fix. It is a very large resort set on the side of a steep hill overlooking Table Rock Lake. The theme is a wooded cedar lodge and fishing resort...probably because it is owned by the same people who own Bass Pro Shops. Do not be afraid of the size of the resort as they have free shuttles on hand that will take you anywhere you want to go (within the resort). Most activities are included in the room rates, canoes, paddleboats, mini golf, shuffleboard, volleyball, 4 swimming pools, several hot tubs, even the paddle boats down at the Marina. Boat and watersport rentals are a little pricey so you might want to consider bringing your own. Horseback riding is available for a fee. It is fun in the warm months because of the pools, hot tubs and lazy river. But it is also fun in the cold months to enjoy the indoor pool and have a fire with movies in the cabin at night. They have plenty of walking trails, too. A small grocery store is about 10 miles away to purchase food to prepare in your cabin. If staying in the lodge rooms, all of their restaurants have fair pricing and good food...especially the breakfast buffet. During the day, it's a 20 minute ride into the strip of Branson. The kids favorite part - a visit from the cookie lady each evening.

BRANSON ZIPLINE AT WOLFE MTN

Hwy 65, seven miles north of downtown **Branson (Walnut Shade) 65771**
Phone: (417) 561-2500 https://wolfemountainbranson.com/
Admission: Ozarks Xplorer (2.5 hour tour)-$89.00-$99.99. Flying Prospector(1.5 hour tour)-$59-79. Avalanche (zip + snow tubing hill) ~$94.
Tours: Schedule changes with the seasons and weekdays vs. weekends. Usually at least two of each type of tour per day.

Using a system that originated in the jungles of Costa Rica, the Branson Zipline and Canopy Tour allows guests to soar in the Ozark Mountains. After learning the simple in's and out's of operating a zip line, you and your party will be escorted to the top of our Wolfe Creek Preserve by way of tram. As visitors "zip" from observation platform to platform, through and over the trees, certified guides accompany participants pointing out unique topographical and historical features of the Ozarks.

Experience the Ozarks Xplorer Canopy Tour® a two and a half hour, interactive tour which features a variety of zip lines, walkways and platforms; or other packages that include shorter tours or a seasonal snow tube park.

The kids take to it well and even middle-aged moms (like me) found it easily manageable and so memorable. Soft adventure, good for anyone who likes mild amusement rides and doesn't have a fear of heights.

TALKING ROCKS CAVERN

423 Fairy Cave Lane **Branson West** 65737

Phone: (417) 272-3366 or (800) 600-CAVE www.talkingrockscavern.com
Hours: Daily, 9:30am-5:00pm. Tours depart frequently.
Admission: $18.95 (13+), $9.95 (4-12). Online coupon. Mini golf extra.

Talking Rocks Cavern near Branson offers guided 50-minute tours of thousands of living crystal cave formations of many different kinds, colors and textures. Perhaps you'll see a glimpse of one of the cave's occupants, the Ozark blind salamander. The main chamber of the cavern is more than 100 feet tall and 600 feet long, and stalactites and stalagmites along the way are a testament to years of water trickling down to shape the brilliant formations. Above ground, you can walk on the nature trail or climb up to the top of the 40-foot Treetop Tower. A crawl through their SpeleoBox maze is always a favorite. Students enter one side and crawl along 150 feet of winding, twisting passage to pop out the other side. This activity is used by "cavers" to practice safe caving techniques in this fun, simulated cave passage. These extra activities are included in admission ticket pricing.

South West Area 181

66 DRIVE-IN MOVIE THEATRE
17231 Old 66 Blvd **Carthage** 64836

Phone: (417) 359-5959 http://66drivein.com/
Hours: Open April - mid-September. Friday-Sunday nights mostly.
Admission: $8.00 adult, $4.00 child (6-12). (includes viewing 2 movies).
Note: No outside food is allowed. See FAQ's on website.

66 Drive-In movie theatre, the last of the original six drive-ins named after this famous road. The screen is 96 feet wide and 44 feet tall, making it one of the largest remaining outdoor screens in America. Get your flicks on Route 66.

BATTLE OF CARTHAGE STATE HISTORIC SITE
Chestnut Street **Carthage** 64836

Phone: (417) 682-2279 https://mostateparks.com/park/battle-carthage-state-historic-site
Admission: The Missouri state park system does not charge entrance fees. However, there are fees associated with camping, lodging, tours, museums and special events.

The battle was the first major land battle of the Civil War. The 7.4-acre tract is the site of the 12-hour battle's final confrontation, which began nine miles north of town on the morning of July 5, 1861. Missouri Gov. Claiborne Fox Jackson commanded the 6,000 Southerners who forced Col. Franz Sigel and his 1,000 Union men to retreat down the stagecoach road to Sarcoxie. An interpretive shelter with displays explains the history of the battle, and the site remains just as it was when the victorious Southern troops camped there the evening after the battle.

DID YOU KNOW ? The nearby town of Marionville is known for one attraction: hundreds of albino (white) squirrels.

CIVIL WAR MUSEUM
205 Grant Street **Carthage** 64836

Phone: (417) 237-7060 https://visit-carthage.com/attraction/civil-war-museum/
Hours: Tuesday-Saturday 8:00am-5:00pm, Sunday 1:00-5:00pm. Admission: FREE

The Civil War Museum in downtown Carthage presents artifacts and information about the Battle of Carthage and the Civil War in southwest Missouri. The focal point is a mural painted by Andy Thomas that features battle action on the courthouse square, as well as mini-displays on Belle Starr, African-American and American Indian contributions to the war. Girls will especially like hearing tales of how townswomen handled the war and how they could be sneaky, too.

PRECIOUS MOMENTS INSPIRATION PARK

4321 S Chapel Road (off I-44, near US 71) **Carthage** 64836

Phone: (800) 445-2220
www.preciousmoments.com/content.cfm/park_chapel
Tours: Daily, FREE Chapel Tours hourly from 9:00am-4:00pm (March-December). 10:00am-4:00pm, (January & February).
Note: A neat video of how they draw, sculpt, mold and paint each new Precious Moments figure is online here: www.preciousmoments.com/content.cfm/how_pm_made. Also, a fun seasonal event happens here in November & December called Carthage At Christmastime.

It all began more than thirty years ago, when Precious Moments® creator Sam Butcher began drawing the endearing teardrop-eye children he called "Precious Moments" as gifts for family and friends. The Gardens, a Christian chapel (50 biblical murals in stained glass and paintings depicting stories from the Bible), art museum, restored Victorian house, and inspirational fountain are all found at this one park. There's a neat island with a playhouse that provokes wishful thinking in all kids. Plus an "upside-down" decorated Christmas tree in the gift shop. Getting hungry? The property has Royal Delights - a small restaurant. Once you know the story behind the figurines and the chapel you understand why so many people love Precious Moments.

MARK TWAIN NATIONAL FOREST - CASSVILLE DISTRICT

Highway 248 East **Cassville** 65625

Phone: (417) 847-2144
www.fs.fed.us/r9/forests/marktwain/ranger_districts/ava/

Visitors to Ava/Cassville/Willow Springs District will find different landscapes, contrasting the typical oak-hickory forests of the Midwest. Open areas of native tall prairie grasses characterized by dry, shallow soils and limestone outcroppings are reminiscent of the historic pioneer trails to the Old West not far away. The unique blending of eastern forest and western desert habitats makes a home for such varied wildlife as the bald eagle and the roadrunner, armadillos and wild turkey, white-tailed deer and black bears. The sunlit balds and deep hollows, narrow ridgetops and steep slopes, secluded pastures and clear streams characteristic of the Ozarks are the trademark of Cassville Area. This is the landscape so eloquently described in Harold Bell Wright's famous book, The Shepherd of the Hills. As you drive through the district, take your time and get out and stop to wander a little on the marked pathways.

For updates & travel games visit: **www.KidsLoveTravel.com**

South West Area 183

ROARING RIVER STATE PARK

12716 Farm Road 2239 (7 miles south of Cassville on Hwy. 112)
Cassville 65625

Phone: (417) 847-2539 https://mostateparks.com/park/roaring-river-state-park
Admission: The Missouri state park system does not charge entrance fees. However, there are fees associated with camping, lodging, tours, museums and special events.

Nestled in the rugged and scenic terrain of the Ozarks is Roaring River, which is stocked daily during trout season. In addition to fishing, the park features a pool, hiking trails, camping, lodging, dining, a store and a nature center. Explore the natural wonders of the park on one of seven trails totaling over 10 miles. Deer Leap Trail is the shortest trail (0.2 miles) that leads to an overlook and boardwalk above the fish hatchery and the spring that is the head of Roaring River. Ozark Chinquapin Nature Center exhibits interpretive displays and park naturalists present programs on the park's natural history. Campers will find 187 campsites ranging from basic to electric hookup. The elegant Emory Melton Inn and Conference Center features 26 guest rooms, a restaurant, gift shop and meeting rooms. Twenty-six secluded, rustic cabins with kitchens. Reservations for the inn and cabins are required.

GEORGE WASHINGTON CARVER NATIONAL MONUMENT

5646 Carver Road (From Exit 18A on I-44, take Highway 59 south to Diamond. Go west 2 miles on Highway V, then south ½ mile on Carver Road) **Diamond 64840**

Phone: (417) 325-4151 www.nps.gov/gwca/index.htm
Hours: Daily, 9:00am-5:00pm.
Admission: FREE.
Educators: http://www.nps.gov/gwca/forteachers/curriculummaterials.htm has a page full of themed curriculum as it relates to Carver. We love the wonderful puzzles and quizzes at the end of each lesson that tie what kids learn into current life application.

The national park covers land that belonged to Moses and Susan Carver, the family who owned George's mother at the time of his birth and who raised him after the Civil War. GW enjoyed freedom early in life. It was at this site, once a working family farm, where Carver's love for science and the outdoors was born. Although he sought to further his education, he often was denied access to schools because of his color. But he persevered and earned a master's degree in agriculture in 1896 – the same year Booker T. Washington asked him to head the Agriculture Department at the Tuskegee Institute.

The GW Carver site tells the inspirational story of the slave child who grew up to become one of the greatest scientists of his day. The monument features the mile-long Carver Trail, the Carver Family Cemetery and the 1881 Carver House. Additionally, park staffers conduct hands-on experiments in plant science at an on-site lab. Kids realize anyone can overcome odds, hone in on their special talents and work to have their dreams come true.

CARVER DAY

Diamond - G. Washington Carver Nat'l Monument - Celebrate the life of George Washington Carver with an fun event that includes storytelling, exhibitors, musical performers, guided tours, interpretive talks, children's programs and more. (July)

PRAIRIE DAY

Diamond - G. Washington Carver Nat'l Monument - Features activities that celebrate early pioneer life, including living history demos, musical performances, wagon rides and hayrides.(September).

CANDY HOUSE CHOCOLATE FACTORY

510 Kentucky Avenue **Joplin** 64801

Phone: (417) 623-7171 **www.candyhouse.net**
Store Hours: Monday-Saturday 9:30am-5:30am, Sunday 12:30-5:30pm. Seasonal hours may vary.
Tours: Tours are free, and available to be scheduled Monday through Friday 9:30am to 2:00pm. (Sorry, no tours between December 1-24 or the week before Valentine's Day and Easter.)

Ever wondered just how chocolates and candies are made? Bring your family on a tour of the Candy House. Visitors will see how peanut brittle and English toffee are made, how candies are enrobed in chocolate (39 feet of chocolate waterfalls) and see chocolates being dipped by hand. Did you know most toffees, brittles and caramels are made from the same ingredients? The best part of the tour comes at the end when you get to taste some of these delightful treats.

GRAND FALLS

Riverside Drive From 1-44 West take Joplin exit 6 (Hwy 86 south)
Joplin 64801

As the largest, continuously flowing natural waterfall in Missouri, Grand Falls plunges over 25 feet down a ledge of solid chert before flowing southward. You can walk on outcrops of this chert to get to the best viewing spots. Missouri's

South West Area

Grand Falls is like a miniature Niagara Falls. On a breezy day, you'll feel the mist hit your face. Phone: (417) 624-4150

JOPLIN MUSEUM COMPLEX

504 S. Schifferdecker Avenue (Schifferdecker Park) **Joplin** 64801
Phone: (417) 623-1180 **www.joplin-museum.org**
Hours: Tuesday 10:00am-7:00pm, Wednesday-Saturday 10:00am-5:00pm.
Admission: $2.00 adult, $5.00 family.

Tri-State Mineral Museum -portrays mining in the Tri-State district where Joplin once led world production of zinc and lead. The Mineral Museum details mining processes and methods used from the 1870s to the 1960s, and houses one of the world's best collections of lead and zinc ores. And best of all, the Mineral Museum sits in a reproduced mine shaft so it feels like you are actually under ground experiencing firsthand the workings of a real zinc mine.

Other rooms in the complex detail Joplin's foundings and history plus areas are spattered with Route 66 memorabilia, Bonnie & Clyde's adventures in Joplin, and the National Cookie Cutter Historical Museum. Afterwards, kids might like to head over to the <u>COUNTRY CABOOSE</u> museum and gift shop inside a real caboose. www.countrycaboose.com.

DID YOU KNOW ? Zinc is the 23rd most abundant element in the earth's crust. The zinc and lead produced in Joplin was 3rd in the world for materials produced from 1850-1950 with more than 500 million tons of ore taken from the ground.

UNDERCLIFF GRILL

Joplin (Tipton Ford) - *6385 Old Highway 71 64804. www.facebook.com/* ***undercliff****. Phone: (417) 623-8382 Hours: Wedsday-Friday 11:00am-9:00am, Saturday 9:00am-9:00pm, Sunday 9:00am-3:00pm. Breakfast is served Saturday & Sunday from 9:00am-11:00am.* The Undercliff is a restaurant built into the side of a cliff that gives you the feeling of eating in a cave. The coolest thing about the space is that it's literally a shack built into the side of a cliff. The back wall of the dark dining room looks like a cave. The interior decor is a mix of old Hollywood and vintage sports stuff. OK, kooky places like this always have something to order that's a little different. Here, it's the fries with cheese sauce. The sauce has a special flavor and it may become you favorite dipping sauce. If the weather is fine, and you're in the mood for less cave, they have patio dining. The Kids Menu is served with drink, fries and a surprise (around $5.00). Adults will want to order make your own burgers starting at $5.99.

HARRY S TRUMAN BIRTHPLACE STATE HISTORIC SITE

1009 Truman (Off U.S. Hwy. 71, 2 miles on Hwy. 160, one block north on Truman) **Lamar** 64759

Phone: (417) 682-2279 https://mostateparks.com/park/harry-s-truman-birthplace-state-historic-site
Hours: Wednesday-Saturday 10:00am-4:00pm. Sunday Noon-4pm (March-October) FREE Tours are offered.
Admission: The Missouri state park system does not charge entrance fees. However, there are fees associated with camping, lodging, tours, museums and special events.

President Harry S. Truman – the only Missourian ever elected president - was born here on May 8, 1884. Truman's family stayed in the six-room home until he was almost 1. Furnishings from the period fill the house. Visitors today can view its four downstairs rooms and two upstairs rooms, as well as the smokehouse, well and outhouse located in the back. It has neither electricity nor indoor plumbing. Guided tours are FREE. The Austrian pine planted the day he was born by his father, a livestock dealer, still stands in the front yard.

PERSIMMON HILL BERRY FARM

367 Persimmon Hill Lane **Lampe** 65681

Phone: (417) 779-5443 www.persimmonhill.com
Hours: (Farm) Daily 7:00am-7:00pm (noon on Sundays) (June and July). Closes at 5:00pm (August-September). Call or vist website for additional store hours in other seasons.

This self-sustaining farm prides itself on its high quality products and ecological practices, including manufacturing its own bio fuels from recycled cooking oils. Among the farm's specialties are "thunder" muffins; blueberry barbeque sauce; spicy raspberry sauce and sweet blackberry glaze; elderberry juice; and the nutty blue goose - a combo of blueberry, gooseberry and black walnut jam. Everything is done in small batches to prevent overcooking and preserve natural flavors and color. The drive to Persimmon Hill Farm will take you through some of the Ozarks' most beautiful countryside.

PRAIRIE STATE PARK

128 NW 150th Lane **Liberal** 64769

Phone: (417) 843-6711 https://mostateparks.com/park/prairie-state-park
Hours: (Visitor Center) Wednesday-Saturday 10:00am-4:00pm, Sunday 1-4pm (April-October). Thursday-Saturday 10:00am-4:00pm (November-March).
Admission: The Missouri state park system does not charge entrance fees. However, there are fees associated with camping, lodging, tours, museums and special events.

For updates & travel games visit: **www.KidsLoveTravel.com**

South West Area

This nearly 4000 acre park is the state's largest public example of native prairie. It protects a variety of prairie grasses, flowers and animals, including bison and elk, and features a visitor center with displays, a prairie diorama, hands-on exhibits, and frequently a naturalist who can answer questions or give the kids an idea for a project. Upon entering the Visitors Center, the large, central diorama depicts the prairie in spring, summer and autumn with the colors and diversity of the prairie. The "Furs and Fence Row" room flows across time and the effects of humans on the prairie. Hands-on items in the "Learning Center" allow everyone the chance to explore the special features of a tallgrass prairie. A 50-person capacity "audio/visual room/auditorium" offers video and more exhibits. If you would like to have a quick snack or taste what people may have eaten more than 200 years ago, try the bison jerky and wash it down with a cool bottle of water. There are also hiking trails and primitive campsites. And, if you're wanting to walk the trails after 4pm Mid-March thru Mid-May, forget it. The trails are closed to protect the greater prairie chicken during its mating season.

LAURA INGALLS WILDER HISTORIC HOME AND MUSEUM

3060 Highway A (45 miles east of Springfield on highway 60)
Mansfield 65704

Phone: (417) 924-3626 **www.lauraingallswilderhome.com**
Hours: Monday-Saturday 9:00am-5:00pm, Sunday 12:30pm-5:00pm (March - mid-November)
Admission: $14.00 adult (18+), $7.00 child (6-17).
Note: Before you go, your family will get so much more out of the visit if you read at least one 'Little House" book or watch a few shows of the same title to "set the scene."
FREEBIES: Pioneer coloring pages, word finds and quizzes are found here: **www.lauraingallswilderhome.com/kids.htm**

Rocky Ridge Farm, in the Ozark Hills, is where Laura Ingalls Wilder wrote the Little House books. The museum exhibits include artifacts from the pioneer lifestyle described in "Little House" books. Laura's daughter, Rose is also featured. Recreations of rooms from both homes, her desks, her manuscripts, and souvenirs from her world travels are also displayed. Many of the rooms were left nearly exactly as if Laura had just left the room. The little homes are so sweet and Almanzo built much of the first home and Laura, Rose, and Almanzo's graves are nearby. Why are the countertops so low? Also, look for Pa's actual fiddle. This is a must for children and adults interested in the early American pioneers and history or big "Little House on the Prairie" fans.

LAURA'S MEMORIES PLAY

Mansfield - Laura Ingalls Wilder Historic Home & Museum. Experience the past with Laura Ingalls Wilder as she reminisces about her childhood, pioneer days, her incredible family, and her beloved Almanzo. Laura's life unfolds through a live theater production that culminates on that momentous day in 1951 when Mansfield dedicated its library in her honor. Laura's Memories captures Mrs. Wilder's journeys through Iowa, Minnesota, the Dakota Territory, Kansas, and finally Mansfield, Missouri where Laura and Almanzo spent their remaining years. Performed by the Ozark Mountain Players, under the starry canopy of the Ozark sky. Concessions are available. Admission. (first two weekends in August and first three weekends in September).

BUSHWHACKER HISTORICAL MUSEUM & OLD JAIL HISTORIC SITE

212 W. Walnut Street (main bldg. Is the basement of the Nevada library)
Nevada 64772

Phone: (417) 667-9602   www.bushwhacker.org
Hours: Wednesday-Friday 10:00am-4:00pm, Saturday 10:00am-1:00pm.
Admission: $5.00 adult, $2.00 youth (12-17), $1.00 (under 12).
Note: The Old Jail Historic Site is located at 231 N. Main Street.

Known as the "Bushwhacker Capital" during the war, learn about "bushwhackers," Confederate guerrillas who played an important role in Missouri's Civil War. Nevada was burned to the ground by Federal troops on May 26, 1863. The city's Bushwhacker Museum and Bushwhacker Jail offer permanent exhibits about the region's Civil War history. Visitors see the cell room in the 1860 stone jail and the sheriff's home. The women prisoners were kept in an upstairs cell room away from the men prisoners. Find out what life was like for the POWs. The final exhibit at the main location- and probably the largest is the Hornback House Exhibit. Dr. Hornback was a physician that worked in Vernon County in 1896.

A short video describes the time period and they are trying to add interactive stations each year. The first such exhibit: incorporating the actual telegraph key from Nevada's old railroad depot. There is a Morse Code guide sheet to help visitors, and they are able to transmit copies of famous telegrams, such as the SOS from the Titanic. A new exhibit on joinery, or the way carpenters put things together, also is ready. Examples of the different kinds of woodwork are available for people actually to take apart and see how they are put together.

BLUFF DWELLERS' CAVERN & BROWNING MUSEUM

954 Highway 59 South (2 miles South of Noel) **Noel** 64854

Phone: (417) 475-3666 https://**bluffdwellerscave.com**
Hours: Daily, 10:00am-6:00pm (March-October). Winters closes at 5:00pm.
Admission: $16.00 adult, $8.00 child (4-11).
Note: The temperature is 56 degrees all year long so please dress appropriately. Pan for gemstones and fossils for extra fee.

This is a guided cave tour and a museum. The same family has operated the cave since its discovery in 1925. The cave entry is almost straight uphill so plan on wear comfy shoes as there are a lot of stairs to navigate to the cave entrance and tour. In the still pools you'll find cave coral, sponges, lilly pads, popcorn and "one of the most striking rimstone dams in the state."

And, for the avid adventuresome families: FLOAT & STAY RESORTS in Noel plus another handful of others:

- **RIVER RANCH RESORT** - www.riverranchresort.com. Campsites and 40 cabins on a full mile of riverfront. You can rent a canoe, raft, or kayak and resort guides will launch you 4 to 8 miles upstream and you can float back to your cabin or campsite.

- **SYCAMORE LANDING** - www.noelrafting.com Float and camp pkgs

DOENNIG SPORT SWINGS & OZARK PAINTBALL

671 Jackson Spring Road **Ozark** 65721

Phone: (417) 443-4444 **www.swingsandpaintball.com**
Hours: Public Session: Friday and Saturday nights only or by appointment. Prices vary. Generally $10.00 per person.

Sports Swings offers jousting, bungee basketball, a mechanical bull, rock climbing, fun cycles, whirly bird and giant inflatables. They even have a goofy Hillmobilly Hayride - wait until you see the "wagon." Paintball with underground tunnels, bridges and trenches. Everything extreme but anyone, any age, physically active can enjoy these sports - even the challenging sport swings. Please wear modest clothing and tennis shoes...no flip-flops.

OZARK FESTIVAL OF LIGHTS

Ozark - Finley River Park. Over 200 displays to enjoy in the drive-thru exhibit. Hours are 5:00pm-10:00pm. There are new exhibits each year. Penguins playing on an ice berg, two reindeer skating, and a train with waving engineer. It's free to drive through but donations are accepted to help pay the expenses and improve the displays for next year. (evenings in December)

JESSE JAMES DAYS

Pineville - Five day event commemorating the fact that actors Tyrone Power, Henry Fonda, Randolph Scott, and Nancy Kelly came to town with a crew from Hollywood to shoot the film "Jesse James" in 1938. Carnival, contests for kids, bingo, food and nightly music. Memorabilia from the film is on display at the McDonald Country Library in Pineville and one afternoon a fake bank robbery at the McDonald County State bank (shootouts, too). (weekend in August)

COLLEGE OF THE OZARKS

1 Industrial Place **Point Lookout** 65726

Phone: (417) 334-6411 **www.cofo.edu**

This 4-year liberal arts college requires all students to work on campus to defray the cost of tuition. There are 80 work areas on campus, ranging from a theater and radio station to a dairy farm and a bakery. Most areas are open to public, including Edward's Mill, where you can purchase whole-wheat flour, cornbread mix, and grits; a weaving studio featuring hand-woven items from pot holders to clothing; and greenhouses where houseplants and flowers are sold.

- **RALPH FOSTER MUSEUM** - 750,000 items pertaining to Ozark history and folklore. See the car from The Beverly Hillbillies television show, a miniature circus, life-sized stuffed animals, a hands-on discovery room for children ages four to eight where kids can crawl thru a cave, try on clothing, examine a wide assortment of crazy objects. Admission: $6.00 adult, $5.00 senior, FREE child (high school age and under). Hours: Monday-Saturday, 9:00am-4:30pm. **www.rfostermuseum.com**

- **FRIENDSHIP HOUSE** - Prepared and served by students, the food here ranges from hamburgers, sandwiches, french fries and dinners to a complete buffet on Sunday. Inexpensive.

ROCKBRIDGE GENERAL STORE AND RESTAURANT

Rockbridge - 65741. The resort sits on 1,500 acres of the scenic Ozarks, sporting to nature trails for hiking and one mile of sparkling, spring-fed creek stocked with rainbow trout. Guests will find a bait and tackle shop, gift shop and a beautiful sitting lounge with a fireplace. There's a pay phone in the lobby, but Rockbridge is an oasis away from the phone and the blare of the television. Rainbow Trout Restaurant is of the finest, specializing in a variety of menu choices: fresh caught trout from the stream, old-fashioned hash browns, handcut chops and steaks, skillet-fried chicken or tender chicken-fried steak and gravy. **http://rockbridgemo.com/?page_id=16**

HISTORY MUSEUM FOR SPRINGFIELD & GREENE COUNTY

155 Park Central Square **Springfield** 65802

Phone: (417) 832-1200 **www.springfieldhistorymuseum.org**
Hours: Monday-Saturday 10:30am-4:30pm.
Admission: $3.00-$5.00.

Located in Springfield's City Hall, this history museum traces local history from prehistoric times through the 1950s. In addition, The History Museum has three hands-on areas for younger guests. These include a Native American grinding stone, a Civil War tent, and a variety of household items similar to those used in pioneer households. These items are historically accurate reproductions, so visitors are encouraged to handle them in order to better understand the lives of our ancestors.

DID YOU KNOW ? The Jefferson Avenue Footbridge (Commercial St. at Jefferson Ave.) is the country's longest. You can watch trains from the sturdy decking. Double-decker trains glide by on 13 sets of tracks below.

DID YOU KNOW ? Officially recognized as the birthplace of Route 66, it was in Springfield on April 30, 1926, that officials first proposed the name of the new Chicago-to-Los Angeles highway. www.missouri66.org.

AIR & MILITARY MUSEUM OF THE OZARKS

2305 East Kearney **Springfield** 65803

Phone: (417) 864-7997 **www.ammomuseum.com**
Hours: Tuesdays & Saturdays

This hands-on environment features a Cobra helicopter, a T-33 jet aircraft, Army Jeeps, trucks and other restored military equipment. Guests can even take a simulated flight in a real Cobra helicopter or have a personalized dog tag made.

DICKERSON PARK ZOO

1401 West Norton Road (Interstate 44 and Missouri Highway 13 - exit 77)
Springfield 65803

Phone: (417) 864-1800 www.dickersonparkzoo.org
Hours: Daily 9:00am-5:00pm (April-September), Daily 10:00am-4:00pm (October-March).
Admission: $14.00 adult (13+), $11.00 senior (60+) & $9.00 child (3-12).

Exhibit themes include habitats from Africa, Tropical Asia, South America, Australia and Missouri habitats. Missouri Habitats area shows animals and habitats native to the Ozarks, including black bears, bobcats, and river otters. The Diversity of Life center houses reptiles, insects and amphibians. A three-car train circles the zoo. The zoo is nationally known for its Asian elephant breeding program.

FANTASTIC CAVERNS

4872 North Farm Road 125 **Springfield** 65803

Phone: (417) 833-2010 www.fantasticcaverns.com
Hours: 8:00am-4:00pm. (open a few hours later in summer) Visit website for current season hours.
Admission: $24.00 adult (13+), $17.00 child (6-12).
Tours: Depart every 20-30 minutes throughout the day and each tour takes about an hour. The temperature inside the cave is 60 degrees.
Educators: a wonderful, easy to follow study guide and quiz about caves is found under Education>Classroom Study Guide online.

Fantastic Caverns is America's only drive-through cave with tours conducted from a vehicle-draw tram in order to protect the delicate formations. Look for cave pearls and delicate drapes. Fragile species of wildlife include cave crayfish and grotto salamanders. Be especially on the lookout for blind Ozarks cavefish - a reclusive little creature no longer than a finger. View sites and formations carved into Missouri limestone one drop of water at a time. Your tram driver gives you a 55-minute talk that combines history, ecology, conservation and geology.

Since today's tour is entirely by tram, with no walking required, families with small children, senior citizens and the physically challenged can all sit back and enjoy the ride. Temperatures inside the cave always hover around 60 degrees making it a wonderful adventure regardless of the season.

South West Area 193

SPRINGFIELD CONSERVATION NATURE CENTER

4601 S Nature Center Way **Springfield** 65804

Phone: (417) 888-4237 **https://nature.mdc.mo.gov/discover-nature/places/springfield-cnc**
Hours: Tuesday-Saturday 8:00am-5:00pm. Trails open daily 8am-dusk.

The park has six hiking trails of varying lengths, a visitor center with exhibits, but camping and fishing are not allowed. Nearly three miles of trails, as short as a fifth of a mile, as long as two miles. A boardwalk goes over the marshy shallows of the lake. Some trails are paved - all are easily accessed. No bikes or pets allowed. There's an indoor bird watching space inside the center. Experience the sounds of the nighttime forest and discover how rainwater becomes spring water, all in the center's multi-sensory exhibit room. Towards evening, you might even catch the eyes of a deer, raccoon, a duck or even bobcats.

DISCOVERY CENTER

438 East Saint Louis Street **Springfield** 65806

Phone: (417) 862-9910 **www.discoverycenter.org**
Hours: Tuesday-Thursday 9:00am-5:00pm, Friday & Saturday 9:00am-6:00pm, Sunday 1:00pm-5:00pm. Open Summer Mondays.
Admission: $12.00 adult, $10.00 senior (60+), $8.00 child (3-15). There may be some additional fees for special exhibits.

This is an interactive hands-on science center for all ages. Imagine, create, have fun and learn with hundreds of exhibits that explore physics, chemistry, energy, health and culture. You can stroll through a giant eyeball, dig for a dinosaur, mix oozing bubbling chemicals in the Exploratory Lab, or be a star on the Evening News. Sense-Sational Hall houses unique exhibits like Big Mouth, Eye Spy, and Brain Central that allow visitors to investigate the workings of the human body through giant-sized anatomic models. Play pretend or be creative in Discovery Town. Next, ride the HighWire Bike or create a dam in waterworks. Every space is designed to draw the kids in on their level to start experimenting. Well done.

SPRINGFIELD LITTLE THEATRE

311 E. Walnut Avenue **Springfield** 65806

Phone: (417) 869-1334 **www.springfieldlittletheatre.org**

The Springfield Little Theatre at the historic Landers Theatre is Missouri's oldest and largest civic theater. Most shows are family-friendly with titles like: High School Musical, Willy Wonka and Disney productions. Tickets run $15.00-$25.00. Wednesday-Sunday evenings and weekend matinees.

BASS PRO SHOPS OUTDOOR WORLD

1935 S. Campbell **Springfield** 65807

Phone: (417) 887-7334 **www.basspro.com**
Hours: Monday-Saturday 7:00am-10:00pm, Sunday 9:00am-7:00pm.

There's a theme park atmosphere in the store including: four story waterfall, indoor bow and arrow range, fish feeding shows in a 140,000 gallon aquarium - one of five large aquariums - with divers and a video. Their newest acquisition ...alligators. Restaurant on premises - Hemingway's Blue Water Cafe.

DID YOU KNOW? This is one of Missouri's most visited attractions.

INCREDIBLE PIZZA COMPANY

Springfield - *2850 S Campbell Avenue 65807. www.incrediblepizza.com/springfield*. Phone: (417) 887-3030   Hours: Sunday-Thursday 11:00am-8:00pm. Friday & Saturday 11:00am-9:00pm (game room stays open 1 hour later). This attraction starts with a pizza, pasta, dessert buffet; bottomless drinks. Go-karts, bumper cars, mini golf, dozens of interactive games.

WONDERS OF WILDLIFE MUSEUM & AQUARIUM

314 S. Campbell Street, downtown **Springfield** 65807

Phone: (417) 868-8181 **www.wondersofwildlife.org**
Hours: Generally daily 10:00am-8:00pm.
Admission: Wildlife: $14.95 adult, $9.95 child (4-11). Aquarium: $29.95 adult, $19.95 child (4-11)

The world-class conservation attraction has been dubbed the Conservation Capital of America with 35,000 fish in a 1.5 million gallon aquarium and the greatest collection of record-setting game animals ever assembled. Its location in Springfield, makes it the perfect jumping off point for your own outdoor adventure, whether floating one of Missouri's numerous rivers or taking in the scenery at Lake of the Ozarks.

For updates & travel games visit: **www.KidsLoveTravel.com**

South West Area 195

SPRINGFIELD HOT GLASS STUDIO
314 S. Campbell Street, downtown **Springfield** 65806
Phone: (417) 868-8181 **www.springfieldhotglass.com**
Hours: Tuesday-Saturday 10am-6pm.

This studio is a working glass-making center, featuring glassblowing and torch-working demos and a gallery of original glass art for sale (look, don't touch). Don't miss continuous glass blowing demonstrations every First Friday.

MISSOURI SPORTS HALL OF FAME
3861 E. Stan Musial Drive (1 mile east of U.S. Hwy. 65 on U.S. Hwy. 60)
Springfield 65809
Phone: (417) 889-3100 or (800) 498-5678 **www.mosportshalloffame.com**
Hours: Monday-Saturday 10:00am-4:00pm, Sunday Noon-4:00pm.
Admission: $5.00 adult, $4.00 senior, $3.00 child (6-15). Immediate Family $14.00.

The Missouri Sports Hall of Fame is a family-friendly environment that includes a museum with more than 4,000 pieces of sports memorabilia, hands-on exhibits and displays. You can feel the speed as you race in the NASCAR simulator, hit your own home run in the batters box against a Major League Baseball pitcher or throw the winning touchdown pass in our football exhibit. All those famous uniforms and signed game balls and quotes...make a young athletes head spin!

GRAY / CAMPBELL FARMSTEAD LIFESTYLE EXPOSITION
Springfield - Nathanael Greene Park. *www.graycampbellfarmstead.org*. The Lifestyle Exposition Activities will include: Blacksmith Demonstrations, Apple Butter Making, Apple Cider Making, Open Hearth Cooking, Lye Soap Making, Clogging, Wagon Rides, Music, Leather-crafting, Fiber Arts, Story Telling and Food from a concession stand. Admission is free - Donations Accepted. (third weekend in September).

FESTIVAL OF LIGHTS
Springfield - *www.itsalldowntown.com*. Twinkling lights atop a 30-foot tree in Jordan Valley Park and fireworks at nearby Hammons Field will light up the evening sky during the kick-off ceremony for the Festival of Lights. The Festival of Lights is a six-week celebration featuring a number of no- or low-cost activities for people to enjoy during the holiday season along with a variety of music and theater performances in the spirit of the season. (starting right before Thanksgiving thru December)

WILSON'S CREEK NATIONAL BATTLEFIELD

6424 West Farm Road 182 **Springfield (Republic)** 65738

Phone: (417) 732-2662, ext. 227 **www.nps.gov/wicr**
Hours: (Visitor Center) Daily 8:00am-5:00pm, Park (Tour Road) Daily, 8:00am-5:00pm.
Admission: The entrance fee to the park is $10.00 per adult to a maximum of $20.00 per vehicle. The receipt is honored for seven days. An adult is defined as anyone 16 years old and older.
Tours: A 4.9 mile paved tour road provides a self-guided auto tour. There are eight interpretive stops at significant battle-related locations. There are five walking trails off the tour road, varying in length from 1/4 to 3/4 of a mile. A seven mile trail system for horseback riding and hiking is accessible from the tour road.
Educators: an excellent Common Soldier/Common Man unit study is found off the main website: **www.nps.gov/wicr/forteachers/curriculum**.

Near Springfield is Wilson's Creek National Battlefield, perhaps the most important Civil War battle fought west of the Mississippi River. Fought Aug. 10, 1861, this battle was the first Confederate victory in the early stages of the war in Missouri, and the battle in which Gen. Nathaniel Lyon became the first Union general to be killed in the Civil War.

This National Park Service battlefield contains a state-of-the-art visitor center as well as a self-guided auto tour of the battlefield itself. Inside the center and the Civil War Museum are camp life dioramas, a fiberoptic map of the battle and a film about the battle.

The Ray House, dating from the 1850s, served as a temporary field hospital for Southern soldiers following the battle. General Nathaniel Lyon's body was brought to the house and placed in a bed for examination. The bed is on exhibit in one of the rooms. The Ray House is open on weekends (subject to staff and volunteer availability), Memorial Day through Labor Day.

STOCKTON STATE PARK

19100 S. Hwy. 215 **Stockton** 65635

Phone: (417) 276-4259 https://mostateparks.com/park/stockton-state-park
Hours: Sunrise-Sunset (year-round).
Admission: The Missouri state park system does not charge entrance fees. However, there are fees associated with camping, lodging, tours, museums and special events.

Located along the rolling Springfield plateau, this park overlooks the Stockton Reservoir. A steady breeze makes it a destination for sailing. Stockton State Park's marina rents a variety of boats ranging from personal watercrafts to sail boats. The park has two launching ramps, making lake access easy.

For updates & travel games visit: **www.KidsLoveTravel.com**

A swimming beach accommodates visitors who would rather play in the water than on it. The park has a marina, a beach, lodging, picnic sites and campsites. The grill is a seasonal restaurant at the marina offering burgers, catfish, chicken, etc. After a fun-filled day of activity, visitors can relax and camp under the stars at one of the park's basic or electric campsites, or rent a camper cabin, cabin with kitchenette or duplex cabin with kitchenette.

HAMMONS PRODUCTS PANTRY & VISITORS CENTER

414 North Street **Stockton** 65785

Phone: (417) 276-5800 www.hammonspantry.com or www.black-walnuts.com
Note: To understand how Hammons processes nuts watch their online video on HOW WE PROCESS/Video Link.

Welcome to Hammons Products Company, the world's largest processor and supplier of American Black Walnuts! Wild, hand-harvested Black Walnuts stand alone in the nut world as a flavorful, nutritional ingredient to some of your favorite baked goods, dishes, and ice cream. Here you'll find everything there is to know about the American Black Walnut. You'll learn how they hand-harvest every year across 15-states, how to use black walnuts in delicious recipes, and how Hammons Products Co. has been a family-owned company for over 60 years. Black walnut harvesting occurs in the fall, when the wild nut crop is hulled, bagged and sold to a network of buying stations, or "hullers," for Hammons Products Company. The Visitors Center is a retail store with some information about the process and, of course, black walnut products to purchase.

WILD ANIMAL SAFARI

124 Jungle Drive **Strafford** 65757

Phone: (417) 859-5300 https://animalsafari.com/MO/
Hours: 10:00am-5:00pm. Open until 6:00pm or 7:30pm spring and summers. The park is open everyday possible but snow, ice, or severe cold conditions do cause them to close as they cause unsafe driving conditions in the park.
Admission: Covers the Drive-Thru and Walk-About. $22.95 adult, $19.95 senior (65+) and child (3-12). Small additional charge for animal feed. Online discounts.
Tours: Tour bus runs spring & fall weekends and Daily in summer.
Note: Safari Grill and gift shop on premises. Note: it's recommended (and we agree) to go on a safari bus/van tour vs. riding your own vehicle. It will be covered with slobber. Also, keep the young kids and squeamish teens sitting in the middle so they don't have to have direct contact with the animals if they don't want.

Have your cameras ready as you embark on this two-part animal adventure. Experience up-close encounters with all sorts of animals. You can drive your own vehicle (or take the complimentary bus tour- seasonal) thru the Drive-Thru safari and get to experience hand feeding the animals. On the safari the exotic animals will literally come up to your car and eat right out of the palm of your hand. Scattered through the park they have approx. 650 animals, (and counting!) including: Rhinoceros, Tigers, Lions, Black Panthers, Spotted Leopards, Kangaroos, Wallabies, Hyenas, Zebras, Camel, Gaurs, Ostriches, Emus, Lemurs, Monkeys, Deer, Elk, Buffalo, Bison, and more. They even have 2 adult and 2 baby "Ligers" for you too see! This is one of those "you have to be there" experiences. For the full experience, it is wise to purchase the feed (giant pellets) so you can get close to animals (they love you more when you give them food). Choose to feed timid deer or aggressive ostrich. Our favorites: the elk, bison (wait til you see their tongues!) and the zebra (like feeding horses).

Hop out of the car and take a stroll through their Winding Path and the Walk-About. Here you will find some of the smaller animals, or the more friendly. You can take a moment and gaze at the Lemurs as they jump around and leap from rope to rope. See the beautiful Peacock spread his feathers and show off. Then, walk through the winding path where you will be able to feed more animals and even pet them as they come up to you. Hand feed a Four-Horned Sheep, an Alpaca, Zedonk, or even a Wallaby!

For updates & travel games visit: www.KidsLoveTravel.com

OSAGE VILLAGE STATE HISTORIC SITE
(6 miles north on Route C, west 3 miles on a gravel road, Vernon County)
Walker 64790

Phone: (417) 682-2279 (c/o Harry S Truman Birthplace State Historic Site)
https://mostateparks.com/park/osage-village-state-historic-site
Hours: Open Daily (year-round).
Admission: The Missouri state park system does not charge entrance fees. However, there are fees associated with camping, lodging, tours, museums and certain special events.

This site was once a Big Osage Indian village occupied from 1700-1775. At its height, the village contained thousands of people and about 200 lodges. Tons of artifacts have been excavated from this land, including many items used in trading. In the late 18th and early 19th centuries, the Osage Indians accounted for more than half of the total trade in furs along the Missouri River. After the United States government took control of the Louisiana Purchase territory in 1804, the Osage Indians were gradually forced to retreat to Oklahoma. Today, Osage Village State Historic Site features a walking trail and outdoor exhibits that help visitors visualize the village and the everyday bustle of this oncepowerful Indian tribe.

Activity Index 201

AMUSEMENTS

- **C** *Lake Ozark*, Lake Ozark Amusements, 19
- **C** *Linn Creek*, Big Surf Waterpark, 19
- **C** *Osage Beach (Lake Of The Ozarks)*, Osage Beach Amusements, 20
- **NE** *Eureka*, Six Flags St. Louis, 36
- **NE** *Grafton, IL*, Raging Rivers Waterpark, 40
- **NE** *Hannibal*, Big River Train Town, 42
- **NE** *Hannibal*, Sawyer's Creek Fun Park, 47
- **NE** *St. Louis (Fenton)*, Swing-A-Round Fun Town, 74
- **NE** *St. Louis (Hazelwood)*, St. Louis Mills Mall, Sportstreet, 76
- **NE** *St. Louis (Maryland Heights)*, Aquaport, 78
- **NW** *Independence*, Adventure Oasis Water Park, 90
- **NW** *Independence*, Cool Crest FamiLy Fun Center, 93
- **NW** *Kansas City*, Crown Center, 99
- **NW** *Kansas City*, Oceans Of Fun, 111
- **NW** *Kansas City*, Worlds Of Fun, 111
- **NW** *Kansas City*, Schlitterbahn Vacation Village Waterpark, 112
- **NW** *Lee's Summit*, Paradise Park Family Entertainment Center, 119
- **SE** *Chester, IL*, Popeye Statue And Park, 140
- **SW** *Branson*, Branson Amusements, 166
- **SW** *Branson*, Dick's Oldtime 5&10, 171
- **SW** *Branson*, Hollywood Wax Museum, 172
- **SW** *Branson*, Silver Dollar City, 175
- **SW** *Branson*, White Water Water Park, 176
- **SW** *Branson*, Fritz's Adventure, 171

ANIMALS & FARMS

- **C** *Warsaw*, Lost Valley Hatchery And Visitor Center, 25
- **NE** *Eureka*, Endangered Wolf Center, 37
- **NE** *Gray Summit*, Purina Farms, 40
- **NE** *Mexico*, Binders Hilltop Apple And Berry Farm, 53
- **NE** *St. Louis*, St. Louis Zoo, 69
- **NE** *St. Louis*, Grant's Farm, 71
- **NE** *St. Louis*, Suson Park, 72
- **NE** *Valley Park*, World Bird Sanctuary, 80
- **NW** *Kansas City*, American Royal Museum & Visitor Center, 96
- **NW** *Kansas City*, Kansas City Zoo, 108
- **NW** *Osborn*, Shatto Milk Company, 124
- **NW** *St. Joseph*, Schweizer Orchards, 130
- **SE** *Cape Girardeau*, Lazy L Safari Park, 139
- **SE** *Eminence*, Crystal Creek Ranch, 143
- **SE** *Potosi*, Sayersbrook Bison Ranch, 150
- **SW** *Lampe*, Persimmon Hill Berry Farm, 186
- **SW** *Springfield*, Dickerson Park Zoo, 192
- **SW** *Springfield*, Wonders of Wildlife Museum & Aquarium, 194
- **SW** *Strafford*, Wild Animal Safari, 198

HISTORY

- **C** *Arrow Rock*, Arrow Rock State Historic Site, 4
- **C** *Blackwater*, Blackwater, 5
- **C** *Boonville*, Boone's Lick State Historic Site, 5
- **C** *Boonville*, Old Cooper Jail, 6
- **C** *Columbia*, State Historical Society Of Missouri, 9

HISTORY (cont.)

- **C** *Columbia*, Boone County Historical Museum & Visitors Center, 13
- **C** *Fort Leonard Wood*, Museum Complex At Fort Leonard Wood, 12
- **C** *Fulton*, Winston Churchill Memorial & Library, 13
- **C** *Jefferson City*, Jefferson Landing State Historic Site, 13
- **C** *Jefferson City*, Missouri State Capitol Complex, 15
- **C** *Lake Ozark*, Bagnell Dam, 17
- **C** *Osage City*, Clark's Hill-Norton State Historic Site, 21
- **C** *Sedalia*, Bothwell Lodge State Historic Site, 22
- **C** *Sedalia*, Katy Depot And Railroad Heritage Museum, 23
- **C** *Waynesville*, Old Stagecoach Stop, 25
- **NE** *Athens (Revere)*, Battle Of Athens State Historic Site, 32
- **NE** *Defiance*, Daniel Boone Home And Boonesfield Village, 34
- **NE** *Eureka*, Route 66 State Park, 36
- **NE** *Florida*, Mark Twain Birthplace State Historic Site & Park, 38
- **NE** *Hannibal*, Adventures Of Tom Sawyer Diorama Museum, 42
- **NE** *Hannibal*, Mark Twain Cave Complex, 45
- **NE** *Hannibal*, Molly Brown Birthplace & Museum, 46
- **NE** *Hartford, IL*, Camp River Dubois, Lewis & Clark State Historic Site, 49
- **NE** *Hermann*, Deutschheim State Historic Site & Museum, 49
- **NE** *Mexico*, Audrain Historical Society Museum Complex, 53
- **NE** *St. Charles*, First Missouri State Capitol State Historic Site, 55
- **NE** *St. Charles*, Lewis And Clark Boat House And Nature Center, 56
- **NE** *St. Louis*, Gateway Arch, 60
- **NE** *St. Louis*, The Old Courthouse, 62
- **NE** *St. Louis*, Scott Joplin House State Historic Site, 63
- **NE** *St. Louis*, Missouri History Museum, 70
- **NE** *St. Louis*, Museum Of Transportation, 71
- **NE** *St. Louis (Lemay)*, Jefferson Barracks Historic Park, 77
- **NE** *St. Louis (White Haven)*, Ulysses S. Grant National Historic Site, 79
- **NE** *Wayland*, Iliniwek Village State Historic Site, 80
- **NW** *Grandview*, Truman National Historic Site, 88
- **NW** *Higginsville*, Confederate Memorial State Historic Site, 89
- **NW** *Independence*, 1859 Jail, Marshal's Home And Museum, 89
- **NW** *Independence*, Chicago & Alton Train Depot, 90
- **NW** *Independence*, National Frontier Trails Center, 90
- **NW** *Independence*, Truman Home, Museum & Information Center, 92
- **NW** *Kansas City*, Arabia Steamboat Museum, 96
- **NW** *Kansas City*, KC Rail Experience, 101
- **NW** *Kansas City*, National WWI Museum At Liberty Memorial, 102
- **NW** *Kansas City*, Thomas Hart Benton Home And Studio State Historic Site, 105
- **NW** *Kansas City*, John Wornall House, 106
- **NW** *Kansas City*, Shoal Creek Living History Museum, 110
- **NW** *Kansas City (Westport)*, Battle Of Westport, 114

For updates & travel games visit: **www.KidsLoveTravel.com**

HISTORY (cont.)

- **NW** *Kearney*, Jesse James Farm & Museum, 115
- **NW** *Laclede*, Gen. John J Pershing Boyhood Home St Historic Site, 117
- **NW** *Lawson*, Watkins Mill State Park & Historic Site, 118
- **NW** *Lee's Summit*, Missouri Town 1855, 118
- **NW** *Lexington*, Battle Of Lexington State Historic Site, 120
- **NW** *Liberty*, Jesse James Bank Museum, 120
- **NW** *Miami*, Van Meter State Park, 123
- **NW** *Sibley*, Fort Osage National Historic Landmark, 125
- **NW** *St. Joseph*, Robidoux Row Museum, 126
- **NW** *St. Joseph*, Jesse James Home Museum, 127
- **NW** *St. Joseph*, Patee House Museum, 127
- **NW** *St. Joseph*, Pony Express Museum, 128
- **SE** *Burfordville*, Bollinger Mill State Historic Site, 138
- **SE** *Cape Girardeau*, John Wesley Powell's Fort D, 139
- **SE** *Cape Girardeau*, Red House Interpretive Center, 140
- **SE** *Davisville*, Dillard Mill State Historic Site, 141
- **SE** *East Prairie*, Towosahgy State Historic Site, 142
- **SE** *Ellis Grove, IL*, Fort Kaskaskia & Kaskaskia Bell St Historic Site, 142
- **SE** *Eminence*, Alley Spring Grist Mill Historic Site, 143
- **SE** *Jackson*, Trail Of Tears St Park, 145
- **SE** *New Madrid*, New Madrid Historical Museum, 148
- **SE** *Park Hills*, Missouri Mines State Historic Site, 148
- **SE** *Pilot Knob*, Battle of Pilot Knob State Historic Site, 150
- **SE** *Prairie Du Rocher, IL*, Fort De Chartres Historic Site, 151
- **SE** *Salem*, Ozark Natural & Cultural Resource Center, 153
- **SE** *Stanton*, Jesse James Wax Museum, 155
- **SE** *Ste. Genevieve*, Bolduc House Museum Complex, 157
- **SE** *Ste. Genevieve*, Felix Valle State Historic Site, 157
- **SE** *Ste. Genevieve*, Great River Road Interpretive Center, 158
- **SE** *Ste. Genevieve*, Ste. Genevieve Museum, 158
- **SE** *Wickliffe, KY*, Wickliffe Mounds, 160
- **SW** *Ash Grove*, Nathan Boone Homestead State Historic Site, 166
- **SW** *Branson*, Titanic, 177
- **SW** *Carthage*, Battle Of Carthage State Historic Site, 181
- **SW** *Carthage*, Civil War Museum, 181
- **SW** *Diamond*, George Washington Carver National Monument, 183
- **SW** *Joplin*, Joplin Museum Complex, 185
- **SW** *Lamar*, Harry S Truman Birthplace State Historic Site, 186
- **SW** *Mansfield*, Laura Ingalls Wilder Historic Home And Museum, 187
- **SW** *Nevada*, Bushwhacker Historical Museum & Old Jail Historic Site, 188
- **SW** *Springfield*, History Museum For Springfield & Greene County, 191
- **SW** *Springfield*, Air & Military Museum Of The Ozarks, 191
- **SW** *Springfield (Republic)*, Wilson's Creek National Battlefield, 196
- **SW** *Walker*, Osage Village State Historic Site, 199

MUSEUMS

- **C** *Columbia*, University Of Missouri, 8
- **C** *Jefferson City*, Missouri Highway Patrol Safety Education Center, 14
- **NE** *St. Charles*, Fast Lane Classic Cars, 55
- **NE** *St. Louis*, Eugene Field House & St. Louis Toy Museum, 59
- **NE** *St. Louis*, City Museum, 63
- **NE** *St. Louis*, Miniature Museum Of Greater St. Louis, 70
- **NE** *St. Louis (Kirkwood)*, Magic House: St. Louis Children's Museum, 76
- **NW** *Hamilton*, J. C. Penney Museum & Boyhood Home, 88
- **NW** *Kansas City*, Union Station Complex, 105
- **NW** *Kansas City*, Toy And Miniature Museum, 106
- **NW** *Kansas City*, Federal Reserve Bank Of Kansas City, 112
- **SE** *Malden*, Bootheel Youth Museum, 146
- **SW** *Branson*, Ripley's Believe It Or Not Museum, 173
- **SW** *Branson*, World's Largest Toy Museum, 178

OUTDOOR EXPLORING

- **C** *Camdenton*, Ha Ha Tonka State Park, 8
- **C** *Columbia*, Finger Lakes State Park, 10
- **C** *Columbia*, Rock Bridge Memorial State Park, 11
- **C** *Kaiser (Lake Of The Ozarks)*, Lake Of The Ozarks State Park, 16
- **C** *Knob Noster*, Knob Noster State Park, 17
- **C** *Lebanon*, Bennett Spring State Park, 18
- **C** *Pittsburg*, Pomme De Terre State Park, 22
- **C** *Warsaw*, Harry S. Truman State Park, 24
- **NE** *Ballwin*, Castlewood State Park, 33
- **NE** *Desoto*, Washington State Park, 34
- **NE** *Grafton, IL*, Pere Marquette State Park & Visitors Center, 39
- **NE** *Gray Summit*, Shaw Nature Reserve, 41
- **NE** *Kirksville*, Thousand Hills State Park, 51
- **NE** *La Grange*, Wakonda State Park, 52
- **NE** *Macon*, Long Branch State Park, 52
- **NE** *Montgomery City*, Graham Cave State Park, 54
- **NE** *Robertsville*, Robertsville State Park, 54
- **NE** *St. Charles*, Katy Trail State Park, 56
- **NE** *St. Louis*, Forest Park, 66
- **NE** *St. Louis*, Missouri Botanical Garden, 67
- **NE** *St. Louis*, Old Chain Of Rocks Bridge, 72
- **NE** *St. Louis (Chesterfield)*, Faust Park, 74
- **NE** *Troy*, Cuivre River State Park, 80
- **NE** *West Alton*, Jones - Confluence State Park, 81
- **NE** *Wildwood*, Babler Memorial State Park, 81
- **NW** *Blue Springs*, Fleming Park & Blue Springs Lake, 87
- **NW** *Cameron*, Wallace State Park, 88
- **NW** *Craig*, Big Lake State Park, 88
- **NW** *Kansas City*, Cave Spring Historic Site And Nature Center, 109
- **NW** *Kansas City*, Longview Lake Park, 110
- **NW** *Kingsville*, Powell Gardens, 116
- **NW** *Laclede*, Pershing State Park, 117

For updates & travel games visit: **www.KidsLoveTravel.com**

Activity Index

OUTDOOR EXPLORING (cont.)

- **NW** *Liberty*, Martha Lafite Thompson Nature Sanctuary, 120
- **NW** *Maryville*, Mozingo Lake And Recreation Area, 122
- **NW** *Meadville*, Fountain Grove Conservation Area, 122
- **NW** *Mound City*, Squaw Creek National Wildlife Refuge, 123
- **NW** *Rushville*, Lewis And Clark State Park, 125
- **NW** *Sumner*, Swan Lake National Wildlife Refuge, 130
- **NW** *Trenton*, Crowder State Park, 131
- **NW** *Weston*, Weston Bend State Park, 131
- **SE** *East Prairie*, Big Oak Tree State Park, 142
- **SE** *Graniteville*, Elephant Rocks State Park, 144
- **SE** *Middlebrook*, Taum Sauk Mountain State Park, 147
- **SE** *Middlebrook*, Johnson's Shut-Ins State Park, 147
- **SE** *Park Hills*, St. Joe State Park, 149
- **SE** *Patterson*, Sam A. Baker State Park, 149
- **SE** *Puxico*, Mingo National Wildlife Refuge, 151
- **SE** *Salem*, Montauk State Park, 153
- **SE** *St. James*, Maramec Spring Park, 154
- **SE** *Ste. Genevieve*, Hawn State Park, 158
- **SE** *Sullivan*, Meramec State Park, 159
- **SE** *Thayer*, Grand Gulf State Park, 159
- **SE** *Van Buren*, Ozark National Scenic Riverways Headquarters, 160
- **SE** *Williamsville*, Lake Wappapello State Park, 161
- **SW** *Branson*, Table Rock State Park, 177
- **SW** *Cassville*, Mark Twain National Forest - Cassville District, 182
- **SW** *Cassville*, Roaring River State Park, 183
- **SW** *Joplin*, Grand Falls, 184
- **SW** *Stockton*, Stockton State Park, 196

SEASONAL & SPECIAL EVENTS

- **C** *Columbia*, For The People Pow Wow, 11
- **C** *Columbia*, Heritage Festival, 11
- **C** *Columbia*, Shryocks Annual Corn Maze, 12
- **C** *Columbia (Hartsburg)*, Hartsburg Pumpkin Festival, 12
- **C** *Knob Noster*, Whiteman Air Force Base Open House, 19
- **C** *Marthasville*, Deutsch Country Days, 19
- **C** *Osage Beach (Lake Of The Ozarks)*, Lake Of The Ozarks Holiday Light Park, 21
- **C** *Sedalia*, Missouri State Fair, 23
- **NE** *Festus*, The Pumpkin Patch, 38
- **NE** *Hannibal*, Tom Sawyer Days, 48
- **NE** *Kahoka*, Clark County Mule Festival, 50
- **NE** *Kirksville*, Shrine Pro Rodeo, 52
- **NE** *La Plata*, Jackson Country Connections, 52
- **NE** *St. Charles*, Fete De Glace Ice Carving Competition, 58
- **NE** *St. Charles*, Lewis And Clark Heritage Days, 58
- **NE** *St. Charles*, Festival Of The Little Hills, 58
- **NE** *St. Louis*, St. Louis Storytelling Festival, 73
- **NE** *St. Louis*, Fair St. Louis, 74
- **NE** *St. Louis*, St. Louis Holiday Magic, 74

SEASONAL & SPECIAL EVENTS (cont.)

- **NE** *St. Louis (Maryland Heights)*, Thies Farm & Greenhouses, 78
- **NW** *Blue Springs*, Dogtober Fest, 87
- **NW** *Independence*, Strawberry Festival At Vaile Mansion, 93
- **NW** *Kansas City*, Festa Italiana, 113
- **NW** *Kansas City*, KCRiverfest, 113
- **NW** *Kansas City*, Faulkner's Pumpkin Farm & Ranch, 113
- **NW** *Kansas City*, Kansas City Ballet, Presents "The Nutcracker", 114
- **NW** *Kansas City, KS*, Renaissance Festival, 115
- **NW** *Liberty*, Carolyn's Country Cousins Farm Pumpkin Patch, 121
- **NW** *Platte City*, Pumpkins Etc, 125
- **NW** *St. Joseph*, Trails West Festival, 130
- **NW** *Weston*, Red Barn Farm, 131
- **SE** *Cape Girardeau*, Cape Girardeau Air Festival, 140
- **SE** *Doniphan*, Civil War Days, 141
- **SE** *Poplar Bluff*, Dunlap Pumpkin Farm, 150
- **SE** *Sikeston*, Beggs Family Farm - Fall Harvest Celebration, 154
- **SE** *Ste. Genevieve*, Jour De Fete, 158
- **SE** *Winona*, Heritage Day At Twin Pines, 161
- **SW** *Branson*, Branson Fest, 178
- **SW** *Branson*, Port Of Lights, 179
- **SW** *Ozark*, Ozark Festival Of Lights, 189
- **SW** *Pineville*, Jesse James Days, 190
- **SW** *Springfield*, Gray / Campbell Farmstead Lifestyle Exposition, 195
- **SW** *Springfield*, Festival Of Lights, 195

SCIENCE

- **C** *Camdenton*, Bridal Cave, 7
- **C** *Camdenton*, Dinospace Adventure, 8
- **C** *Jefferson City*, Runge Conservation Nature Center, 15
- **C** *Jefferson City*, Missouri Vet, 16
- **C** *Versailles*, Jacob's Cave, 24
- **C** *Warsaw*, Harry S Truman Dam & Reservoir Visitor Center, 24
- **NE** *Alton, IL*, National Great Rivers, 32
- **NE** *Clarksville*, Clarksville Visitor Center, River Heritage Center, 33
- **NE** *Hannibal*, Cameron Cave, 42
- **NE** *Imperial*, Mastodon St Historic, 50
- **NE** *Kirksville*, Still National Osteopathic Museum, 51
- **NE** *St. Louis*, HealthWorks, 67
- **NE** *St. Louis*, St. Louis Science Ctr, 68
- **NE** *St. Louis (Ferguson)*, Challenger Learning Center - St. Louis, 75
- **NE** *St. Louis (Kirkwood)*, Powder Valley Conservation Nature Ctr, 77
- **NW** *Blue Springs*, Burr Oak Woods Conservation Nature Center, 87
- **NW** *Kansas City*, Science City, 103
- **NW** *Kansas City*, Lakeside Nature, 108
- **NW** *St. Joseph*, Remington Nature Center, 129
- **SE** *Cape Girardeau*, Cape Girardeau Conservation Nature Center, 138
- **SE** *Marble Hill*, Bollinger County Museum Of Natural History, 146
- **SE** *Rolla*, Mineral Museum, 152
- **SW** *Branson*, Dewey Short Visitors Center, 170
- **SW** *Liberal*, Prairie State Park, 186
- **SW** *Noel*, Bluff Dwellers' Cavern & Browning Museum, 189
- **SW** *Springfield*, Springfield Conservation Nature Ctr, 193
- **SW** *Springfield*, Discovery Center, 193

For updates & travel games visit: **www.KidsLoveTravel.com**

Activity Index

SPORTS

- **C** *Lebanon*, Lebanon Midway Speedway, 19
- **NE** *East St. Louis, IL*, Gateway Grizzlies, 35
- **NE** *St. Louis*, St Louis Blues Hockey, 64
- **NE** *Wildwood*, Hidden Valley Ski, 82
- **NW** *Kansas City*, College Basketball Experience, 98
- **NW** *Kansas City*, Negro Leagues Baseball Museum, 102
- **NW** *Kansas City*, Kansas City Chiefs - Arrowhead Stadium, 107
- **NW** *Kansas City*, Kansas City Royals - Kauffman Stadium, 107
- **NW** *Weston*, Snow Creek Ski Area, 131
- **SE** *West Plains*, Legit Speedway, 160
- **SW** *Ozark*, Doennig Sport Swings & Ozark Paintball, 189
- **SW** *Springfield*, Bass Pro Shops Outdoor World, 194
- **SW** *Springfield*, Missouri Sports Hall Of Fame, 195

SUGGESTED LODGING & DINING

- **C** *Columbia*, Shakespeare's Pizza, 9
- **C** *Jefferson City*, Central Dairy, 13
- **C** *Lake Ozark (Four Seasons)*, Lodge Of The Four Seasons, 18
- **C** *Osage Beach (Lake Of The Ozarks)*, Tan-Tar-A Resort, 20
- **C** *Williamsburg*, Crane's Museum And Country Store, 26
- **NE** *Eureka*, Yogi Bear's Jellystone Park Camp Resort, 37
- **NE** *Hannibal*, Mark Twain Dinette, 45
- **NE** *Hannibal*, Ole Planters Restaurant, 47
- **NE** *Hannibal*, Paddlewheel Popcorn & Candy Company, 48
- **NE** *Monroe City*, Mark Twain Landing, 54
- **NE** *St. Charles*, Embassy Suites, 57
- **NE** *St. Charles*, Little Hills Restaurant/ Winery, 57
- **NE** *St. Charles*, Llywelyns Pub, 57
- **NE** *St. Charles*, RT Weiler's Restaurant, 57
- **NE** *St. Louis*, Flamingo Bowl, 58
- **NE** *St. Louis*, Eat-Rite Diner, 59
- **NE** *St. Louis*, Union Station, 64
- **NE** *St. Louis*, Soulard Market, 64
- **NE** *St. Louis*, Crown Candy Kitchen, 65
- **NE** *St. Louis*, Ted Drewes Frozen Custard, 66
- **NE** *St. Louis*, America's Incredible Pizza Company, 72
- **NE** *St. Louis*, The Hill, 73
- **NE** *St. Louis (University City)*, Fitz's American Grill & Bottling Co, 79
- **NW** *Kansas City*, Arthur Bryant's Barbecue, 95
- **NW** *Kansas City*, Fiorella's Jack Stack Restaurants, 95
- **NW** *Kansas City*, City Market, 97
- **NW** *Kansas City*, Crayola Café, 98
- **NW** *Kansas City*, Fritz's Railroad Restaurant, 100
- **NW** *Kansas City*, Coco Key Water Resort, 109
- **NW** *Kansas City, KS*, Great Wolf Lodge, 114
- **NW** *North Kansas City*, Chappell's Restaurant And Sports Museum, 124
- **SE** *Black*, Koinania Cottages & Cabins, 136
- **SE** *Cape Girardeau*, My Daddy's Cheesecake, 139
- **SE** *Cape Girardeau*, Port Cape Girardeau Restaurant, 140

KIDS LOVE MISSOURI

- **SE** *Salem*, Bo's Hollow, 152
- **SE** *Sikeston*, Lambert's Café: Home Of The Throwed Rolls, 154
- **SW** *Branson*, Branson Campgrounds, 165
- **SW** *Branson*, Billy Gail's Café, 169
- **SW** *Branson*, Tribesman Resort, 178
- **SW** *Branson (Ridgedale)*, Big Cedar Lodge Resort, 179
- **SW** *Joplin (Tipton Ford)*, Undercliff Grill, 185
- **SW** *Rockbridge*, Rockbridge General Store And Restaurant, 190
- **SW** *Springfield*, Incredible Pizza Company, 194

THE ARTS

- **C** *Osage Beach (Lake Of The Ozarks)*, Main Street Music Hall, 20
- **NE** *East St. Louis, IL*, Gateway Geyser, 35
- **NE** *Hannibal*, Mark Twain Boyhood Home Complex, 43
- **NE** *Hannibal*, Mark Twain Himself, 46
- **NE** *St. Louis*, Bob Kramer's Marionnette Theater, 65
- **NE** *St. Louis*, St. Louis Art Museum, 68
- **NE** *St. Louis (Kirkwood)*, Laumeier Sculpture Park, 77
- **NW** *Independence*, Puppetry Arts Institute, 93
- **NW** *KAnsas City*, Coterie Theatre, 99
- **NW** *Kansas City*, Kaleidoscope, 101
- **NW** *Kansas City*, Kemper Museum Of Contemporary Art, 104
- **NW** *Kansas City*, Nelson-Atkins Museum Of Art, 105
- **NW** *Marceline*, Walt Disney Hometown Museum, 121
- **SE** *Ste Genevieve*, ASL Pewter Foundry, 52
- **SW** *Branson*, Branson Theaters, 167
- **SW** *Branson*, Dixie Stampede, 171
- **SW** *Branson*, IMAX Entertainment Complex, 172
- **SW** *Branson*, Shepherd Of The Hills, 173
- **SW** *Branson*, Showboat Branson Belle, 174
- **SW** *Branson*, Sight & Sound Theatre, 174
- **SW** *Carthage*, 66 Drive-In Movie Theatre, 180
- **SW** *Carthage*, Precious Moments Inspiration Park, 182
- **SW** *Point Lookout*, College Of The Ozarks, 190
- **SW** *Springfield*, Springfield Little Theatre, 194
- **SW** *Springfield*, Springfield Hot Glass Studio, 195

TOURS

- **C** *California*, Burgers' Smokehouse, 7
- **C** *Columbia*, The Candy Factory, 10
- **NE** River Ferries Over The Mississippi River Into Illinois, 31
- **NE** *Glencoe*, Wabash Frisco And Pacific Steam Railway, 33
- **NE** *Hannibal*, Hannibal Trolley, 43
- **NE** *Hannibal*, Mark Twain Riverboat, 46
- **NE** *St. Louis*, Double Key Treasure Hunts, 58
- **NE** *St. Louis*, Gateway Arch Riverboat Cruises, 61
- **NE** *St. Louis*, St. Louis Cardinal's Busch Stadium Tours, 61
- **NE** *St. Louis (Hazelwood)*, Big Foot 4 X 4 Inc, 75
- **NW** *Belton*, Belton, Grandview & Kansas City Railroad Co, 86
- **NW** *Independence*, Pioneer Trails Adventures, 91
- **NW** *Jamesport*, Amish Community Of Jamesport, 94

For updates & travel games visit: **www.KidsLoveTravel.com**

Activity Index

- **NW** *Kansas City*, City Hall Observation, 97
- **NW** *Kansas City*, Chips Chocolate Factory, 98
- **NW** *Kansas City*, Hallmark Visitor Center, 100
- **NW** *St. Joseph*, First Street Trolley, 126
- **SE** River Ferries Over The Mississippi River Into Illinois, 136
- **SE** *Bonne Terre*, Bonne Terre Mine, 137
- **SE** *Jackson*, St. Louis Iron Mountain & Southern Railway, 144
- **SE** *Leasburg*, Onondaga Cave State Park, 145
- **SE** *Stanton*, Meramec Caverns, 155
- **SW** *Branson*, Helicopters Tours, 168
- **SW** *Branson*, Branson Landing Cruises, 169
- **SW** *Branson*, Branson Scenic Railway, 169
- **SW** *Branson*, Ride The Ducks, 172
- **SW** *Branson*, Shepherd Of The Hills Fish Hatchery And Conservation Cente, 174
- **SW** *Branson (Walnut Shade)*, Branson Zipline And Canopy Tours, 180
- **SW** *Branson West*, Talking Rocks Cavern, 180
- **SW** *Joplin*, Candy House Chocolate Factory, 184
- **SW** *Springfield*, Fantastic Caverns, 192
- **SW** *Stockton*, Hammons Products Pantry & Visitors Center, 197

www.ingramcontent.com/pod-product-compliance
Lightning Source LLC
Chambersburg PA
CBHW052024070526
44584CB00016B/1893